AWAY FROM

ZANN RENN

AWAY FROM
By Zann Renn

Published in the United States of America
Restless Winds Publishing
Nashville, Tennessee

Cover Design by Chad Smith

ISBN-13: 978-1499628975

978-1499628975

DEDICATION

For B.J.

Thank you for fighting in the trenches with me.

ACKNOWLEDGMENTS

Many thanks to Frank Breeden for his hard work on behalf of this book and to Premiere Authors for your support and belief in me. Thanks also to Dr. Andrew Hayes, Joy MacKenzie, Dr. Joani Brandon and Anita Bergen for editing expertise. And thanks to John Harricharan for catching the vision and helping me put a dent in the universe.

And absolutely much gratitude to Chad Smith for the outstanding cover art.

Thank you to my two amazing sons who are now world beaters. Stay close to the heart of God, no matter what it costs you. Thanks, most of all, to God, author of all great stories. You can wake me up again in the middle of the night any time!

Chapter 1

Any monumental movement toward change invariably begins with a declaration:

"I have a dream. Four score and seven years ago.... The only thing we have to fear is fear itself. That's one small step for man, one giant leap for mankind. We the people of the United States in order to form a more perfect union.... Die Fahne hoch."

"Let there be light."

The words, "In this new day of vast diversity...," had now been added to that long list of declarations. The men and women in the Capitol rotunda all dressed in black suits, white shirts and ties smiled as the last one signed his name to the final page of a stack of papers, and a swarm of photographers pushed in with cameras flashing for the photo op of the century. How John Beckett had found himself witness to this significant event, he did not know, and though his feelings on the document and the ramifications of what it all meant left him ambivalent to say the least, he knew that he was witnessing history in the making and that his presence in the room at this significant hour would be something he would tell his grandchildren some day in a story that would begin, "I was there when...." He thought of John Trumball's painting of the signing of the Declaration of Independence which his son, Jesse, had hanging in replica form in his room. He thought about how earnest they all looked, those original framers, Benjamin Franklin and Thomas Jefferson staring off into some ideological distance; everyone of them as determined as they were serious. This was no photo op for these patriots; this was the very soul of an infant nation written out on parchment and signed with fear and trembling by each one, the ink still drying as they took their seats.

He remembered how excited Jesse was the year he had gotten the painting for Christmas. Patriotism had sprung full bloom in the heart of that eight-year old boy; he had memorized all the traditional songs, could recognize every president by his picture, and was fiercely defensive any time anyone would make a negative comment about the United States of America. His innocence and ignorance made his convictions all the more endearing; for Jesse country was at the apex of his idealistic priorities. John never had the courage to tell him to aim higher.

John left the Capitol later that day and boarded a plane back to Kansas. As Special Assistant to Senator Rydell, he spent half of his week in D.C. and the other half in Topeka. Opening his briefcase after take-off, he pulled out the printed copy of the controversial document whose signing he had witnessed earlier. He focused on the words in bold print at the top of the page: "Proposing an amendment to the Constitution of the United States..." "This one has been coming for a long time," he thought. Slowly and scrupulously he began to read:

"Resolved by the Senate and House of Representatives of the United States of America in Congress assembled (two-thirds of each House concurring therein), That the following article is hereby proposed as an amendment to the Constitution of the United States, which shall be valid to all intents and purposes as part of the Constitution when ratified by conventions in three-fourths of the several States:

Section I

No act, petition or reference to any divinity or object of worship shall be spoken or written in Congress or in any government forum; nor shall prayers or petitions to any "divinity" be exercised at any event led or sponsored by any Government officials.

Section II

When ratified by each state, no prayer, petition or reference to any name relating to any object of worship shall be spoken or written in any public education forum. No place of public education shall teach science from any theories deemed "nonscientific" by the State.

Section III

No employees of the State may profess or adhere to any one faith or religion.

Section IV

Any assembly of more than fifty attendants may be monitored regularly by State authorities to insure peaceful assembly. Any act deemed violent, radical or disruptive by State authorities will be reported, and sanctions may be enforced by each State.

Section V

Any forum of education that professes any religious bias is hereby to be stripped of accreditation and terminated as a learning institution. United States education must be uniform in intent, purpose, curriculum and ideology. All educational facilities will hereby become instruments of the State and will be run, operated and staffed by sanctioned government educators and employees.

Section VI

All public acts of expression will hereby be tolerated, unless the State deems that such an act infringes upon the civil liberties of others.

John had engaged in debates and discussions over the past several months about the subjective nature of the terms of this amendment. What exactly do the words tolerance, disruptive, offensive and cleansing mean to people, to each individual person—thousands of interpretations. Who would be classifying certain acts as "intolerant?" How would the amendment be enforced? How would violators of the terms be punished? The penal system had so many problems of its own, one of which was overcrowding in the prisons. He had mentioned this point last Tuesday to Senator Hadley from Ohio who said that there was some discussion on the Hill of state-funded "rehabilitation centers." The centers would serve as learning institutions to reform the behavior of violators by means of re-education and operant conditioning in the style of B.F. Skinner. The goal would be to modify the thoughts and actions of violators so that they would behave more moderately and less "radically" and "militantly" and so that they might become more gender, racially, and religiously neutral. These institutions would also offer remedial reading and tutorial services for any American free of charge as well as physical therapy for veterans. John had suggested once again that the powers that be were altering the meaning of the age old phrase "freedom of religion" by insisting we have "freedom from religion." Hadley had simply laughed and said, "Oh, John, evermore the idealist. Don't be naïve; this is a good thing—rest in it. In the end it will protect us as people. It's all about majority rule, democracy—you know that. What the majority says it means is the law, and these discussions on semantics have already been decided. It's what the people want."

"Not all the people," John muttered under his breath. He closed his eyes, clicked off his overhead light, and put his seat back. He clinched his fists around the ends of the armrests. The next few years were going to be a bumpy ride.

Chapter 2

Jesse and Andrew Beckett awoke to the smell of bacon and fried eggs. Andrew was especially lethargic since his teenage hormones had kicked in a few months before causing his body to demand more sleep than usual. Rachel almost had to drag him out of bed. Flicking on the nightstand light, she said, again, "Andrew. You've got to get up and get ready for school. C'mon. Long sleeves, long pants—it's chilly today."

There was a groan and some rustling arising from the lump under the brown comforter. Rachel smiled. When she walked back into the kitchen, John Beckett was standing there with dark circles under his eyes and a cup of steaming coffee in his hand. He was wearing khaki pants, a white shirt with the "Brown's Hardware" logo on the pocket, and a tie.

"Gotta go, Honey," he said.

"Don't you want breakfast?" Rachel asked, draping her arms around his neck.

"Don't have time. We open early today for the sale. If this goes well, I may be late. Everything is 40% off. Oh, are we meeting tonight?"

"Yes. Hannah just called. Everyone can come except the Millers. Sick kids."

"Okay, "John said kissing her forehead and attempting a slight smile. "I'm out."

Rachel slid the eggs on two plates, buttered some toast and called out, "Jesse! Andrew!"

Jesse, who was now eleven came lumbering down the stairs. "I need to feed my frogs, real quick!" He grinned mischievously. He dropped three crickets into a ten gallon tank and watched as one of the orange bellied frogs leapt out from behind a stone and caught the bug in his mouth. "Got him," Jesse whispered.

The two boys and Rachel sat down at the table. Rachel took the brown Bible from the counter, opened to the marked page where they had been reading, and began, "Consider him who endured such opposition from sinful men, so that you will not grow weary and lose heart." Rachel prayed the Lord's Prayer together with the boys and rushed them off into the bathroom. "Teeth, hair and pits!" she shouted, hoping they'd remember the "pits" part as they were at the age where deodorant was the first line of defense in an odorous middle school world.

"I wish we didn't have to walk today," Andrew complained. "How bad would it be to get the stupid chip so we could get a car? Everyone thinks we're weird."

"I don't care what everyone thinks, and you shouldn't either. We've talked about the chip a hundred times, Andrew. It goes against what we believe."

"I know," Andrew said lowering his head and pulling on his jacket. "It just gets cold walking sometimes." He smiled at his mother who kissed him on the nose.

"I think you'll live through it," she responded sarcastically. She watched from the window as Andrew and Jesse walked down the street, backpacks strapped to their bodies and lunch bags in their hands. "God, help them," Rachel whispered. They walked, heads down past the "Welcome to Remington" sign, past the giant billboard which read: "Get the chip! Get a life!" On it was a picture of a man's hand, the chip shown magically under the skin, gleaming like a diamond. From the window of one house, the boys heard the thumping beat of slam music. They had grown used to the repetition of profanity in the music and talked to each other to tune it out. From one window the deep voice of a newscaster on a chip screen stated, " A grand slam for President M today as Homeland Security announced that security breeches have been reduced 85% since the chip, introduced three years ago today, has been required of all U.S. citizens. Congress will be voting on an upcoming bill to unify state law regarding the chip. People would then be required to have the chip not only to fly ride in motorized water vessels but also to drive or ride in any automobile."

"I wish I had a chip," Andrew said to Jesse as he stepped over a discarded escort service flyer.

"Why? I don't. Martin has a chip already, and Mom would die if she knew what kids can get now on that thing. Did you know that if you're sixteen now you can download porn for free on your chip and watch it on any i-screen? You can go to strip clubs on it, too."

"That's not true!" retorted Andrew.

"Yes it is! They just lowered the age! You know Vance Degan? He went last week, and he's sixteen. "

"I just want it for the music," said Andrew.

"What music? That music?" Jesse pointed to the second house they had come to playing the slam music.

"Uh, not exactly. You know, like classic rock," said Andrew.

"Do they even have that anymore?" asked Jesse. Andrew rolled his eyes.

"C'mon. We're going to be late. Don't look up. It's that new sex club billboard. I'm not kidding; don't look or I'll tell Mom."

John had just finished taking inventory of a new shipment of handsaws, when Mr. Brown came up to him with his paycheck.

"Hey, John. Did you get that paint order in?"

"Yes, just finished it."

Frank Brown fiddled with the sign display. "Did you catch the news?"

John stopped and looked at Mr. Brown. "How am I going to catch the news without a chip?"

"Just wondered if you heard it somewhere else. They're talking about making all U.S. businesses convert to chip by January."

John slammed down his clipboard. "You've got to be kidding! You know, I get why they needed . . . something, you know to expedite hospital check in, all that information you always have to

7

fill out and people sitting there literally dying trying to get it filled out. Really, I get it. But why a chip under your skin? Why not a card or something? You'd think they were deliberately trying to destroy . . . . "

"People might lose . . . "

"Yes, yes, I know. People might lose it. But people might lose their jobs, too. People might lose their respect and their jobs and their income and their life." John's voice cracked and he dropped his head.

"I'm sorry about the state job, John. I'm sorry you have to live in Remington; I know it's not D.C. Hell, it's not even Topeka. And I'm sorry, in a way, that you have to work here. I know you're not happy. But I'm grateful for the help. Really. It's just that . . . a law's a law. They've been doing it in Japan and Europe for years. It's not so bad really. I just don't understand why you won't just . . . ."

"I know you don't understand, Frank. Maybe you never will. I just don't know how much more I can 'downsize,' if you know what I mean."

At the end of the day, John was utterly exhausted. He totaled out the cash drawer at the hardware store and walked slowly home. He had been battling depression again for weeks, especially since the cool autumn weather had moved in. The thought of going through another Kansas winter working at Brown's was almost unbearable, but he didn't want to go back on medication and he didn't want to bother Rachel and the children. They had enough adjustments and difficulties without the additional yoke of his personal cloud. All of a sudden he remembered the grainy sand on the North Shore of Oahu. His family had gone there several years in a row just after Christmas when the humidity was lowest and the sunsets were most spectacular. He recalled waking before dawn to hike to the point for a breakfast picnic and horseback riding with Andrew through the wooded areas around the resort. He thought about slow dancing with Rachel on the terrace of the "Blue Dolphin" overlooking the volatile waves of the Pacific. For him, Kansas had come to represent stagnation—no more dreaming, no more traveling—just a land-locked, immobilized existence. The only hope he had of visiting Emerald City was a good, old-fashioned Kansas tornado.

He turned reluctantly into his driveway. He could tell by the porch lights and the muffled sounds of conversation that the meeting had already begun. Walking in the back door, John could smell spiced cider and warm pumpkin bread. Soft music was playing and there was fire in the fireplace. He thought how much he loved Rachel for trying so hard in spite of their circumstances to make their times at home an escape and an oasis from the world. He was greeted by his sister-in-law, Hannah, a beautiful, thin blonde woman in her thirties who, along with her husband Tim taught in the Washburn University Theater Department. They were both gifted teachers and actors; their three children, Thomas, Maggie, and Simon, had grown up with Jesse and Andrew. Thomas and Jesse were only two weeks apart in age, and though they were competitive and sometimes bickered, they were hard and fast friends. Maggie, who loved horses, was eight and Simon was three.

"Hey, John," Hannah said, giving him a hug and a half-hearted smile. "I think Rachel left you some dinner in the oven. It won't offend us if you want to eat while we talk." Grabbing his plate out of the oven, John could hear Shane Peterson in the living room. "I heard another one was shut down this week—First Baptist—it's not even that big. Fairly soon, I think, all of us will be meeting in homes. It's the only place left where the authorities don't disrupt worship."

"I know," said Sharon, a friend of Rachel. "It's getting almost humorous. The Methodists have a 'book club;' the Lutherans have a 'lodge meeting,' and we have a 'get together.' And these abandoned churches! It's starting to get ridiculous! So many of them have been vandalized, but I hear now that businesses are buying them and turning the bigger ones into malls and stores and

God-knows-what. I actually heard that they are turning 'Our Lady Catholic Church' into a strip club and calling it 'Believers!'"

"Are you serious?" asked Tim.

"As a heart attack," said Sharon. "What's next—McCarthyism?"

"What I cannot stop worrying about until it almost makes me sick is all this publicly displayed pornography. Have you been by Crater Park lately? What people are doing now in the broad daylight—it's unfathomable. I mean gay couples, straight couples, young couples....VERY young couples. I'm glad my grandmother is gone. She would have died all over again seeing what I see every day. How in the world did we as a country decide that THIS was okay, I mean, in public?"

"All part of the Tolerance Amendment. If it's not hurting anyone . . . "

"I think that statement is certainly up for interpretation," Rachel said biting into an apple.

"And how does Wicca get away with it?" asked Hannah setting down a cheese tray. "Why is it okay for them to meet in the schools? I asked Thomas's principal about it, and he said that the state officials said they could as long as they were monitored and weren't in groups larger than ten. They actually registered as a nonreligious organization so they could meet on school property. They had a freakin' bake sale last week! I heard they even work spells and repeat incantations in their meetings, and the authorities just find it funny. They are recruiting kids at his school right and left. Thomas said he walked by their room the other day and they were getting in touch with 'the powers of darkness within' and 'harnessing the powers of nature.' They were probably doing all this over milk and cookies!"

Louis Chen said, "We finally got rid of our computers and TVs last week. I just got tired of playing Gestapo. There are so few things that our family can even watch anymore. It wasn't worth it, and you know me—I'm not a prude. But I kept trying to find the actual dialogue in between all the profanity and sex scenes . . . even on the networks. The news is all skewed one way or another.

We're just over it! I kept an old DVD player and a small screen for older movies. And that's about it."

"We pawned our TVs a year ago," said John. "I'm not even sure what's on anymore. Wouldn't know a movie star if I saw one."

"It's that word 'tolerant,'" said Jack. "I think if I hear it one more time . . . . I'm all about understanding where people are coming from and for understanding their struggles and not judging them. But is it just me, or are we almost getting away with murder, literally, in the name of tolerance?"

John sighed, "Let's get started," he said opening his Bible. "Any thoughts on the readings before we do?"

The children were in the basement playroom reading their scripture lesson and doing a craft. The room got quiet as John read the lectio divina. There was a time of silent meditation, then each person in the room began to share his prayer requests and concerns—the list was long. Two people in the circle worked for businesses that were in the process of transferring to the chip. They were trying to look for new jobs and face the likelihood that they would be unemployed for an indefinite period time.

"I hear that by this time next year, all businesses will be required to go to the chip for income tax purposes. Walmart and all the big corps have already gone chip because it streamlines payroll," said Shane Peterson. The Sarios requested prayer for their neighbors who were taken to a "center" just the day before and separated from their children who were put into a state run boarding school. They were Episcopalian Christians whose home church had been discovered and disbanded because they were planning to picket the school in opposition to the recent ruling on dissemination of sexually explicit material to high school students as part of their sexual education courses.

"What exactly goes on in those centers?" Sharon asked sipping a cup of green tea. "No one is ever allowed to say, but the people who come out of there certainly have no more religious convictions—even the most impassioned believers step out of there moderate as politicians."

"I'm afraid it's only going to get worse," Tim interjected. "Eventually it will come to blows with anyone who has any moral or spiritual lines. Or should I say any 'lines' that aren't in 'line' with the federal definitions . . . or lack thereof."

Louis Chen who had spoken little throughout most of the meeting finally said, "We're struggling." Shifting around in his seat and staring at the floor he cautiously proceeded, "I think May and I are going to get the chip." The rest of the group focused on Louis who was still looking at the floor. "We've read and reread the part in Revelation about the mark of the beast, and we're just not sure that this is it. We have no money left—we're unemployed. The children are suffering—our marriage is suffering because we can't do the things we need to do without having the chip. We've decided to get it. We can't believe that God would want us to let our family suffer like this and we're not convinced that this scripture and the chip are related in any way."

Shane Peterson finally spoke up, "You know, I've got to admit I've been conflicted about this whole thing. There's no denying that this is that way the world is going. But are we called to be that set apart? We're called to be in the world and not of it. But we are definitely in it. I guess for us it's just wait and see. Keep doing what we're doing until we get a clearer picture."

A nervous silence fell over the room as if there were no more words. The fear in the air was palpable and real.

"Let's pray for a perfect love that will cast out some of this fear," Hannah suggested grinning. "Tim and I are on the verge of losing our positions, too. We just got word today that in two weeks all American universities will be on the chip. Those without chip will be let go."

Everyone joined hands and one by one each person prayed what came into his or her heart. Fran Sario whispered a prayer in tongues while Sharon Phipps interpreted its meaning. Most everyone in the circle began to weep as the spirit of fear lifted from the room and was replaced by a feather-light peace. The meeting ended with hugs and handshakes at the door. No one actually said it out loud, but the pervading thought in the minds of these believers was "Will I ever see you again after tonight?" These days nobody ever knew.

Chapter 3

Two weeks passed before John's boss, Frank Brown, in an unusually low-key manner told John that within the next month the hardware would be converting to the chip for payroll purposes, and if John wanted to stay employed there he had to have the implant by next Friday. Mr. Brown explained that he could not pass up the new tax break incentives that the government was offering to small businesses that would convert to the chip. On the same day that he received this news, Thomas James, Tim and Hannah's oldest son, was suspended from school for taking up for a Jewish boy who was being harassed by two older boys for wearing his kippah to school for Rosh Hashanah. In the altercation, Thomas had apparently gotten so upset that he blurted out the fact that he and his parents also said prayers aloud and took the sacraments in the home church where they met and that was no basis for a person to pick on another person. "I LOVE GOD, TOO!" he had yelled at the boys. Unfortunately, the minute the word, "God," came out of his mouth, teachers flew at him like a flock of crows and whisked him to the principal's office. The principal grilled Thomas most of the day about the house church, how big it was, how often the people got together. Rachel met John at the door of their house to tell him this news and that their home church was now on the "list" for potential investigation.

Later that evening Tim and Hannah met John and Rachel at the Park Café. The place, run by a friend of Tim's, was almost empty at this time as it was known primarily for its lunch and breakfast family style menu.

"We'll have to disband. It's not worth the hassle or the risk." Hannah was crying and wiping her eyes with a dinner napkin. "We can't end up in a center."

"We've got to do more than that. John, I heard on the news this morning that for the sake of records they are preparing to initiate a mandatory chip requirement for all current or past state or federal government employees regardless of race, religion or creed. It won't matter that you had to quit to avoid getting the chip. You stay here and you'll have to get the chip—no way around it," Tim commented.

"We've talked about this before, but we've got to get out of here and soon. This is a police state for believers. I can't compromise my family or my relationship with God for this crap anymore," John stated firmly. "I've been thinking about this for weeks. I've always been one to find a logical solution to problems." He paused and looked into the eyes of the others. "There's no way around the solution for this one."

"How will we do it, John?" asked Rachel, leaning in and whispering. We can't get in a car—we'll be scanned on most roads and highways. We can't ride with someone else, either or we jeopardize the driver. We can't fly—we can't take a bus. Nothing. What are you going to do—beam us out of here with five kids?"

"There's gotta be a way—a way that is quick and non-motorized that would go undetected. Perhaps something more associated with recreation than travel," said John.

"Could we find a boat, a Mark Twain/Huck Finn sort of thing?" said Tim.

Hannah smirked, "Tim, c'mon. We're in Kansas. I don't think that would get us far unless we hit the Mississippi and headed south."

"Where do we want to go?" Rachel asked seriously.

John spoke up, "I think the Atlantic Ocean is our best bet. There are a few European countries and several African ones that are still open to American refugees. The Atlantic is a shorter trip than the Pacific where we could end up on some island... or in

Japan where we definitely would not be welcome. What about Virginia? That coast has several ports with lots of boat options. Let's think seriously about Virginia. I'll research the exact spot."

Tim interrupted, "Yes, but that still does not answer the question about how we get there. We definitely can't use anything with GPS with all the standard tracking devices they put in them these days."

Hannah, who had been deep in thought finally said, "What about a balloon?" The other three turned to look at her. Tim started to say something snide then closed his mouth. His eyes narrowed. Hannah continued, "Last summer we took the kids to the Gibson County Air Show. They were giving hot air balloon rides, and there were so many balloons lined up getting ready for the annual race, beautiful balloons. We watched them as they took off, lifted up into the sky. Then we took a ride. You've never felt anything so calm and serene. I talked to the man who runs the tournament. They house several of the balloons in the hangar all year round. I know it's possible to go cross-country. The man told me that in back in 1999 two men took a balloon clear around the globe in 19 days and 21 hours. Another guy did a flight, Fossett I think, in 14 days and 20 hours nonstop around the globe! There's no motor—we wouldn't get scanned. And this time of year we could get away with it since this is when most of the big fairs take place. We could even travel at night."

Tim thought for a minute, "I wonder how hard it would be for us to learn how to navigate one."

"The man said he trains people all the time," Hannah continued.

"Could we get the kids and all of us in a couple? How many would we need?" asked Rachel.

"I'm guessing 3 or 4 for all of us with kids and some luggage," Hannah added. "I'm sure it depends on the balloon and the gondola. Scientific balloons can carry up to 4000 pounds, but those are the NASA super-pressure types and I'm fairly sure we can't get our hands on one of those."

"Let's meet tomorrow at ten," said John. "We'll go talk to the guy. See how long it takes to train. Hopefully, it won't take too long to learn the basics and be certified. We should all learn. All of us will end up navigating more than likely."

That night not one of the four of them slept. But while everyone else was battling anxiety and detailing "to do" lists in their heads, John was, for the first time in years, at complete peace. The decision to leave, as dangerous and uncertain as it seemed, released him somehow. The heaviness he had endured since the passing of the Tolerance Amendment had lifted, and his tired heart found an energy that he thought he had lost under the bricks of spiritual oppression. When he finally drifted off to sleep in the wee hours of the morning, he dreamt for the first time in a long while not of pressures, obligations, and worries about his family and their well-being, but of lying in an open meadow, the sparse clouds floating above his head, the sun on his face, and the brush of a cool breeze. Whether it was safe or sensible or smart, the decision the four of them had made that afternoon was right. And in the depths of his soul, John knew it.

The air was unseasonably cool for Kansas in October, and the wind swept across the plains with a determined force. Regardless of that fact, Tim, Hannah, John and Rachel decided to bike out to Blanchard Air Field. The wind cut like tiny needles into their cheeks as they rode under a cloudless sky. Rachel thought about all the times she and the boys had gone biking up the same, flat stretch of road every summer, Jesse complaining of side stitches and Rachel saying, "Make yourself do it—just a little farther. It's good for you." There were so many memories in this town. Rachel put out of her mind what they were about to do. She had gone again and again through the mental gymnastics of finding a way around it. The mind works overtime when its habits and addictions are being threatened, and Rachel was addicted to the American way of life so much so that when she really stopped to think of all that she had compromised and rationalized, a strong,

Zann Renn

heavy guilt washed over her putting her in a funk that took days to rise above.

The cyclers rode up the long driveway to the airfield. An older gentleman emerged. He was stalwart and bald though he wore a black Panama Jack hat. He had on a red sweatshirt with the Blanchard logo on it and a pair of jeans. "You guys call about the balloons?" he asked.

"Yeah, we did," said John. "I'm John Beckett; this is Rachel, my wife, and Tim and Hannah James."

"My name is Bob Ledger. I'll be trainin' ya. Might take a few weeks, dependin' on how much time you wanna spend and how quickly ya catch on. I've been flyin' these babies for the past fifteen years. Before that I was a martial arts instructor, Go-Ju Ryu. Then my knees went bad and I had to retire." He stopped to shake John's hand. "Nothin' like the feelin' you get in the balloon though; peaceful at it gets."

Thus began the routine. The kids would walk to school in the mornings then the James and the Becketts would head to the field to learn to navigate the balloons. The four of them would cart the strong, wicker baskets and the balloons, which Bob called envelopes, to the open field. They would then gently remove the nylon envelopes from the canvas bags, attach them to the baskets, and spread them out on the ground, taking care not to lay them on anything that might puncture or rip them. These particular balloons and baskets were bigger than most as they could hold and carry up to four people. After the inflation fans were turned on, the balloons began to inflate, rising and breathing like colorful giants, until they were nearly three-fourths full of cold air. Tim and John would then squeeze the blast valves on the burners so that the propane would come exploding out sending eight-foot flames into the balloons with a ferocious roar. Hannah and Rachel would hold the crown lines to control the rise of the balloons and to keep them from swaying. The colors were magnificent; Rachel could never get quite used to seeing the billows of reds and yellows and blues—the

18

spectacle always took her breath for a moment and she had to fight the temptation to rush home to tell the boys every afternoon.

Then came the hard part. Usually the pilot and crew of a balloon also have a ground crew that helps them with lift off. The couples knew that in their situation this scenario would not always be possible. So they devised a plan so that the pilot would already be in the basket and the ground assistant would hold the crown line until the last minute. Then the assistant would quickly and precariously board the gondola as the balloon was lifting off. They all practiced this maneuver dozens of times until they finally created workable options, sometimes using props. All four of them took turns piloting. John began to realize that ballooning was nothing like flying an airplane since the pilot of a balloon is always at the mercy of the winds. In this respect it was more like sailing, except in the skies there were more advantages. He discovered that air flows in different directions depending on how high or how low one flies, and fortunately for them, most air currents during this time of year and in these weather conditions blew them eastward every time. Navigation was certainly the most difficult aspect of ballooning, and the wind speed was notoriously unpredictable. One day they spent an hour in the air only to discover they had covered just five miles. Yet they knew that winds of great velocity were dangerous to the passengers. On the plus side, the pilots learned the ease and tranquility of a balloon flight, no wind noise, no motor noise. On the minus side, trees and especially power lines were extremely hazardous and sometimes fatal for passengers. Travel, they learned, is best conducted over treeless fields and plains avoiding power lines that are particularly difficult to see at dusk and dawn.

Since John had given Mr. Brown his notice and quit work at the Brown's Hardware, John and Rachel had resorted to living on stashes of cash they had been squirreling away since 9-11, and the children who were oblivious to the entire chain of events never missed a beat or noticed any change in their standard of living or in their routines. At the end of their training, the Becketts and the

James decided it was time to tell the children. In a family meeting over scones and tea, Maggie's favorite snack, John began to articulate, in a way they could understand that the time had come for their families to do something new and exciting that would require saying goodbye to their house and traveling to some interesting places. They had worked out the absence from school by signing up for a "home school sabbatical" which the government allowed for up to six weeks for the purpose of learning enhancement or transition to another system. Due to the state's ruling on home schooling and the prohibition of Christian schools, the children could no longer be removed from the public system indefinitely, but there were still some loopholes, especially for transitioning to another system which did not accept new enrollees until semester break or other such situations. Six weeks would buy them the time they needed to travel without investigation or at least that was their hope.

"So . . . we have learned how to fly in balloons," John said to the children. They all just looked at him blankly as if he had just said he was now working on Mars. "We, that is all of us, are going to take a trip in balloons, at least at first. I know what I'm going to say will be hard for you, but we need to leave Kansas." Again there was silence as the truth of it began to register on the faces of the older children. "We have always told you that if we ever did anything that involved all of you that we would wait for God to tell us it was right. And now is one of those times. We feel it is necessary for us to leave in order for us to have the kind of life that God wants us to have. But the good thing is that we are doing all of this together." Again there was silence, though Jesse's lip began to quiver a little.

Finally after a long pause Simon said, "I want a red balloon." The rest of the children began to laugh which broke the ice for questioning.

Andrew asked, "When will we leave?"

Maggie asked, "What will we do with our dogs, and can I bring my Barbies?"

Jesse wanted to know about all of his toys and collections. Thomas asked, "How far will we go in the balloons?" John, Rachel, Tim and Hannah answered all the questions the best way they knew how even though for them there was so much that was unknown. Finally Andrew asked, "Is it really that bad here?" The children got quiet and looked at John with curious eyes.

"I don't think you realize, Andrew," Rachel said taking him aside, "how much you've been desensitized, how much we've just had to live with it and grin and bear it. There was a time not so long ago when you could walk all the way to school without having to look at the ground the whole way to avoid all the obscene billboards and advertising and the nasty things people do in the parks. We used to be able to turn on a radio or a TV set and find programming that was decent to watch, what didn't fill our minds with profanity and violence and pornography. Andrew, groups like Wicca that meet in your school that give you the "willies," as you say, never used to be permitted to meet in schools. Our rules of decency, how we treat others and respect their property, how we value individual freedoms had at their core the guidelines of the Ten Commandments and the teachings of Jesus, especially teachings about loving your neighbor, doing good to those who persecute you, and being a servant. It is where we get the idea in government of being a 'public servant.' And I don't believe that even the founders of our nation saw this country ending up this way. They just didn't want a state-run religion—they wanted people to worship God in their own ways, but there was an underlying belief that many people would always worship God in some way or another. They didn't foresee a day when the worship of God or saying the name Jesus would be so offensive to people that there would have to be laws to stop it."

John sat down next to Andrew and continued, "You see the revolutionary thinkers felt that man truly desired to co-operate with others, that he naturally loved liberty and goodness, you know, basic human decency, and that he had some degree of rationality. They believed that there were some negative traits, too, that men and women had the potential to become selfish, thinking of his or her own good or gain over the common good, that they could become depraved, or full of sin, out of control with their passions, that means their anger and lusts and hatred, that they could become morally lazy and corrupt. But all these ideals they were talking about, they had to get them from somewhere; they didn't just pull them out of a hat. And that somewhere had at least something to do with the Bible, whether anyone wants to admit it or not. That is why they prayed together and consulted the Bible for ways to behave and govern. That is why their tax dollars paid for missionaries to the Indians. That is why there is a Bible verse on the Liberty Bell and why they hired a chaplain for Congress. Some of them believed more strongly than others, and some didn't profess to be Christians at all. But they all agreed on the laws of human decency, and those laws came straight from Biblical principles. Kids, this is only going to get worse. We have all prayed over you all since you were born that you would follow God with all your hearts, but I'm afraid we are in a place where it is nearly impossible for you to do that. We refuse to sacrifice what we believe is right for anyone or anything. We believe that God has protected this nation this long only because there are a few of us left who hold on strongly to what we know and feel and believe. But we believe it's not safe for us any longer here. We believe it's unsafe in the worst kind of way."

The children were silent. Thomas and Maggie began to cry. Tim and Hannah put their arms around them. For several moments no one said a word. All of a sudden Simon jumped out of his chair and said, "I want a red balloon."

"Me, too," smiled Tim.

Chapter 4

All five children stood in the foyer of the Beckett house each with a medium-sized duffel bag containing a few changes of clothes, an extra pair of shoes, toiletries and some small mementoes: stuffed animals, toy cars, pictures, games, one or two books—the rule was that they had to be able to carry it on their own. Jesse and Maggie wept as they looked around at their beloved home and the things they were about to leave behind. Hannah held them in her arms, trying to comfort them as best she could. The plan for the houses was that they were to stand empty until the families reached Virginia. From there the deeds to the houses would be sent to the Sarios who would be responsible for selling them and auctioning the contents and dividing the money among all the members of the home church. Sam, the dog, was given to an obliging neighbor who had small children as was Maggie's cat, Robin. Maggie reluctantly handed the furry animal to her friend, Shelly, who promised to take care of it. The cat watched Maggie over Shelly's shoulder as the little girl, bouncing him up and down, walked away.

The goal for the families was to take care of business as much as possible while still keeping everyone they knew in the dark in regard to their plans. All the money the families had gathered together for the trip and the purchase of the balloons ended up covering less that they had hoped it would. They were able to purchase only two balloons. It was decided that Hannah and Tim James, who had the most travel and acting experience would "improvise" a way to meet up with everyone, including their own children, in Virginia. There would be no way to maintain communications since all cell phones were now on chip; short-range communication would be limited to old fashioned two-way radios that John had purchased at an antique store. The couples arranged a series of checkpoints based on home church groups whose members they knew across the country. The Becketts and all five children would travel together, checking in with families along the way; when the James arrived at that destination, they would do the same, and that way each group could keep tabs on the progress and status of the other group.

There were tears in the eyes of all the children, as they closed the door of Becketts' house; even Andrew who was older and rarely showed his emotional cards, was visibly sorrowful. Thomas held his jaw at a stiff defiant angle as the tears rolled freely from his dark eyes. The entourage biked through the brisk autumn wind to the airfield. Tim pulled a wheeled cart with Simon in tow. Maggie cried all the way to the field, with Petey, her stuffed kitten, tied with a ribbon to the handlebars of her bicycle.

The wind had died down somewhat when they arrived at Blanchard. Bob was there to greet them. "Excellent day for balloonin'," he said. "Perfect wind, cloudy, not too terribly cold."

"We want to thank you for everything you've done. You have been a Godsend for us," Hannah said, hugging his neck.

Hannah and Tim took their children to the edge of the field. Simon, who did not fully comprehend what was happening, was grinning and pointing to the two huge balloons lying on the ground in front of them. Maggie was in tears worrying about her parents, asking them how long it would be until they were together again, sad about leaving her house and her room. Thomas simply refused to speak. When Hannah tried to hug him, he yelled, "Don't!" and pulled away. Tim tried to talk with him awhile, tried to assure him that though things were changing it would be for the best, but Thomas stared at the ground with a sullen look on his tawny face.

"This is going to be like a long vacation with your cousins," Tim finally said. "You don't need to worry about us. We'll be fine and excited to see you in Virginia."

Hannah added, "You just mind Uncle John and Aunt Rachel. Everything will be okay. It will be just like the time you went to visit Grandma a few years ago. It wasn't so hard to be away a couple of weeks once you started doing all the fun things Grandma had planned for you. Do you have everything you need?"

"Yes," Maggie said. "It doesn't seem like much, though." She sniffed and wiped her nose with a tissue.

"I've packed some special snacks for each of you. Just eat one a day. Uncle John will see that you get regular meals, and Aunt Rachel will tuck you in at night. I love you." Hannah turned her head to wipe away a tear. She hugged each child so tightly that Tim was afraid they might break. Tim and Hannah helped John and Rachel inflate the balloons. Andrew, Jesse and Thomas had taken a few lessons from Bob on how to help inflate and hold the crown line for take off. Tim and Hannah loaded Simon and Thomas into Rachel's balloon along with Jesse, and Tim helped Maggie into John's balloon along with Andrew. Forgetting their parents momentarily, all the children became mesmerized by the expansive balloon and the kaleidoscopic colors as they peered inside. Tim and Hannah helped control the crown line as the balloons slowly lifted off the ground.

"Bye Mommy," Simon said. "Bye Daddy." Simon waved his little hands, and Tim, putting his arm around Hannah, waved back.

"We'll see you soon! We love you!" they yelled, watching the children, their heads growing smaller against the sky, drift off into the morning light.

For the first hour the children were lost in their fascination of the event—the weightless feeling, the quietness of the breeze, the landscape from this bird's eye perspective, the rush of the flames from the burners. But after awhile they grew tired and sat down crossed legged in the bottom of the gondola. Simon soon fell asleep. Jesse and Thomas took out a deck of cards and started to play War. In John's balloon, Maggie pulled out two Barbie dolls and began to dress them in party clothes. Andrew found his Fling and launched into Super Dodger. John kept his eye on Rachel in the distance, who, thanks to the deliberate westerly winds was keeping on course with him without much difficulty. Balloons, they learned, were fickle. Even the best pilots fall to the mercy of the winds. But Rachel, especially, had taken to flying like a pro; she had an almost instinctive ability for finding the exact currents. John grabbed his two-way radio and holding it to his mouth spoke into it, "Hey, Baby, wanna date?"

Rachel laughed at the other end, "Sure. This is what I'd call a long distance relationship."

"You look good, though," said John.

"Yeah, that's what they all say at this altitude," Rachel smiled. "Everything okay over there?"

"So far," John responded. "How about your crew?"

"Piece of cake, but give Jesse and Thomas another thirty minutes before World War III."

"Well, throw some snacks at them and give them ear buds when that happens. We've got to cover some ground while we've got this great weather," said John.

Rachel wasn't sure if it was the novelty of the balloon ride or the gentle breeze or simply the grace of God, but the rest of the day was extremely peaceful and without incident. Flying conditions were ideal, and the wind was just strong enough to push them along at a good pace but not too strong to be dangerous. The children, with the exception of a couple of short-lived arguments were getting along extremely well, and Simon took a long nap curled up on Gila monster pillow under a down blanket.

After six hours of traveling the children in both balloons began to get restless and fidgety. Tim, always the "plan man," had left John and Rachel an E-exercise he had made himself to be used at an opportune moment such as this one. On the E were specified arm and leg exercises set to music that he had chosen from favorites of each child. So listening to everything from A-List to Zapo, John and Rachel endured forty minutes of calisthenics in a balloon, a novel experience to say the least. They even joined in a couple of times, lifting their legs and swinging their arms to the music. Afterwards, Rachel and John gave each child a sandwich and a package of small carrots from the cooler and a box of juice. Rachel thought she'd give anything for a Cuppa Chai, but that miracle was not going to happen. Even Cuppa whose goal it was to inherit the earth one street corner at a time had not discovered how to serve up a latte in mid air.

"How far should we go?" Rachel asked John after they had been riding about ten hours.

John replied, "By my calculations we are about to cross into Missouri. I've been tracking all these rivers and landmarks Bob showed me on this map, and we seem to be making good time. I'd like to see how far we can to before we touch down. Just inside of the Missouri border in an airfield near a small town. Claire, I think. Bob says they have inflation fans—he knows the guy there. And it's five miles from a house church family."

"Sounds good to me. Let's hold this current as long as we can. I'm not into power lines in the dark," Rachel shivered.

Chapter 5

Just as the sentence was out of her mouth, Rachel saw an ominous looking cloud looming in the distance. "Are you seeing this, John?"

"Yes, I'm on it. Let's head down." Slowly the balloons began to descend, which at first was not noticeable to the children who were preoccupied playing games. The readings on the variometer and the altimeter confirmed the descent was as it should be. Rachel pulled the maneuvering vent line allowing the hot air to escape periodically. She was eyeing a field—clear pasture land dotted with a few cows, but very few trees—it was perfect. Keeping an eye on the horizon and glancing down toward the field she said in a firm tone, "Kids, brace for landing." The children had practiced standing and anchoring themselves, Thomas and Jesse both holding tightly to Simon who was also on a restraining harness. One bump, then a slight jerk. Dragging itself along the ground for a few seconds, the gondola finally came to a stop. Rachel pulled the rip line, and the air began to escape rapidly from the vent. Once she had gotten everyone out safely and the envelope was lying on the field like a colorful sheet, she searched the skies for John. The last time she had seen him was slightly to the south and descending. She didn't want to pull his focus at this crucial landing time, but as the moments passed worry began to rise up in her like a flood. She took the radio from her hip belt.

"John." No answer. "John, do you read me?" Nothing but static. She adjusted the knobs on her radio, but could hear nothing. Gathering Jesse, Thomas and Simon together, she said, "Hey, guys, let's pray for John. I don't know where he is." She began, "Jesus, you know where John is. Keep his balloon safe. Guide him to land.

Be near Andrew and Maggie. Please, God, let us hear something from them. Amen." Simon stood by his aunt looking up at the sky. Jesse and Thomas ran in opposite directions looking skyward, too.

The darkness, heightened by the heavy cloud cover, was moving in quickly. Finally, there was crackle on the radio. Rachel grabbed it, holding it close to her ear. Then, "Rachel?"

"Yeah, John, where are you?"

"I'm still coming down. We got....thermal....slightly southwest of the field...you are." The radio was cutting in and out, but Rachel got the gist of what he was saying. Suddenly she saw him, bobbing up and down, not far from land.

"JOHN! Watch those power lines!" She saw a burst of flames from the burners in John's gondola and the balloon lifted slightly, just missing a set of power lines along a country road. The gondola was skimming the trees in the corner of the adjacent field. The balloon was coming down too fast and choppy. Rain began to fall gently and there was a thunderclap in the distance. She could no longer see John. Between the line of trees, the rain and the lack of light at this hour, John was no longer visible. She prayed again silently that he would be okay. One minute passed, two minutes, five. No word from John.

"Rach...."

"Yes, where are you?"

"We have landed. We need you to roll up your balloon, leave your gondola and get here quickly." Rachel gathered the children and their bags and put the coolers and bedding on a plastic pulling sled they had brought. With the help of Jesse and Thomas she covered the gondola and the rest of its contents with a thin vinyl tarp and secured it all to the ground. All of them, including Simon, began to trek across the field in the rain, climbing the fence on the other side and passing everything over until people and supplies alike were heading toward what looked like a basket lying on its side. As they closed in they could make out Maggie running around a tree and John sitting against the trunk with Andrew lying across his lap. Rachel quickened her pace.

"Is he okay? What happened?"

"Rachel, he's hurt his ankle. It happened when we landed. Come see what you think." Rachel raced toward them hugging John and Andrew, who winced as she did.

"What's wrong, Baby?" asked Rachel looking at his leg propped up on a rock. She pulled up his pant leg carefully, unlaced his shoe and took it off.

"Mom, it hurts," groaned Andrew. The ankle was already red and blue and beginning to swell.

"Dear God, how did this happen, John?"

"I couldn't get control after we hit the thermal pocket. I tried so hard to avoid those power lines that I hit a tree as I was coming down. One of the lower branches must have toppled us. Maggie and I were anchored fairly tightly, but just before touchdown, about nine feet up, Andrew fell out, tried to land on his feet. I'm not sure about the envelope either. It's lying flat now, but I think I caught some branches in the nylon on the way down," sighed John.

Rachel looked around. "We've gotta get out of this rain. There's a barn over there," she pointed. "You kids help me fold this envelope and cover John's gondola. Let's get Andrew in your pull sled." All the children, including Simon, carried more than their share. The barn was about two hundred yards away. They walked for what seemed like an eternity. The barn was dark and dry for the most part. Under their feet lay a thick layer of straw or hay, they couldn't see to tell. John pulled his flashlight out of his backpack. The barn was full of cobwebs and old straw. It had obviously been abandoned or at least was not in much use. There was no house near that they could see. In one corner was a section where the roof had caved in. Rainwater was pouring down into a sepia puddle on the floor. There was a loft with a couple of bails of straw on the other side. John began to move the straw around into piles. Underneath was a dirt floor. He took the small Coleman catalytic heater from the sled of supplies along with the aluminum lantern. The warm glow from the light illuminated the interior of the barn. The children with the exception of Andrew were standing in a huddle in front of John looking like drowned rats. Andrew looked pathetic, his leg swollen to the size of a grapefruit, mud on his face and arms.

"First things first," said John. "Let's make Andrew a palette and get that leg wrapped and propped up. I can't tell for sure, but I don't think it's a break. Either way, we need to brace and elevate it. Do we have any ice packs?"

"Right here." Rachel handed him a travel-sized ice pack from the cooler.

"The rest of you kids get out of your wet sweaters and jeans. Hang them over there on that railing above the feed trough." The children slowly began to peel off their wet clothes, hanging them piece by piece from the wooden railing so they could dry. They riffled through their duffels for something dry, dressed and sat in a row on three rectangular bails of straw. Rachel had been heating some water on the camp stove and soon everyone had a cup of hot soup in his hand.

"John, I'm not sure I can walk another step after standing all day and trekking around in a field for an hour or so. I vote we bed down here for the night. I've got an extra tarp. We could cover this straw and make palettes on top. Andrew, do think you can get through the night like that?" asked Rachel.

"I think so. My ankle still really hurts, but it feels better to have it elevated. Could I have some aspirin or something?" Andrew pleaded.

Rachel grinned, "Absolutely."

"I'm not sure where we are exactly," John injected. "We're not far from where we need to be, and I think we're definitely in Missouri, but I know I can get a better idea in the morning, and I don't think we'll bother anyone here tonight, especially under the circumstances."

Rachel and John in recent years had become quite adept at camping. Because of the situation with John's job and income and the restrictions for travel, the Becketts had resorted to camping as an adventurous and inexpensive vacation option. Over the past three years they had procured all the necessary equipment and had learned how to use it well, how to hike with a large pack and how to make do in less than ideal circumstances.

"It was good, all in all, today. Seriously, no one got fried on a power line, we made good time, the kids were angels comparatively speaking, and thank God Kansas is pancake flat. Fewer obstacles that way." Rachel smoothed out the blankets over the tarp. John grinned at her optimism that was definitely her best quality. She looked like Caroline Ingalls on Little House on the Prairie making up beds on straw, except she had on a pair of distressed jeans and a sweatshirt with a guitar on the front that said, "Rock On." John laughed at the juxtaposition. Somehow she knew what he was thinking, gave him a "Power to the People" fist, and went back to work. Rachel found some mild pain medicine that the doctor had prescribed for her when she had oral surgery. She had stashed it in at the last minute in case of an emergency. She gave half a tablet to Andrew who, in no time, was sleeping like a baby. She tucked in the other four children, prayed with them, and kissed each one on the nose.

"We're sleeping in a barn," whispered Simon as she fixed his covers under his neck. "No room in the inn." He giggled.

"I know. Isn't this fun?" she whispered back.

"Yeah, pretty fun," and Simon closed his eyes and turned over, hugging his stuffed bear. John crawled under the covers with Rachel pulling her in close.

"I was just checking the envelope. It does have a tear in it, vertical, about two feet long. We'll have to see if someone in town can replace it. Please tell me again why the balloon thing was the best idea?" John spoke in hushed tones into Rachel's ear.

Rachel took his face and ran her fingers through his hair. "John, God's been with us today. The weather was perfect. We're in Missouri...I think." She turned over with her back to him wrapping his arm around her waist. "And anyway, no one stopped us. The kids are alive and happy. Andrew's going to be fine. No one is hungry and we've got a place to sleep for the night. The plus side's looking pretty good to me. John.... John."

John had fallen asleep.

Chapter 6

"Excuse me, ma'am, sir...."

John squinted. Slightly disoriented, he could see light coming in through the slats in the side of the barn. Propping himself up on his elbows he rubbed his eyes. With the sun rising behind him all he could see was a black figure.

"Yes...." John answered.

"I don't mean to be nosey, but what are you folks doin' in my barn?"

John shook his head and pulled himself to his feet. Standing before him was an older man, about seventy-five or eighty, short and stocky with a full head of gray hair and a toothpick in his mouth. He wore a pair of overalls and a flannel shirt.

"My name's George. George Allen," he said quietly.

"Sorry, yes, hi. My name is John Beckett and this is my wife Rachel and our five....children." John was trying not to give too much away, even though it was too early for thinking. He ran his fingers nervously through his tangled hair. "We came in last night in a hot air balloon just before the storm hit. Ballooning is kind of our hobby, I guess you would say. But we have an injured boy here, and we didn't think it was smart to haul him around before we found out exactly what was wrong. Anyway, we want to thank you for the use of your barn. If you'll give us fifteen minutes, we'll get outta your hair."

George looked around at the children who were stirring under the covers and at Simon who was already sitting up grinning at him. "Well, no hurry," said George. "In fact I got my truck and my house is about five miles down the road. I own several hundred acres here that I lease out to farmers, but I kept the old barn for

34

sentimental reasons. It was part of my grandfather's old home place. Anyway, I'm glad you could use it. Let me help you with your things. Looks like you could use a shower and a descent breakfast." John winked at Rachel who was already up folding blankets and rousing children.

George Allen's house had been built in the late 1800's and renovated several times, but upon entering the mud room through the back door, John could have swore he was stepping back in time. The cabinets in the kitchen were made of thick barn wood; the oven and refrigerator looked like something his ancestors used in the 60's, and the wallpaper, which was smattered with yellow and brown daisies, was faded from the sunlight, as were the yellow curtains that hung in the window over the sink. There was a smell in the house that John could not quite identify, like sulfuric water, onions, and Johnson's Baby Powder all mixed together. On the walls in the living room were photographs from every decade starting with the 1910's on up, and they were situated on the wall in such a manner that John had to surmise that they had been hung there by George himself, probably late one night after a long work day in the fields.

"My wife died four years ago. It's just me and this dog here. I'm not good at cookin'. Get all my meals at Paige's Café. But I've got some fresh eggs and a loaf of bread, ma'am, if you'd like to make yourselves something. I'll run down to the market real quick and get some more juice. Bathroom's down the hall on the left. Towels are in the linen closet in there. Help yourselves." And with that George Allen grabbed his hat and keys and shuffled out the door.

The children all took quick showers. Rachel helped Andrew bathe while he moaned and groaned holding onto the sides of the tub. She rewrapped his leg noticing that the swelling had gone down somewhat. As Andrew relaxed on the couch with his leg propped up, the children ran outside. Within seconds, Jesse and Thomas were arguing about which trees were better, oaks or maples, and Simon and Maggie were sitting opposite each other on

35

an old seesaw swing singing at the top of their lungs. John and Rachel took showers. Rachel dried her hair with an antiquated dryer she found in the linen closet. Just as Rachel had broken a couple of eggs into an old iron skillet, George reemerged from the outside through the back door.

"I ran into Doc Bowers' nurse in the store. She said she'd put your boy on the schedule this afternoon if it's not too full. Said she'll call and tell us what time later on. Hope that was okay to do," George added.

"Yes, that was okay. Thank you for taking care of that," said John. "I don't think it's a break, but we need to have somebody look at it. The weather isn't looking all that promising anyway. These cumulous clouds spell doom for balloons."

"Where are you from," asked George clearing his throat and jostling the ring of keys in his pocket.

"We're from Central Kansas. Having a little adventure with the kids. The boy Thomas and the girl and the little one are my brother-in-law's brood," John explained.

"Kind of a long way from home, aren't ya?" George smirked impishly.

"Yeah, looks that way. Balloons are unpredictable like that. Plus we tore one of them on the way down. Do you know where Heights Air Field is?"

"Yep. About twenty miles north of here. You need a ride up there?" asked George.

"Yes, but I don't have the chip," said John.

"I got one. Besides in Missouri you only have to have the chip if you're on a state highway. We'll take the back roads. You'll be fine," George answered.

"That would be wonderful. We've got two gondolas out in that field that need to be taken there, too."

George stood up, "That's not a problem for a pick up. I don't have much to do today seeing as it's supposed to rain. After breakfast, I'll take you in there. Your wife and kids can hang around here in case Doc Bowers calls. Yeah. Okay." George nodded and walked out the door toward the mailbox, opened it, pulled out a newspaper and some catalogues, and walked back down the driveway to the house. Rachel smiled as she watched him out the window. She thought about her dad who had died the year before and how much she missed him popping in for coffee.

The eggs and toast tasted like a banquet to everyone, especially to George. Maggie helped Rachel and Jesse clear and wash dishes by hand since there were no contemporary appliances to be found.

"Do you know a family named Covas?" John finally asked George.

"No, don't know any Spanish families. But Doc Bowers will know. Ask him when you go there. Are they friends of yours?" George questioned.

"In a manner of speaking, I guess they are," answered John.

Tim and Hannah didn't sleep at all. The emptiness of their two-story farmhouse was oppressive. Hannah dozed off only once then wakened abruptly after dreaming that Simon, who had the tendency to be accident-prone, had fallen from the gondola when Rachel wasn't paying attention. She woke up crying. Wiping her eyes, Hannah stumbled into the bathroom to wash the sweat off her face. She looked into the mirror. The past few years had taken a toll on her body, her face, on everybody she knew. She smoothed out the crow's feet by pulling back the corners of her eyes, which made her look like a blond Asian woman. She shook her head in disgust and turned out the light. About an hour later after much tossing and turning, Tim sat straight up in bed, switched on the light and announced, "I'm over it. Let's make a plan!"

"Good grief, Tim," Hannah said, pulling the hair off her face and squinting at her husband who was already pulling on a pair of sweats.

"Make some coffee, woman!" he said in a purposely playful misogynistic tone that he knew would irritate the feministic sensibilities of his wife of fifteen years.

"You're sick! You're one sick critter, that's what," said Hannah slowly moving out of the bed and pulling on her robe. Tim spent the next four hours in the kitchen marking sites on actual paper maps and jotting plans on actual yellow legal pads that were spread out all over the kitchen table. He worked with the focus of a plow horse with blinders on. Eventually he moved into the living room, typing frenetically and hurling wadded pieces of yellow paper on the floor as he went. Finally he burst back into the kitchen. Hannah was eating a bagel and reading her latest copy of "The E-New Yorker."

"Okay, I'm ready for you now," announced Tim.

"Well, thank God. I've just been sitting here on go hoping you'd be ready for me soon," Hannah remarked sarcastically.

Tim, so caught up in his enthusiasm, totally dismissed this last comment and pulled her by the arm into the living room. On the coffee table in front of her he laid sheet after sheet of paper—maps, charts, directions, spread sheets with numbers that looked like Greek to Hannah, and itineraries.

"We bike!" Tim said decisively as if he'd revealed the resting place of the lost Ark of the Covenant.

"Yeah?" said Hannah. Tim just stood there with that "so-what-do-you-think" look on his face. "Are you telling me you spent all this time and, and . . . paper coming up with 'we bike?'"

"Yes, but Honey, it's not just the biking, here. It's the routing and the stopping and the spending and the eating, all mapped out with minimal cost to us, minimal wear and tear on our bodies, minimal chances of getting stopped by authorities and maximum nights of sleep, mostly in places where there are home churches that will take us in." Tim began to hand Hannah several sheets of paper. "Okay, let's go over this."

Hannah rolled her eyes and smiled, "Okay, let me at least get my coffee."

Doc Bowers sighed, "I'd like to scan it at the free clinic. It's just down the street. I'll call ahead so you can get right in. We should get the results back fairly quickly. Looks like a sprain, but I'd like to make sure." Rachel and Andrew exchanged looks of relief. "He's fortunate. If he had landed any other way, it would have been a break for sure from that height."

Rachel asked, "What do we owe you? We're here from outta town and..."

"Nothing. This one's on me. You can pay cash for the scan down there, which won't be much. One good thing the government has done—free clinics and inexpensive scans helps so much with the families around here. Good to see health care improving some. Plus any friend of George Allen's is a friend of mine," Doc said putting his large hand on Andrew's shoulder.

The scan confirmed Doc Bowers' suspicions. It was only a sprain. The leg was wrapped, and the nurses at the clinic gave Andrew a free pair of crutches.

In the meantime, George and John had returned from Heights Air Field. The manager there had agreed to store the gondolas until John was ready to leave and had replaced John's envelope with a slightly used one at half the cost. Both of them felt that getting a new envelope was better than taking a chance in the air with a faulty repair. The new envelope had a huge image of a cartoon monkey on the side. John thought it was the goofiest thing he'd ever seen, but at that point he wasn't going to be picky. Plus, he reasoned that it might work to his advantage since no one, not even the authorities, would take a balloon seriously that had a monkey on the side of it. John also got the weather report for the next several days. At least the next two days were supposed to be clear with winds between 10 and 15 mph, not bad for ballooning.

Rachel had asked Doc Bowers about the Covas family, and, just as George said, he knew them, the couple, whose names were Bart and Isabel and their daughter, Maria, who was twelve. John found them in the phone book and called, explaining to Bart his situation. After everyone had eaten a lovely meal that Rachel had prepared, George drove them out to the Covas's address. The Covas's lived in a ranch style house at the edge of the county near Bristol, Missouri.

John rang the doorbell and Isabel came to the door. She was about four feet eleven inches tall, a small-framed woman with dark brown hair, snappy chocolate eyes and an award-winning smile. "You must be the Becketts," she said. "Come on in."

John introduced everyone in his entourage then turned to George who was standing quietly on the front porch with his hands behind his back. "George, I don't know how to thank you enough. I wish we had something to give you."

"Don't mention it. You don't have to give me nothing. It was good to have the company. Good luck with your travels." George shook John's hand, shifted the toothpick to the other side of his mouth and walked to his truck looking at the sky. "Yep. Them clouds are clearing off. It'll be nice tomorrow, I reckon." Then he pulled the door shut and drove off without looking back.

Chapter 7

The interior of the Covas' house was festive—colorfully painted in yellows, reds and greens. Memorabilia from South America decorated the walls and end tables, and the large picture windows let light into every corner. The first time that John saw Bart emerging from the den removing his reading glasses, he was surprised. He had imagined Bart to be only slightly taller than his wife with a well-proportioned build. Instead the man was huge; his hands were massive and brown as a Stetson hat; his shoulders were broad and thick as slabs of beef. He had a full mustache and curly hair. But the one feature he and his wife had in common was an unforgettable smile. Bart's happy face set off against the exotic room in which he was standing along with the jovial arrangement of the Covas' possessions made John want to chuckle as he reached out his hand to meet Bartolome´ Covas.

"So glad you made it this far. You're welcome in our house as long as you need to be here. Have you and your family eaten yet?" Bart asked with the hint of an accent.

"Yes, we have. Thank you. Your house is beautiful," said John eyeing a collection of antique crosses on the wall.

"Those are from Columbia. That's where my family originated. I moved here to study to become a priest. Isabel was working as a receptionist in the seminary where I attended. We located here close to the parish where I was assigned out of school."

"Oh, so you're a priest?" John asked excitedly.

"Yes, not practicing now, but in my heart I will always be, I guess," Bart sighed. John could tell there was something deeper, something Bart was not saying. He was eager to find out more about these fascinating people.

Bart and Isabel invited Rachel and John into the living room. Then calling down the hall in a commanding voice he said, "Maria, vena aquí y conoce a este gente." Sounds of rustling came from a back room, then a beautiful, little girl with long, black hair and wearing an orange jumper came down the hall with a mystery novel in her hand.

"Toma, Papito," she said in a melodic tone.

"This is Maria; she's eleven. How old are your children?"

John began, "Simon is three; Maggie is eight; and Thomas is eleven as well. They are my brother-in-law's kids. Our two are Jesse, here, who's eleven and Andrew who is all of thirteen and has a sprained ankle." Bart and Isabel continued talking with John and Rachel about their adventures so far, but no one noticed Thomas who, ever since he had seen Maria walk down the hall, was in a state of smitten euphoria and had not spoken a word. Jesse, who finally noticed Thomas staring intently, elbowed him in the ribs and giggled under his hand at which Thomas frowned and whispered without moving his lips, "Stop it!" then returned to obsessive staring. Bart suggested that Maria take the children downstairs to the recreation room where there was a pool table, a table hockey game and a ping pong table as well as an antique working jukebox which, much to Andrew's elation, was loaded with classic rock selections.

Isabel made fresh coffee, imported from Columbia, and pulled a flan from the refrigerator. John enjoyed the coffee almost as much as the fellowship.

"It's interesting how these laws differ from state to state. The chip isn't so much of a problem here. You can actually have a life without a chip, and our diocese really doesn't have a problem with it like some protestant churches do. We're not chippers yet simply because we don't travel out of state much, and we don't really need it around this area, yet. But where it's been difficult here is in the churches, or what used to be the churches. It seems like the authorities here have a personal vendetta against Catholics, especially. First it was their presence in all our services, you know, just standing there waiting for something offensive or controversial," Bart sipped his coffee.

Isabel spoke, "Yes, then it was the Eucharist. It was offensive and radical. They thought what we said about the host was cannibalistic and cultish. Good grief! Then it was the FDA. I'm serious! They called in the damn FDA because the priest was administering the sacraments in an unhealthy manner. And the common cup had to go, of course. It wasn't long before three parish churches closed down because attendance got so low. Nobody wanted the disruptions interfering with worship and mass. These are traditions we've had for centuries! And now they are radical and . . . unhealthy?"

Bart continued, "Since the recent terrorist attacks, you know, worldwide, the crack-down on all religious sects have been under such scrutiny. I understand them wanting to be fair about this. Can't crack down on Islamic groups without looking at everyone. But when they made us finally remove our confessional booths because they could not be properly monitored, well that did it for me. I left the parish and formed a house church, got a job teaching Spanish at the local high school. Mi Dios, ¿ qué está pasando en este mundo."

John and Rachel explained to them how and why they had decided to leave Kansas. They told the Covas about their convictions regarding the chip and how limited their life had become. They explained how they had prayed about it both as a couple and with Tim and Hannah and how they had decided that God was telling them to leave the country.

Bart and Isabel listened intently. The conversation, which included the history of politics, Catholic and Protestant theology, and the pluses and minuses of separation of church and state, lasted until after midnight. Bart had been discussing his utter disapproval of mandatory health classes at the school which handed out condoms and birth control pills like candy, free of charge, and which taught that abortion was a woman's inalienable human right not to be questioned by a civilized society or by liberated, intelligent women.

"I get so sick," he said. "I can't dwell on it much."

"Can I ask a personal question?" Rachel posed.

"Certainly,"

"Why is it that you feel this way about contraception and yet you only have one child?"

"Good question," Bart smiled. "Easy answer. Just after Isabel had Maria, the doctors discovered a tumor in her uterus. It was malignant. Our doctor felt certain that it was contained and thought that a hysterectomy would insure a long life for her if she took the proper follow-up treatments. So that's what we did. We always wanted a big family, but now I've got to say that if we could only have one, Maria is a gem. She's like an angel with a beautiful heart for God and a passion for service. That is why I am frightened. I don't want her in that high school. I don't want her encouraged to devalue the sanctity of marriage as if that is the mature way to behave. I don't want her to have a chip at sixteen that gives her unlimited access to pornography. I don't want her to be silenced every time she doesn't agree with a policy or a rule. We thought that being in a small town would make a difference—but I don't think there is any difference anymore. I really worry about her. She's all we've got."

They had only just met Bart and Isabel, but for John and Rachel it seemed they had known them since the dawn of time. Rachel felt they should get the kids in bed. She discovered Simon asleep on a bean bag on the basement floor and carried him up to the roll away bed in Maria's room. All the boys slept in Maria's room, two in the bunk beds and one on the floor. Maria and Maggie bedded down in the living room in sleeping bags. Maria could not stop giggling, as she was so delighted to have company. Bart and Isabel showed Rachel and John the guest room and bathroom. Standing in the hallway, John asked, "Father Covas, would you say a prayer for us tonight?"

"You got it," he said laying his large hands on them. "Blessed are you, Lord God, King of the universe for bringing us to the end of another day. Thank you for your patience and your continued inspirations. Thank you also for the crosses which became occasions for our following your divine Son, willingly bearing them out of love both for him and for you. Enable us to express our gratitude by following him even more closely tomorrow." Then Bart made the sign of the cross over them both saying, "In the name of the Father, the Son and the Holy Ghost, Amen."

As John slid under the down comforter next to Rachel he realized this was the first time they'd been together alone without the burdens of their old life weighing on them. The financial stress as well as the fear of their house church being discovered by the authorities had taken its toll on their intimacy. But John, having been in the company of these kindred spirits and feeling safe for the first time in awhile, felt a fresh freedom surging through his veins. It was as if the conduits of communication and emotion had been unclogged, and he pulled Rachel in close to him.

"I love you, Doll, so much. I want to feel you close to me. Is that okay?" Rachel removed her gown and moved in next to John so that they were on their sides face to face.

"I love you, too. I feel like we can relax a little here, don't you?" Rachel asked stroking his face.

Without answering, John pulled her face in next to his and kissed her soft lips. Rachel gave herself into his tender kisses, responding by moving her mouth around the familiar curves of his. John looked deep into her eyes. It was as if he could really see her, see into her soul. Overwhelmed by the emotion, he almost cried. The love he felt for her had a depth he could no more put into words than he could describe the Grand Canyon to someone who had never experienced it.

He ran the palm of his hand down the skin of her tanned arm, past her elbow and down the side of her body and thigh. Bringing his hands back up to her face he kissed her again. She circled her

45

fingers around the front of his chest. He had always had hair on his chest, which she loved, but in recent years the hair had begun to turn gray, and Rachel thought it made him even more seasoned and desirable. They moved as if after many years of trial and error they had discovered how to best serve each other, how to be the most tender, how to selflessly please each other. John was athletic and knew how to use the strength in his legs to pace himself, letting Rachel enjoy the experience. Slowly Rachel began to lose herself, to let herself go into another place, a familiar and safe refuge, her body tingling with pleasure. She felt a love for John, for the purity of his newly released spirit. She found herself wishing it would never end. Inside of John a dam was breaking. The waters of his soul, his heart and mind, his body rushed freely now from places that had been pent up and stagnant for so long. He began to weep, holding on tightly to his remarkable lover. Rachel's body responded to his every touch, to every move.

As they lay in the silence afterwards holding one another, there were no words, only the satisfaction of a profound and sacred love that drifted eventually into peaceful slumber.

Just before dawn John began to dream. He was walking in a breathtaking meadow when he came to the foot of a mountain. From where he stood the mountain seemed to reach through the clouds into eternity and the distance gave the peak a lavender hue. John was taken in by the magnificence of it all feeling so small and insignificant next to this monolith. But as he watched, it appeared to him that the mountain was changing color, darkening, first to a medium violet, then to a deep purple. Clouds began to move in from all directions toward the mountain blocking all the sunlight, darkening the sky as the mountain turned charcoal. Black. The ground around the mountain began to rumble and people all around commenced to screaming and running, fleeing in terror from the monstrosity. John looked around and saw Rachel and the children, Tim and Hannah and the Covas as well as several others he did not know running towards him.

"Quick, we've got a way out," said Rachel. John ran after them, helping the younger ones hurry to a plateau in distance. Eventually the family and the others crowded onto the plateau. Appearing at first as a mesa, the flat area on which they were standing began to turn into a colossal hand. The hand, full of people of all sizes and ages, began to ascend bit by bit until it was in mid air. From that vantage point, John could see below him the mayhem of fleeing people and the black mountain, now quaking so violently that even the people in the hand had to brace themselves against the fingers. Chunks of the mountain began to crumble and fall upon the people below, instantly killing hundreds, injuring others. John had to look away. Sobbing uncontrollably he could not bear to watch the destruction. He held his family close in a huddle for what seemed like forever. Then the quaking began to subside. Eventually John stood up. The mountain was no more; rubble lay all around as far as he could see, smoke and dust rising up from it and the strong smell of burning ashes.

John woke up drenched in a cold sweat.

Chapter 8

Rachel and Bart were in the kitchen making breakfast. "Good morning," Rachel said kissing John as he came in looking like a drunk at the end of a three-day binge.

Bart dried his hands. "I'm glad to see you're both up. Isabel and I would like to talk with you about something." Bart called to Isabel who was folding blankets in the living room, and they all sat down at the table. John could hear the children playing ping-pong in the basement, Simon squealing with delight every time someone made a point. "We were up most of the night talking, and Isabel and I have decided that we'd like to come with you; I mean if you don't mind us tagging along. We would drive our car and take Maggie and Simon if you'd like following you in the balloons to the Illinois line. We've got a four person maximum per car here in Missouri. From there we'll figure out something. That way you'll have a ground crew to track you and help with lift off, and you won't have to worry about two of the kids falling out of the basket at least."

John looked at Rachel. Caught completely by surprise by Bart's offer, he responded, "Well, I don't know. I mean, it would be great to have the help, but I'm not sure how I feel about it." John paused. Rachel was thinking, too.

"John, I know you don't know us from Adam, and it would be a hard call for me if I were in your shoes. But I've got a fairly good sense about people after all of my years in ministry. Isabel and I feel like this thing that you are doing is a divine thing. We want to be part of it. We're so weary of life here. We're worried, so worried about Maria," Bart said earnestly to John.

John thought for a moment. Then he remembered his dream. A peace began to settle over him when he thought about the Covas family coming along with them. "You know, something tells me this is no time to over-analyze this situation as I am prone to do. Yes. Please come with us. What do we need to do to help you get ready?" Rachel hugged John's neck as if she'd been hoping that he would say "yes."

The next couple of days were hectic, all of them running around trying to make preparations for the Covas's departure, getting papers ready for friends of the Covas to proceed with the selling of their home in two weeks. The money from the sale was to be divided among three struggling parishes in neighboring counties. Maria was full of joy and relief. School for her was a perpetual battlefield where she was ridiculed and ostracized for her brave choices and her naturally innocent outlook. She enjoyed the company of the boys who were beginning to feel like the brothers she never had and Maggie who she began to call, "Sis," when no one else was around. Thomas was especially elated at the decision as this was his first crush on a girl, and Andrew who was inherently social was always up for a bigger party.

The days over Missouri in the balloons were clear, but there were more crosswinds, which were menacing even for Rachel who had become nearly professional at finding better currents. On one day a crosswind took Rachel's balloon off course for about three hours, and another day John's balloon veered south for about 45 minutes then just as abruptly northeast again for an hour or so. The Covas had purchased a radio so they could maintain communications with both parties. They spent two nights in house churches on their list, one night in a family campground in tents they had purchased, and one wakeful night in an abandoned shoe factory in which every pebble, drop and gust which hit the steel building reverberated as loudly as a train wreck throughout the hollow structure. Ten miles west of the Illinois line they made the decision to sell the balloons for whatever they could get for them and continue on some other way. They found a retired air force sergeant who was willing to pay them nearly full price as ballooning was a passion of his and these gondolas were in mint condition.

"What's Illinois like? Have you heard anything?" asked John as they ate meatloaf and mashed potatoes at Sims Car and Truck Stop.

I've heard they're stricter there on the chip than they are in Missouri," Isabel answered. A sarcastic laugh came from the booth behind them. Isabel wheeled around to see who had spoken to give him a dirty look.

"Sorry, it's just that there's all these jokes about Illinois being so strict. 'You can't piss without a chip in Illinois.' That's what they always say. Crack down hard, too. Ever since they broke up those two big terrorist cells near Chicago, they won't let you buy, sell, eat, drive, or . . . piss. I'm serious--at least not in public restrooms."

"Crap," Rachel said tactful as ever. "We don't have time to bypass it either. Not without losing days, and we still don't know how we're going to travel. We can't use Bart's car, that's for sure."

"You guys Christians or something?" asked the trucker.

"Why do you ask?" Isabel retorted.

"It's just that if you're Christians, you're in for it double. Seems a lot of Christians lately are trying to emigrate, most of them without going through the proper channels. A lot of them countries over there in Europe, especially England, don't want no more American refugees. They're putting all this pressure on the government to crack down on these Christian folks trying to escape." The trucker gulped his coffee and shoved a fork full of lemon pie into his mouth. "They're even starting to check trucks and trailers at weigh stations for stowaways." He glanced over at Maggie and Maria sitting in the next booth. "St. Louis ain't great either. Getting stricter all the time. Hell, with all these stops, how are we supposed to haul a load cross country in time to deliver?"

Rachel and John let the children look in the gift shop while they discussed with Isabel and Bart their next move. Simon and Andrew were fixed on a shelf of die cast cars. Maggie and Maria were spinning a display of assorted candies discussing which was their favorite. Jesse and Thomas were in a section with plastic weaponry arguing about which one would "really hurt you." Finally Rachel called the children over to where she was standing with Isabel near a display rack of sex toys. John and Bart had gone out into the parking lot where lines of gas pumps were illuminated against the dark countryside and rows of semi trucks stood lifeless as cadavers.

"Kids, it's getting late, I know," Rachel said in hushed tones. "But if you'll bear with us a bit longer, I think we have an idea. You all may pick out one treat as long as it is under five Euros, and everyone needs to pee right now before we leave." The children's eyes grew wide when she said the word "treat," and they headed first for the restrooms then for the candy aisle. Isabel and Rachel made one last restroom stop, too. Rachel laughed at the condom dispensers on the wall, extra ribbed, extra, extra ribbed, glow-in-the-dark sold in one machine along with samples of perfume. She loved all the ironies of American life.

As they came out of the restroom they saw the boys with Simon at the counter.

"Where are Maggie and Maria," asked Isabel.

"Don't know," said Andrew. "They were just here."

Isabel and Rachel walked up and down the aisles, but could not find the girls. They looked out the window toward the parking lot. They saw John and Bart walking along the rows of trucks, but no girls. Moving quickly into the restaurant, they glanced into every booth, walking between the tables, looking underneath.

"Wait," said Isabel. "Listen." They heard a little voice say, "I don't know." It was Maria. Walking hurriedly toward the voices they spied them down a dimly lit hall beside the kitchen. The trucker, down on one knee, was there talking with them. He had Maggie's arm in his hand and was rubbing it as he spoke to them. Just as he said, "How would you girls like a ride in a big truck?" Isabel and Rachel were standing beside him. Rachel grabbed both girls by the arms pulling them away from the startled man. Rachel was asking Maggie if she had been hurt when suddenly out of

Isabel came, "¿Qué piensas que está hacienda? ¡Enfermo pervertido! ¿Tienes que divertirte con las minitas. Tienes suerte de estar vivo. ¡Si mi esposo estuviera aquí estarias muerto!"

Rachel had never seen Isabel like this. Her five foot eleven frame instantly was filled with a kinetic energy like a coil spinning tighter and tighter. Her brown eyes blazed with fury; her wavy hair bounced up and down with every word. As the last sentence hurled itself out of her body, she grabbed the trucker's shoulders with both hands and proceeded to knee him repeatedly in the groin with a force that would have impressed Chuck Norris. Then she spun around, grabbed Maria by the hand, and marched in to the store where she paid for treats for the girls and a twelve-pack carton of bottled water. Rachel turned back only once to look at the trucker who was lying on the floor holding onto his crushed testicles for dear life and calling out, "They are consenting minors. It's legal if they're consenting, bitch!" Rachel snickered behind her hand, and Maggie looked up at her smiling and shrugged her shoulders. Rachel picked up Simon who was sitting on the floor eating Sour Boingz and took him and Maggie to the restroom to wash their hands.

Meanwhile, in the parking lot John and Bart were sauntering in and out of the rows of trucks searching for . . . something. If no one was looking they would climb up on the side of the cab and peer inside. Mostly what they found was predictable—coffee thermoses, candy wrappers, sacks from fast food joints, E-sticks, Playboy and Penthouse Magazines, crack vials, leather driving gloves, half empty grass pouches, gum and cigarettes. However, in the next to the last row of trucks toward the back of the lot they found something unusual. The cab had a clean appearance like it had been recently vacuumed. In the seat rested an ancient contraption that played round, compact discs with some recorded sermon CDs from the nineties strewn around it. In a clear plastic pouch attached to the side of the driver's seat was a pocket Bible, an old paper and leather version, the kind John used to receive as a child at Vacation Bible School and a tattered copy of Oswald Chambers' My Utmost for His Highest.

"This is it," announced Bart. "Now we wait." About ten minutes later a man in a blue tee shirt and jeans and a brown bomber jacket approached the semi. He had a Diet Zot in one hand and a bagel in the other.

"Excuse me," John said, emerging from the shadows. The man was startled by the sight of the two men, especially Bart.

"Yes?" he said tentatively.

"We mean no harm. Just wanted to talk with you," John explained. The man relaxed somewhat but still seemed reticent to get too close. "Is this your truck?"

"Yes. It passes inspection. I haul furniture for a company in Atlanta."

"I know this is going to sound like a strange question," Bart paused, "but are you a believer?" The word was carefully chosen. Usually the authorities and the media used the word "Christian" when they interrogated people. The man could tell that these two men were not police or reporters by their use of the word "believer." Still he was cautious.

"What makes you think that I am?" the man asked.

"Well, to be honest, we've peeked into all these trucks here and all those sermon CD's and real books were a dead giveaway." John said looking a bit embarrassed. The man was obviously debating on how to respond, as he was visibly shocked that strange people were peering into his vehicle. He waited several seconds glancing back and forth at the two men, then burst out with a hearty laugh.

"Okay, you got me."

"You ever haul anything but furniture," John stared directly into his eyes as if he was fishing for something bigger.

"Yes, on occasion. Who wants to know?"

"John Beckett," John said extending his hand, "and this is Bart Covas. I'm originally from Kansas. Bart's from Missouri. Our families are inside. We're heading for a little ... vacation in Virginia.

Problem is we've only got one car and that won't fit all of us, and we couldn't drive it through Illinois anyway. We don't have chips."

Daniel found John's wavelength and glanced up after kicking a flattened Zot can from the pavement, "How many are we talking?"

"Four adults and six children, used to traveling, and ...making adjustments."

The man stood thinking. Scrutinizing the faces of John and Bart with his head half cocked, he said, "I'm Daniel. Daniel Barnes. The route I take through Illinois passes three weigh stations. They search every nook and cranny in Illinois so here's how I play it. Two miles before each station, I stop on the side of the road to check my tires. I won't open the trailer door very wide, so you step out one at a time when the traffic is scarce. You get into the wooded or shadowed areas off road and start walking east. You stay at least half a mile south of the weigh station when you come to it. Then I pick you up on the other side at another stop. I'll tell you where. John, you ride up in the sleeper with me, close the curtain, and we'll talk. There are cameras about every few yards on all the roads here, highways and back roads. Discourages terrorists driving without ID. If they get a photo of you in the passenger seat, you'll be scanned for chip."

"Where will the others ride?" asked John.

"In the trailer. It's not warm, but there's no wind. The kids can't mess with the furniture at all. Gotta have your word on that. Most of it is covered and anchored for the haul. All the way to the back of the trailer I got some furniture pads. They can use those to sit on or to rest, but they won't get much sleep with all the stopping and starting and walking."

"How far can you take us?" Bart's thick voice was sounding hopeful.

"I'll take you into Southern Indiana or Kentucky, whichever, but after that it's gonna seem strange to my boss if I don't start heading south. Indiana and Kentucky aren't so strict, Kentucky's less so. You may even be able to find lodging without a chip."

Away From

As they were talking, Rachel and Isabel walked up with the children. Bart introduced everyone to Daniel. "He's giving us a ride through Illinois. Everyone follows his instructions without questions or complaints. Got it?"

As Bart spoke, John glanced over at Isabel's face , which had the appearance of a violent somnambulist who has just been awakened from her wandering slumber and was eager for retribution. Walking to the rear of the trailer, he leaned into Rachel and whispered, "What's up with Isabel?"

Rachel answered, "Tell you later. But just take my advice. Don't piss her off."

Bart and John used their flashlights to maneuver the children around the furniture. All the way in the front lay a stack of dusty pads the color of a smoggy sky. A covered armoire loomed like an ogre on the left side. Each of the children chose a pad and, shaking the dust from it, plopped down and unzipped their backpacks. Bart exited the trailer long enough to park his car behind the truck, remove the license plate and registration, and give the key to Daniel.

"I'll take care of it for you when I come back through here. I'll see if I can sell it and I'll send you what I can get for it to this house church in Lynchburg, Virginia."

"Thanks for all this," said Bart.

"Let's just get through Illinois and I'll tell you if it was worth it or not," Daniel smirked, jokingly. John crawled into the cab of Daniel's truck and stretched out in the sleeper. Bart went back with Isabel, Rachel and the children. Daniel shut and locked the door and they were off.

The shifting of gears, the release of the air brakes and the rumble of the engine was almost soothing to the children. In the darkness they had no alternative but to sleep. Exhausted from their experiences over the past week, the children, Isabel, Bart and Rachel drifted off more easily than predicted by Daniel, though it was an ordeal at first trying to find comfortable positions amongst the furniture. Simon and Maggie fell asleep on Rachel's outstretched legs. She, herself, dozed off propped against a divan covered with a quilted, green pad.

Chapter 9

John and Daniel talked into the night. Daniel, as it turns out for all his isolation in the cab of his truck, was an animated conversationalist. He had been raised Church of God, Cleveland based, in South Georgia. His father, a tobacco farmer and self-taught biblical scholar, had raised him on an apocalyptic theology that focused on a literal interpretation of scripture—Revelation was his favorite. He had laid out for Daniel through the years his analysis of prophetic passages and his own brand of eschatological thinking that had both frightened and allured him into the faith. Daniel had always had an intuition for things of the Spirit since he was a small boy, though his mother's superstitious and purely experiential religion and his father's coldness toward him juxtaposed to his rigid religiosity had left a bitter taste in his mouth and for awhile after he had left home he had "run wild" for a number of years until he was able to find his own Jesus, a Jesus that was real to him. Though it was against all he had been taught, he had gotten the chip because, pragmatically speaking, being a truck driver was impossible without it, and he had long since thrown out the speculative thinking on God's prophetic word and stuck to what he knew about God through his own experiences. He did have misgivings, however. Often when he was driving alone listening to the news on his radio he would begin to feel like a foreigner in his own country and had even considered leaving a time or two. The idea of escape was never far from his mind, and he turned to it for comfort when life was difficult. His mother who was ninety-six kept him close to Atlanta for now, and when he was not hauling a load, he was with her at the assisted living center where she resided. He had been divorced and never remarried and had three daughters, two in Canada and one in California, who were married with families of their own.

Eventually they came to the first stop.

"Okay, this time you're lucky. Just east of the weigh station is a Stop-n-Go—first exit down there about two miles. I'll meet you in the parking lot there. I'll leave the back unlocked with the trailer facing the south field. Tell your gang to be sure nobody's watching when they get in. The place has great doughnuts, a real cop magnet, so we may have company. Think the young ones can keep up?"

"Yes, I think they can. Keep your passenger side unlocked, too and park next to something inconspicuous. I'll slip in after everyone is loaded," said John. "Let's do it." Sliding out the passenger door, he moved along the shoulder of the road; unlocking the back of the trailer he saw Thomas peering out from the crack in the door like an owl in a dark barn. Opening the door slightly John unloaded bodies one by one when there was a pause in the highway traffic. Rachel took the first group to the woods beside the road; the second group went with Isabel. Bart and John both helped Andrew, crutches and all, off the back, then shut and locked the door giving Daniel a signal with the flashlight that all was clear. The two men girded Andrew on either side and lifted him up and over the ravine and into the woods with the others.

"Okay, guys, we need to move quickly. Andrew, are you faster with the crutches or with the two of us on either side of you?" asked Bart.

"Let's try it with crutches. I'm doing pretty good with them now," answered Andrew shoving his crutches under his arms.

"That's fine, now let's move. Maggie and Simon, you hold onto Aunt Rachel," John added. "Andrew, watch out for pot holes and branches." They lumbered along through the woods at a fairly steady pace, fast enough to cover the ground but slow enough that the younger children could keep up. In the distance they saw the weigh station. John began to lead the entourage slightly to the south leaving some distance between them and the station. At one point just before they were parallel with the station's west parking lot they came to a chain link fence. Rachel and John went over first to help the children as Bart and Isabel boosted them over. Andrew had an arduous time maneuvering his wrapped leg over without the pressure and the awkward angles causing pain. Straddling the top of the fence he scraped the inside of his upper thigh on a protruding wire and on his descent down the other side ripped a wound into his skin about seven inches in length. He could feel the warm blood seeping from the wound, and it throbbed when he put his weight on it again. Bart saw him struggling, and, giving his crutches to Jesse and Thomas to carry, he and John braced Andrew around the waist and helped him the rest of the way.

The woods got increasingly dense until they could no longer see the glow of the highway lights or the weigh station at all. John halted to paw through his back pack for a compass. They had been walking south instead of east. Gauging his direction with the compass, John headed the group due east for about a half of a mile, then they marched back north. John thought it would be better if he could actually see the lights of the station. Conversation was minimal, even among the children. The inherent danger of the situation compounded with the pitch blackness of the woods and the crackling sticks beneath their feet forced up a fear in them that kept them silently forging forward. Simon, wide-eyed and alert, could sense the gravity of the situation. Occasionally whispering questions, he held tightly to Rachel's hand and trudged over the floor of the thick woods, lifting his stubby legs twice as often as everyone else.

John suddenly stopped, "I hear something," Everyone came to a standstill behind him. Stepping through a coarse thicket, John plowed directly into the rear of a building. He edged his way down the side so he could peer around it, and, much to his shock, he was standing immediately behind the restroom facilities of the weigh station. A muscular man in a security uniform not twenty feet from him was lighting a cigarette. Slowly John backed up in the direction he had come, vigilant not to step on dry sticks although the sounds of the trucks and people milling around the drink machines were loud enough to work in his favor. He ducked back into the woods, motioned to everyone to be absolutely quiet, and began to lead them south toward the heart of the forest. Rachel, sensing the seriousness in John's demeanor cupped her hand over Simon's mouth until they were about half a mile into the brush.

"Whew, that was close," said John exhaling a long breath. "Let's go another mile east before we head back north again." The entourage kept advancing, crossing another fence with Andrew hobbling up and lumbering over. Eventually they saw the green sign in the distance that read: Stop-n-Go. Walking toward the lights they came to a clearing and began moving faster, taking cues from Bart and John on direction and pace. They could see Daniel's truck on the west side of the building with the back of the trailer grazing the field. Rachel and Isabel hurried along and glancing around to make certain they were not being watched loaded the children onto the trailer. Rachel noticed that Andrew's pant leg was stained with blood as she hoisted him up.

"We'll take a look at that when we get going, Honey," she whispered to Andrew. "I've got the first aid kit in my pack. Don't worry. You did great." After everyone was aboard, John locked the trailer and walked slyly around to the passenger side, running straight into an officer with a cup of coffee and a doughnut.

"This your rig?" the officer asked John.

Thinking fast John responded, "No, it's my buddy's rig. I came down to see him off. Live right over there," he said pointing over the hill.

"What were you doing out there in the field, then?" the officer asked sipping his coffee.

John coughed, pondering his response, "Well, sir, to be honest," he leaned into the officer's ear, "I've had diarrhea all day and the restroom was kinda full. Sort of embarrassing, but when you gotta go, you gotta go. I just grabbed some tissues and headed for the field." He conjured his most sincere expression hoping the story was convincing enough.

"Well, I know how that is," the officer said, at last. "You take care." Then he walked off toward his car and drove away. Daniel emerged from the Stop-n-Go a few minutes later with a box of doughnuts and a thermos of coffee.

"You made it. I was hoping something didn't happen. Been talking to another trucker in there from Vegas. Dullest man I've ever met. I was about to run out of topics—you know, there's only so much you can say about Vegas," Daniel grinned.

"I nearly got caught just now so stand guard while I get in the rig. Make sure the coast is clear," John said, his eyes darting back and forth across the parking lot.

The next weigh station was two hours away. John got some sleep in the berth while the others dozed off again in the trailer. The wound on Andrew's leg, as Rachel discovered, was long but deep only in one place. Rachel applied some butterfly bandages to the deepest cut and disinfected the rest, wrapping it in white gauze. The next stop was easier. No woods lined the highway, but only an open field with some bushes tall enough to crouch down behind if they needed cover. Because there were no convenience stores or gas stations close to the weigh in area, Daniel just pulled over about a mile past the station, pretended to be checking his tires, and the entourage scrambled into the trailer one at a time when no cars were in sight.

The children were more fatigued on the second trek than they were on the first, complaining when they had to wake up and walk again. Jesse moaned annoyingly the entire walk to Daniel's trailer, and Simon never did wake up, which made the journey more difficult for John who ended up carrying him the entire hike. Maggie could hardly keep up. Though she did not complain, she walked as if she were emerging from the grave, her steps erratic and directionless. Rachel had to guide her back in line with the others several times, grinning all the way as she watched her niece weave deliriously in and out of the company.

Ninety miles down Interstate 64, they came within a mile of the next weigh station. Just as Daniel had pulled over on the shoulder of the road and was ready to hop out, he saw the red flashing lights of a police car in the side mirror.

"Stay put, John," cautioned Daniel. "We've got company. Might wanna tell the others." Daniel jumped down from his cab and shut the door. John radioed Rachel in the trailer and told her what was happening.

"This is serious, Rach. Keep everyone absolutely silent." A paunchy man in a navy blue uniform strode toward the cab, taser gun in hand and a wad of chewing gum in his jaws.

"Hello officer, what's the problem?" Daniel asked as the man approached him.

"You having problems with your truck?"

"Actually, yeah, I kept feeling like it's riding a little low on the left front side."

The officer studied Daniel's eyes, "We've been following you Mr. . . . ?"

"Barnes. Daniel Barnes."

"Yes, we've been following you Mr. Barnes for awhile now. You pulled over before the last weigh station, too, then again after you weighed in. That tire must really be giving you trouble." Daniel could not tell if the man was being suspicious or sympathetic.

Daniel shifted, and then said, coolly, "I thought it might weigh funny if something was wrong. Then I checked again afterwards because I knew it was several miles to the next truck stop. Didn't want to get stranded with a flat too far from a truck stop." Inside Daniel was petrified. A trucker carrying passengers in a trailer, some of which were children, all without a chip, would certainly result in a minimum 2-year sentence in a county prison. However, Daniel who was used to dealing with these types of law enforcement people, gave a stellar performance, and said, in a calmly solicitous tone, "Maybe you could help me. Wanna see what you think about these front tires?"

The officer followed him over to the cab. "Yep, it might be a bit low—not enough to throw you off, though. May be the alignment." He paused running his hand over the rough grooves of the tire, "Care if I look inside the cab, just to be safe, you know?"

Daniel nodded holding his breath. The officer opened the cab door, shining his flashlight around the interior. John remained still, even trying not to breathe. He had pulled the curtain of the sleeper together and zipped it shut, remaining toward the back in the shadows. Suddenly John's radio blared, "John, John, you still there? How's it going? John, do you read?" John's heart raced. Stealthily he ran his thumb down the volume switch of the radio, turning it off. The officer listened for a moment, then shut the door and stepped down.

"Can I see your hand, sir?" he asked Daniel pulling out a portable reader. The policeman scanned the back of Daniel's hand, then read the screen. "You say your name's Daniel—that's what it says here. Is that what people call you?"

"Yeah, most people anyway."

"Well, someone, a woman, was trying to reach you on a radio in your truck. Kept saying 'John.'"

"Oh," said Daniel, "that's my ex-wife. Never liked the name Daniel. Always insisted on calling me John. Drove me crazy. Guess you never stop paying alimony, even when you're way outta the picture, do you?"

Whatever Daniel had said seemed to resonate with the officer who responded, "Got that right. I'll follow you to the weigh station. My mechanic friend there will take a look at your tires." The policeman walked back to his car and waited for Daniel to pull out. Speaking quickly to John, he said, "You're not gonna believe this one, but we're not stopping. Tell your wife and the others to cover themselves with those furniture pads and let's all pray that we can pull this off. Tell them to sit real still—this might take awhile." John radioed Rachel who, along with Bart and Isabel began to work quickly covering the children. Thankfully, all of them except for Andrew were fast asleep. They then draped a longer pad over themselves hoping that they would appear to be something long and narrow like a coffee table or a sofa, instead of human beings. The trailer came to a halt. They waited.

They could hear people talking just outside. A man's voice said, "You do the trailer, I'll do the cab this time." They heard a rattling and the trailer door flung open. Two long, narrow beams from flashlights skimmed the contents.

Peeking under one pad another man's voice said, "Yeah, it's furniture—packed tight, too. Might be causing the problem." They began walking back, touching all the covered pieces, searching under others. Beneath the pad, Isabel, Bart and Rachel were praying, their lips moving without emitting a sound. They could sense the light sweeping over them. "Looks like smaller pieces back there and a few loose pads." Then they heard nothing for several seconds. Maria shifted her leg and yawned, but luckily the light was in the opposite corner and the engine noise drowned out her muffled sound.

Finally a voice said, "I can't get back here without moving some of this stuff around. Looks okay to me anyway. It's late and I'm gettin' cold. Let's go in now." Bart and Rachel smiled and gave each other a smooth high five. They had thought of the idea of moving the furniture to create an obstacle just after John had called her on the radio. In the cab a man was searching the seats. John was pretending to be asleep in the berth. The man parted the curtain and showed his light around the sleeping quarters.

"Oh, excuse me," he said softly. John did not move. Jumping down from the cab, the man walked up to Daniel who was standing near the scales. "Who you got in the bed?"

"Oh, that's my partner. Been awake for two straight nights. He's grumpy as hell when he's trying to sleep so I just left him. Between this last shift and finishing his judo program last week, he's plum wore out," Daniel said without so much as a blush.

"Well, I think it would be best not to bother him then," the man said. "Oh, and we filled up that front tire some. It was riding a little low."

"Thanks a bunch," said Daniel, hurrying to get back in the truck. They were about three miles down the road before Daniel burst into nervous laughter. "Whew! Everything cool back there?"

John chuckled, "Yes, how about you?"

"Well, I gotta say that was the closest I've come to something scary in awhile. How are the troops? The officer didn't hang me up by my ears or anything so I assume all is well."

John got on the radio, "Rachel?"

"Man, John, that was frightening. We're all okay. The kids slept through most of it, thank God. We blocked the way to the front of the trailer with some end tables and a desk. Worked like a charm," Rachel said with relief.

"Babe, you were incredible. You guys get some sleep now if you can. I feel like we've been protected here. My heart is racing, but I'm gonna try to sleep, too."

Daniel drove into the auburn sunrise and across the Kentucky state line. He found an out-of-the-way motel near a truck stop, left a note for John on the seat and checked in to sleep for a while.

Chapter 10

Riding into the eastern sky early in the morning watching the sun peeking over the plain was the best part. Tim loved the scarlet peach hue just before the first sliver of the sun pushed up from the ground of the horizon. Hannah and Tim were getting used to the pace and building endurance. Though they were sore for the first few days and struggled to adjust to sleeping outdoors or wherever they could find inexpensive lodging, they were now beginning to feel at home on a bicycle and out in the elements. Sometimes it would rain, prickling the skin on their faces with frigid needles and chilling them to the bone. Yet they would always end those days by a warm fire in a family campground, and the taste of hot coffee brewed over the open flames burned off any chill the windy weather could dish up.

Tim had decided to pull Simon's cart behind his bike for two reasons. First, it provided a means to carry the tent, sleeping bags and food they needed for the journey. Secondly, the authorities tended to look less critically at a "family" out for an afternoon bike ride, and from a distance it appeared as if Tim were pulling a small child. For the first several days they were never pulled over or questioned.

They stayed the night at a couple of the house churches on the way, and the families there told them about Rachel and John— when they had stayed with them, how the children were faring, what they had planned to do next. The news and stories of their children were reassuring to both of them. Hannah spent many nights crying, desperately missing the children, praying for their safety. When they arrived at the Covas' house, they found an envelope taped to the front door that said: "Tim and Hannah

James." Opening it, they found a note that said, "Under the frog on the back porch." Circling the house, they discovered a quaint, screened-in porch with potted plants that needed watering and several wooden statues of saints. Saint Francis of Assisi stood slightly slumped by a birdbath in a circular landscaped garden in the center of the back yard. He held a wooden sparrow and appeared peacefully somber. By the backdoor was a porcelain green speckled frog. Hannah picked it up. Taped to his belly was a key. Hannah fitted the key into the lock on the backdoor, and Hannah and Tim entered the house cautiously calling out, "Is anyone home?" and glancing around the festive rooms. When they came to the kitchen table there was a note from the Covas' explaining what had transpired and a manila envelope that said, "Mommy and Daddy" on the front in Maggie's handwriting. Hannah held the envelope, gliding her fingers over the writing. She opened it. Inside were three cards, one from each of her children telling their parents how much they loved and missed them. Simon's card had a picture of three odd looking people, two tall ones and one short one. They had no bodies, but they all had unusually large eyes, mouths and chins. Simon had written his name in enormous red letters at the top. The "S" was backwards, and Rachel began to weep.

"I'm ready to find them, Tim. I can't take many more days without them."

"I know," said Tim reading Thomas' letter and wiping his eyes. "I'm missing them more everyday. I keep seeing their faces in my head. You know, we'll catch up with them soon. I know it. We'll find a faster way, I promise."

The note from the Covas' had welcomed Tim and Hannah to stay in their house, to use their kitchen, and to get a good night's sleep. Hannah savored the feeling in the Covas' house. A positive, holy reverence permeated every corner, in the furnishings, in the dog-eared books on the shelves—it reminded her of the Cloisters in New York. She wanted to sit among the collection of antique crosses, light some candles, and meditate on the Word of God in the Bible that lay open on an oak lectern. Neither Tim nor Hannah realized how exhausted they were. Hannah put on some Oriental meditative music, lit a stick of incense, and brewed a pot of herbal tea. She found some dry pasta and made an Italian dish she remembered from home. Tim read aloud from the scriptures after they had eaten and also from the evening vespers. The presence of peace in the house was palpable and began to sooth the rough and damaged parts of their psyches. They slept that night more soundly than they had in weeks and awoke the next morning with a fresh hope.

"Everything's gonna be alright," Tim said waking with the sun coming through the bedroom window. He scooped his arm around Hannah.

"I know. I feel like it will be," Hannah sighed.

The temperature began to drop as they traveled through Missouri. Tim and Hannah had to add layers of clothing to barricade their bodies against the brisk wind. A couple of days they had the good fortune of a strong tail wind that made the pedaling effortless and pushed them along at a lively clip. But other days the winds were against them and they pumped their weary legs until fatigue won out and they were forced to bed down for the night.

On one such night Tim was unable to locate a family campground anywhere in the vicinity. He searched his notes and maps, but there was nothing for miles. The hour was getting late, and all of the hotels were full for the night because of a Quarter Horse Convention. Hannah's legs were nearly giving out with each step. "Tim, I'm not sure I can walk much farther," she said. "Let's just crash somewhere, please."

Tim studied the map. "Well, there is a public park at the edge of town. It has camper and RV hook-ups. How bad can it be in a town this size? Let's at least check it out." Hannah gave him a leering look. They located the park without difficulty. Full of old black walnuts, pin oaks, and sugar maples, the park seemed quiet enough. A few people were walking the trail, but no one appeared suspicious. Four campers were parked for the night in the upper section and two women were setting up a tent.

"Let's stake up here in this wooded area so we can have some privacy from the other campers," said Tim. He unloaded the tent and staked it down quickly. Hannah threw the sleeping bags and pillows inside, locked the bikes to a tree, and stumbled into bed mumbling something about stray dogs.

At about forty-five minutes past two, Hannah awoke with a full bladder and a dry mouth. She sat up and felt around for her water bottle. Finding it she took several gulps, then, emerged from the tent rubbing her eyes and looking for a secluded place to relieve herself. She squatted behind a white birch, smoothing her hair away from her face.

She heard a sound. Listening closely and quickly pulling up her sweats, she heard it again. It sounded like a wounded animal. Under the yellow overhead lights she weaved in and out of the trees toward the sounds. She surmised that a dog or cat had been injured in a fight, and she was a sucker for defenseless animals. The sounds grew more pronounced. Crouching behind a thick oak, Hannah gingerly peered around. The light from the full moon shone down on a clearing. What Hannah saw made her gasp. Two men and a woman entirely naked were writhing and moaning on the grass. The woman was bent over with her face in the groin of the taller man who had a wad of her matted hair in his fist. The other man, the shorter one, stood behind her, grinding his thick pelvis into her. The bodies were covered with grime from the earth, mud running down legs, arms, elbows, feet, torsos, smudges of mud on their faces. No one made eye contact with each other. The taller man clutching the woman's hair kept chanting, "Yeah, bitch. C'mon, bitch. Do it bitch." Finally, the man behind her reached into a tree and broke off a pliable branch about two feet in length which he began to use on the woman's buttocks, striking hard until her skin began to bleed. He smiled deviously with satisfaction at the sight of the blood and moved himself animalistic-like into her mercilessly, striking her repeatedly with the switch in his hand until he gave a final brutish groan. He pulled away from the woman without a word, walked back to a pile of clothes on the ground and dressed himself. The woman, feeling the welts on her back side finally stood up abruptly much to the disappointment of the taller man. "Hey, bitch!" he said. "You finish this shit right now."

"No, I can't do it, damnit. I'm bleeding," she said wiping her face with the back of her bony hand. For the first time since Hannah had been watching, the taller man looked directly into the woman's eyes. He was red with rage, and he drew back his coarse hand and slapped the woman's face. "Dumb bitch!" he said and walked over behind a tree to finish the job himself.

The woman just stood there alone, naked in the moonlight. The blood from her backside mixed with the mud trickled down her thighs. She shivered. For a moment she turned and stared in the direction of the tree where Hannah was standing. Mascara had run under her eyes. Her hair was colorless. But when the light from the moon hit her face, Hannah could see that this worn creature was no more than fourteen years old. This young girl took a deep breath, closing her eyes. Then she found a pair of ripped jeans and a black sweater in the wet grass and clumsily got dressed. She pulled on a tattered pair of cowboy boots, and found a pack of cigarettes in her back pocket. She lit one, sucking in the gray smoke and blowing it into the biting air. Stealthily, she disappeared into the bushes.

Hannah had been frozen, unable to move. Finally, she turned around with her back against the tree. Her whole body trembled uncontrollably. Trying to breathe, just breathe, she bent over with her hands on her knees and vomited on the ground. Wiping her mouth, she tore back through the woods to the tent. "Get up!" she commanded Tim.

"What? What is it??"

"We've gotta go. We gotta get out of here." She gulped down the rest of the water in her bottle and recklessly rolled her sleeping bag, throwing it into the cart. Tim knew his wife well enough to realize that something horrifying had happened and that this was not the time to discuss it.

He only asked, "Are you hurt? Did anybody touch you?"

"No," she said. "Please, let's go." They loaded the bikes and rode through the dark streets of town and down a back road. Neither of them spoke a word. Hannah could not quiet her mind—she wanted a bath, but knew it was out of the question. Finally they came upon an abandoned Presbyterian Church. Most of the windows had been boarded up and there was a laminated sign on the door that said: "Closed Until Further Notice." They left their bikes in the lawn. Tim followed Hannah as she walked around and around the church. Eventually, she stopped in front of a rectangular stained glass window. The prismatic panes separated by black rims formed the image of a hand reaching down from the sky to a man and a woman in a variegated garden. Hannah took out her flashlight so she could see it better. She ran her fingers over the transparent couple. Then she noticed that there was a hole in the glass about the size of a fist in the lower corner of the pane. Reaching in cautiously, she found a metal latch against the frame and shifted it up. Slowly she pushed open the right window panel.

Tim who had been standing quietly behind her spoke, "What are you doing Hannah? This is private property. We're trespassing here. Why don't we find another place?"

Hannah said simply, "No, this is the place," and she pushed the other side of the window open, threw her leg up on the ledge and crawled in. Tim, not knowing quite what to think, followed her with the sleeping bags in tow. They found themselves standing at the front of the sanctuary by a long maple altar rail. Walking slowly down the center aisle toward the back, they were startled to find there were people lying in the pews, some asleep, and some who scrutinized them warily in silence as they passed. There were two small pup tents behind the last row of pews, and in the narthex four more tents stood still as statues. Hannah found a place in the hall near a door marked "Pastor's Study." She rolled out her sleeping bag. Tim followed suit, shaking his head and looking around. As they lay in the darkness among strangers, Hannah pulled him in so close to her he almost felt smothered. In seconds she was breathing deeply, and Tim knew she had fallen asleep.

Tim awoke with a prickly pain in his arm, staring at blue and yellow blotches on a wall. He couldn't remember where he was. He turned over to see Hannah sitting up smiling. The morning light shining through the tall stained glass windows splashed a rainbow on the wall that in contrast to the tempestuous night they had experienced made him feel like Noah after the flood. All around them people were folding blankets, taking down tents, drinking canned juice and packing up clothes. No one spoke. Tim felt as if he had gone stone deaf in the night as he watched these people go about this silent routine. He whispered to Hannah, "Good morning. Why is nobody talking?"

She whispered back, "I don't know. It's been this way since I got up. It's fascinating." She stood up and tiptoed into the sanctuary. The scene was much the same—people folding blankets, packing belongings, except when they finished, one by one each person made his way to the front of the church, knelt at the altar for a few minutes, then slipped quietly out the open window. The hush was almost deafening and absolutely awe-inspiring. Some of the people would go to the altar and raise both hands as they prayed. Others would bow their heads and make the sign of the cross on their chests. One man lay prostrate in front of the baptistery. Hannah was bursting with curiosity. She touched the shoulder of an older man in a navy parka who was about to leave and asked, "Why are they so quiet?"

"They're always quiet," he answered softly.

"What do you mean, 'always?' Do you come here often?"

"Not just here," the man said, "Everywhere."

"Everywhere?" Hannah was enthralled.

"Yes. We're all travelers who have discovered . . ." He trailed off.

"Discovered what?"

"Well, sometimes they're locked up too tight or the signs out front let you know you're not welcome. But if you can find one with a broken lock or an open window, well, honey, it's the weary man's best kept secret."

"Are all these people . . . believers?"

"Some of them are. Some of them are simply tired. Others just know this is a safe place to be." With that he pushed open the window and threw out his backpack. Straddling the ledge he turned back to Hannah and said, "You take care, Darlin'. Winter's coming. It could get rough out there. Now that you've been here, I mean, now that you know, I may even see you again." The man jumped down and walked off across the dewy lawn whistling.

Chapter 11

At John's request Daniel dropped the stowaways at a dilapidated YMCA in a town called Ridgewood. They had not made a habit of staying in hotels first of all, because most of the major chains required a chip for check-in, and secondly, because they had so many in their group that even one night in an inexpensive place would deplete them of their precious cash reserve. However, this YMCA was one of the few across the country that remained open and offered inexpensive room and board to travelers and discounts to members.

John handed Daniel a box. "What's this?" asked Daniel.

"Nothing much, but I wanted to give you something. You risked your livelihood for us these past two days. It's the best I could do and something I brought from home."

Daniel opened the box. Inside was the entire New Testament on CD. His eyes welled up with tears. "Thanks, man," he said hugging John's neck. "God bless you guys, all of you." Shaking hands with Isabel, he said, "Don't let anyone give you any guff, girl." He winked at her as if he had known about the incident at the truck stop all along. Daniel picked up Simon. "You are a trooper," he said. "Never seen a little guy get through a woods so fast. You must have super powers." Simon showed Daniel his muscles and giggled. Daniel handed John his card. "If you ever pass this way again, look me up, brother."

"You got it," said John.

The middle-aged woman behind the welcome counter at the YMCA had a thick southern accent. "May I help you?"

"Yes, how much for three rooms for the night?" John asked.

74

"Are you a member?" she asked, punching in numbers on her computer.

Bart stepped in, "Yes, I used to be before they shut down in Missouri. Does that count? I still have the card."

For the first time, the woman looked up at the ragged, grungy group of people standing in front of her. They appeared as if they had been rolling in dust for about a week. Simon, who had smudges of dirt on both cheeks, cupped his hand to Rachel's ear and said in a voice that the woman could hear, "Aunt Ray, I'm hungry."

The woman's eyes darted back and forth around the adjoining offices and lobby. Then leaning into Bart and John she said, "I'll tell you what. We've only got three rooms booked for the night so I'm gonna cut you a little deal. I'll give you the rooms for fifteen Euros each. Plus, there was a business party in earlier that had a pizza party, and they way over-estimated on the number of pizzas. Our custodian just put six untouched pizzas in the freezer. You interested?"

John had never been more excited about the prospect of pizza. "Yes, we are. And, thank you."

"It's nothing really. Maybe everyone else here forgot what that 'C' stands for, but I haven't," the woman said in a whisper. The children were jumping up and down excitedly. "You kids," said the woman raising the timbre of her voice, "We've got a gym and some basketballs if you'd like to play awhile." The six children screamed so loudly that Isabel began to laugh.

"We won't bother the other guests, will we, Ma'am," John asked tentatively.

"No, I don't think so. We don't have any more classes scheduled for tonight and the overnight guests are not the type to be very bothered, I don't think. You'll see them in the cafeteria."

The rooms were tiny and clinically white, no décor, no color, and the wood floors were also white washed and appeared slick. Yet it was clean, and everyone was given a towel and samples of soap, shampoo and toothpaste. John and Rachel took Simon and

Maggie; the three boys shared the adjoining room, and Bart, Isabel and Maria took the room down the hall. They all showered and put on clean clothes. Rachel made good use of the washer and dryer at the end of the hall. It was an altogether different group, smelling like lavender soap and toothpaste, which entered the cafeteria. The custodian had already heated up the pizzas and put out napkins and paper plates. John handed each child a couple of Euros for the drink machine, and the children, chatting noisily, ripped into the pizza boxes like ravenous wolves.

At one table sat a man who seemed to be in his late forties or early fifties. He wore a pair of faded, ripped jeans and a pale green t-shirt with the image of a pine tree on the front. His shoulder-length hair was greasy, the color of wet straw and he had a three day beard and wire-rimmed glasses. Andrew nudged Jesse, "Look, it's John Lennon's lost twin." Jesse snickered.

At another table, four young people most likely in their late twenties were engaging in a focused discussion. The only male in the group, African American and exceedingly animated, was gesturing with both hands as he spoke. Beside him sat an African American woman with long beaded braids and no make-up though her natural beauty was stunning and unique. She nodded periodically at the man and interjected comments as she was able, the man being so effusive the task was nearly impossible. The other two women were blonde, which was their only similarity. One woman was dressed in loose fitting, dark slacks and a leather jacket, full-figured, with a very manly round face and green eyes; the other woman was petite and frail, though strikingly attractive. She wore a long floral skirt, cream –colored Mary Janes, and a pale pink sweater with a string of simple pearls. They were finishing off the last of a cheese pizza and listening intently to the man as he spoke. Every now and then, John overhead a word or a phrase: "Inalienable rights of all people," "republic versus democracy," "evangelicals," "inherency of scripture." These phrases piqued John's curiosity, and he turned his ear in an attempt to pick up more of the conversation.

All of the children, except for Maggie and Andrew, raced into the gymnasium when they had finished eating and began bouncing balls and shooting baskets. Andrew, who was gaining mobility everyday with his injured ankle, was playing an old pinball game in the corner of the cafeteria. Maggie wandered around the tables staring at the other guests, her fingers laced behind her back.

"That's a redwood, you know—tallest tree in the world," she said confidently. The man with the straw-like hair and wire-rimmed glasses turned around to see Maggie, pointing at the image on his t-shirt.

"Oh yeah, how do you know?" he asked.

"You can just tell by the shape, although it could be a Giant Sequoia. I'd have to see the needles. Sequoias are even scarcer. Redwoods are protected by law. Good thing, too because the California Gold Rush about killed them all!"

The man was so visibly amused by this miniature conifer expert, he said, "Are you an environmentalist, too?"

"Yes, I'd say that I am, for sure," answered Maggie.

"Well, nice to meet you, then," he said extending his hand. "My name's Micah Shaw. And you are..."

"Maggie James," she said shaking his hand firmly. "Are you staying here all night, too?"

"Yes, it looks that way. How about you?"

"We're all staying here," she said pointing to the children in the gym and to Rachel who was keeping a close eye on her. "We're going to Virginia," she whispered to him, "but I can't say why, so too bad about that."

"Did you drive here?" he asked glancing over at John and Rachel.

"Well, sort of. Somebody drove us in a truck 'cause none of us have chips."

"I don't have one either. I like it better that way," the man smiled at her.

"We do, too," Maggie responded.

Rachel, sensing the conversation had gone on long enough, approached the table where the man sat and took Maggie by the hand. "Maggie," Rachel said, "this man may want some peace and quiet." Then she addressed Micah, "I hope she isn't bothering you, sir. She always enjoys a good conversation."

Micah answered, "No, on the contrary. She's very interesting and quite a little environmentalist. I'm impressed by her knowledge of trees."

"Well, I'm afraid she gets that honestly. Her parents are environmentalists, too. We all are, actually. Kinda feel a responsibility to protect all the amazing living things these days, especially trees," Rachel said.

"She tells me you aren't chippers. I don't meet many of our kind anymore." He extended his hand, "My name is Micah Shaw, fellow non-chipper."

"I'm Rachel Beckett; that's my husband John and our friends the Covas. Not many places to stay these days without a chip."

"I know," Micah agreed. "I've had to get good at camping when I travel."

"You travel a lot?" Rachel asked noticing that the antique book he was reading was one of her favorite novels by Joseph Conrad.

"I used to before I quit my job. I'm was a screen writer from Anaheim, California."

"Wow! Why, may I ask did you quit that job?"

Micah chuckled and said, "Bureaucracy. After awhile I just got tired of compromise, you know."

"Yes, I know," Rachel responded shaking her head.

Micah continued, "I'd write about what impassioned me, what moved me, and without fail it always ended up watered down once it was computed through all the opinions of focus groups and government agencies. Finally, I just said, 'To hell with it!'"

Rachel thought for a moment, then said, "To be honest, I don't think there's anything in the world worse than having the things you are most passionate about compromised." This man was interesting—he was an intellectual, that was obvious, but there was something else. She wanted to know more, more about what made him tick. "Can I ask you a question?" she said reluctantly.

"Sure," Micah answered.

"Are you . . . a believer?"

"In what?"

"In God. I mean are you a follower of Jesus?"

Grinning Micah answered, "I'm a follower of no one. That's why I became so unpopular in Hollywood. I did grow up in church, Sunday school, the whole bit, but once I got old enough to see through the facade of it all, I left the illusion behind. I'm a believer in unadulterated humanity, that is, I was before it was contaminated by materialism, big business, and corrupted government. I believe there are still places in the world where that kind of humanity exists. It's just not here in the good ol' U. S. of A. So are you Christians?"

"We prefer to be called believers nowadays, but yes, we are, and ironically, we're frustrated with the 'good ol' U.S. of A.' for some of the same reasons that you are. So why don't you have a chip if not for religious reasons?"

"Simple. It's controlling. We're always talking about our nation's freedoms and our civil liberties. Well, where's the freedom in being tracked everywhere you go? Where's the freedom in everyone knowing everything about you all the time? They make you think you have a choice when it comes to the chip. Yet you can't work, stay in a hotel, drive a car. Where's the 'choice' in that? Does that make you or me feel a sense of security?"

"No, not really."

"So . . . Virginia, huh?" Rachel glared at Maggie who shrugged her shoulders and threw her aunt a guilty smile. "You aren't deserters, are you?"

"What?" Rachel asked.

"You know, draft dodgers.... emigrants."

"I'm not sure how to answer that," Rachel said cautiously.

"Well, I am. Like to see them try to stop me, too. They certainly are not going to rob me of my choice to leave."

"I definitely appreciate your courage. It seems like most people would rather stick with the status quo, even when it comes to their most cherished beliefs than to alter their lifestyles."

"And I respect you, too, especially, you know, traveling with all these children," Micah winked. "So what are your ideas on getting to Virginia?"

"We haven't exactly worked all that out, yet," Rachel said.

"Well, when you're ready to discuss it, I came across a great idea recently. I've been looking into it—seems solid. Well," he said standing, "it was a pleasure to meet you, Rachel. And you, too, Maggie. Oh, I almost forgot," he said reaching in his pocket and pulling out something he had clinched in his fist. In Maggie's hand he placed a large, brown seed.

"Ohio buckeye," said Maggie turning it over and over, ". . . or horse chestnut, depends on what you want to call it."

"Wow, you ARE good. Found it yesterday," said Micah. "See you all later."

Chapter 12

Upon her return to the table, Rachel noticed Bart and John in a heavy discussion with the four people at the next table. Approaching John, Rachel was introduced to the African American man, Samuel Bradley and his sister, Deborah. The two other young women were friends, Sarah Tucker and Miriam Cook. All four were former students of Bob Jones University which had been closed down, along with most other religious universities which refused to convert to state institutions and thus were stripped of their accreditation. The studies of each of these young people had been truncated. Samuel who had been studying history and had planned to pursue a degree in law was ousted when he was nearly concluding his studies and had since become extremely disillusioned by the entire system, abandoning his idealistic notions about making a difference in the world. The other women were in the same boat. Deborah, two years Samuel's junior, had been studying medicine; Sarah, the woman in the leather jacket, was working towards a BA in Christian Ministry hoping to get a Masters of Divinity and serve as a missionary in India. Miriam had opted for a double major in Theology and English. Her dreams of being a professor on the university level subverted, she had been working on a novel ever since the university's door had been forced to close.

Though their doctrines and philosophies were extremely right wing as John had surmised (and certainly inconsistent with Bart's ideologies), there was something about their passion for the Truth and their unabashed resoluteness when it came to the things they believed in. In the current climate of compromise and lethargy, it was for John, to say the least, refreshing.

"So, here's the burning question," John proposed in a sarcastic tone. "What were two intelligent, African American young people from Detroit doing at a university which until the early seventies would not admit black students, and even then, because of their strict interracial dating policies, only married black students?"

Samuel, evidently accustomed to answering that question, responded, "We come from an Independent, Fundamentalist Baptist church back home, and we both sought after a university which would reflect our strong beliefs in the 'fundamentals' of our faith. The decisions that institution made in the past were of no consequence to us when we applied, and I am certain that they believed they had been adhering to biblical principles by admitting whites only years ago, but all that was repealed when they fully understood the truth, and I've got to hand it to them for their willingness to admit error on that issue. I hold no more against that university for their past decisions than I hold against you because your great-great-granddaddy owned my great-great-granddaddy."

"You are a long way from Detroit. What are you doing in Kentucky?" asked Bart.

"We've all been doing much soul-searching. We took a trip to Denver where we met with some other Baptist brothers and sisters to discuss what we could do as a group to effect change. But there is so much division these days in our denomination, so much fragmentation that we couldn't reach any conclusions for all the arguing over doctrine. And our numbers are rapidly decreasing. So many of our families and friends have been arrested for everything from picketing abortion clinics to passing out flyers to marching around public schools in protest of the dissemination of pornographic material to students. We Baptists have never been good a keeping our mouths shut," Samuel joked.

Deborah said, "I think about seventy-five percent of the people in those rehabilitation centers are Independent, Fundamental Baptists who won't quit talking."

"Have you heard much about those places? What goes on in there?" asked John.

Sarah spoke up, "Truthfully, I've heard they are fairly humane, at least from the standpoint of physical abuse. Of course there is an occasional Gestapo every now and then who thinks he knows everything and wants to throw his weight around. But all in all I think they just want to wear people down, keep them from their kids and families, interrupt their lives so long they'll do anything to get released. It's not much different from prison—separate a person from his life, his family and his free will long enough, he'll be putty in your hands eventually."

"What will you do now?" asked John.

Miriam replied, "We don't know. It's so hard when you feel that you've been called by God into an area of service and then told that you can't follow through with it by a country which touts itself as being 'the land of the free and the home of the brave.'"

Sarah added, "I think all of us are about all 'braved' out."

"You ever thought about leaving here, John Becket?" asked Samuel.

John was taken back by the question, "What?" he asked buying some time to think of a competent answer.

"Do you remember when Jesus was sending out the disciples in Luke 9. He was giving them authority to cast out demons and cure diseases. He told them to stay in the houses they enter until it was time to leave that town. Then he says something interesting. He says, 'And whosoever will not receive you, when ye go out of that city, shake off the very dust from your feet for a testimony against them.' I guess what I'm asking is, 'What if an entire nation no longer welcomes you?'"

Bart, Isabel, John and Rachel all looked at one another knowingly. Leaning into Samuel and the students, John said, "You want in on a secret?"

They continued with their discussion which involved an extrapolation from Samuel blaming the breakdown of society on Christians who refused to adhere to the strict moral and doctrinal codes of the Bible, on Catholics whose papal hierarchy and abstinence requirements invited power abuses, sexual misconduct, and sins of pride; Samuel blaming Pentecostals for their unbiblical experiential religion and prosperity theology which inevitably led to several highly publicized media scandals; and Samuel blaming the Jewish people for taking Christ out of everything from Christmas to Easter. Around ten o'clock Rachel and Isabel decided they had had enough fun for one evening and took the sweaty children to their rooms for more showers. They tucked each one in, then folded the clothes from the dryer and crawled into bed themselves.

"So how are you traveling from here?" asked Samuel.

"We're not sure yet. We're going to pray about it tonight. God will provide a way for us," John answered gulping some stale coffee.

"And you are a Catholic priest?" Samuel asked Bart.

"Yes, I am," Bart responded in a matter-of-fact tone.

"And you don't mind praying together with him?" said Samuel directing the question to John.

John answered, "Bart is my brother in Christ. We pray to the same Jesus. We ask for direction from the same Holy Spirit. Our execution and forms may look different, but our 'fundamentals' are one and the same."

"And when he prays to Mary...?"

"I've never heard him pray to Mary. But if he wants to recite the rosary in my presence, and it is an integral part of who he is becoming in Christ then he may do so without my judgment," said John.

Samuel shook his head, "How do you call yourself a Christian? It seems to me there's nothing set apart about you at all. You have no lines. Looks like all your tolerance has made for a lukewarm Christianity."

John took a deep breath, "When the apostle Paul says that our unity is paramount, that we who believe in Jesus are all parts of the body Christ and must work together as a body, doesn't that shake you at all?"

"Yes, I'm just not sure Mr. Covas here is in the same 'body' as I am. Therefore, I'm not sure all Paul's talk about unity applies in certain situations."

"So you're saying that if we all look and act like you, if we were all African American Yankees who attended fundamentalist universities and refused to listen to worldly music or to watch any movie that is not rated G we could be part of your 'body of believers.'"

"Not quite. I think you're being facetious."

"Yes, I am. Because no matter how much I monitor my rock and roll intake or my movie ratings, it won't in the end, change my heart. Only God can read that part of me. I'm afraid, Mr. Bradley, that although our nation has abandoned its spiritual roots which has obviously taken a toll on all of our lives, part of the reason we bear these crosses which you failed to mention earlier is because of people like you who think so narrowly that they leave out the number one thing Jesus called us to be: lovers. You have excluded people based on standards that are so unlike the thinking and example of Jesus they are ridiculous. People like you are not of the world, I think you've established that, but they are not in it either. If each person is made in God's image, we've got to be able to see the 'God' in everyone, without exception."

"That's new age blasphemy!" screamed Samuel scooting back from the table and standing abruptly.

"I'm sorry you feel that way." John said standing. "I have moral lines, too. So does Bart, which is why our families are leaving the country. But when it's all said and done, I guess I'd rather err in the direction of loving people first and keeping every letter of someone's narrow interpretation of the law second."

John offered his hand as a truce to Samuel and to the women who seemed to desire a good night's sleep more than to participate in Samuel's polemics. "God be with you on your journeys."

Bart, shaking their hands added, "Blessing to you all." Samuel just stood there as the three women pushed back from the table and headed to their rooms.

"Are you coming to bed?" asked Rachel yawning.

"Yes. " John was folding his pants. "Intense, isn't he? I wish we could help Samuel and Deborah and the others. I think they desperately want out, too. I just don't think they're comfortable being with other believers who do not think exactly as they do."

"Well, John, you can't force them or change them. Only God can do that," Rachel said turning over in the bed.

"I know, but they're really just kids, just idealistic kids. I worry about them. In spite of all of their dogmatic rhetoric, I think they have sincere hearts for God. Those types are probably in the most danger of all." said John crawling into bed.

Chapter 13

The windowpanes of the YMCA were unusually thin. John could hear cars whirring by on the main thoroughfare; he could hear a train in the distance. Eventually he heard the muffled voices of men talking in the parking lot. By the sheer volume of the conversation, John could tell that the men were having an argument; voices raised, expletives hurled; names called. Then he heard a shot. John and Rachel jolted out of bed, rushing to the window. They saw a man being severely beaten by two dark figures in hooded sweatshirts.

"That's Samuel!" John hurriedly pulled on his jeans and shoes, threw on a coat and ran out the door, meeting Bart and Micah in the hallway. Dashing through the dimly lit building and out the front door, they saw the two dark men jabbing Samuel repeatedly in the torso. One man sent a powerful right hook into his ribs. The other man pummeled his nose, the blood exploding profusely. They were yelling, "That'll teach you to cock off, Nigger!" The two perpetrators were oblivious to the approaching men just behind Samuel. Suddenly, one of the men looked up and saw Bart looming like a member of the Hispanic mafia in back of Samuel, glaring angrily at the two men. John had picked up a gun on the pavement that had evidently been misplaced during the skirmish and was aiming it at the face of one of the men.

Calmly John said, "Back off, boys." The two men, terrified with fright, turned and ran with uncanny speed into the shadows of a nearby neighborhood. Micah and Bart helped Samuel hobble, hunched over, back into the building. John woke up the caretaker, and turning the gun over to him, explained what had happened.

Zann Renn

The caretaker called the police department, and John described the assailants to the officer on the phone.

"What were you doing out there, Samuel?" asked Bart, laying him down gently on a couch in the lobby.

"I wanted to clear my head," Samuel uttered weakly. "After we talked, I took a walk around the building and those brothers jumped me. They wanted money. I told them to leave me alone, that I had no money, and they fired a gun, mostly to scare me, I think. They started hitting me . . . ." Samuel held a damp towel to his bloody nose. "I think my nose is broken, maybe a rib or two cracked, too—my whole body hurts. Honestly, if you had not come out I think they would have killed me." Then with the intensity of the situation subsiding, Samuel began to cry. "I just want out of here. I hate what this country has become. I'm tired, tired, tired of fighting. I'm tired of everything!"

"Samuel, you can come with us. You can all come. We want you to come. We're all tired, too. This is too much for anyone with convictions. There's no justice in it," John said with his arm around Samuel.

Micah finally spoke, "I'm not a Christian like all of you, but this kind of thing is why I'm leaving, too. We live in a country that encourages violence at every turn, violence in government that they call defense, violence glamorized in the media that they call entertainment. Then they wonder why kids beat up innocent people on the streets. It's a double standard, a hypocritical manipulation. You're right. There's nothing just about it," Micah said grabbing another towel for Samuel.

John looked up, "I'm sorry, but thanks for helping us here. We didn't catch your name."

"I'm Micah. I talked to your wife and niece earlier."

"It's good to meet you," John said. Then he introduced Bart and Samuel.

"Are you going to be okay? Maybe we should get you to a doctor and have those ribs checked out," Micah said to Samuel.

"No, I don't do doctors. My sister will wrap these ribs. There's nothing much you can do for cracked ribs anyway . . . or a broken nose. Believe me, I know."

Micah addressed John, "I told your wife earlier that I have an idea. Fast travel, no chip scanning, inexpensive, if we do it right. We could get clear to Pennsylvania within ten days. I know it's not Virginia, but it's closer than this," Micah said.

"I'm game for anything," said Samuel. "Tell us your idea."

"I picked up a brochure a couple of weeks ago about steam engine locomotives, how they are refurbishing them and making them operational. They have repaired a few of the old routes, created some new routes, and put some of the old engines back in working order. In a few places they are offering a cross-country steam engine experience for people who want to step back in time and take an authentic train trip. Not far from here, in Owensboro, they just opened one up that goes from there to Scranton, Pennsylvania to the Steamtown National Historical Site. And because they did not want to alter the integrity of the original trains, they have refused to install scanners on any of them—not even on the railroad. I've checked it out, been out to the station a few times. Every train carries at least two extra empty cars, mostly to appear more impressive, but also because they do have to haul a load of something now and then. Here's the catch: This thing is a complete historical travel experience, sleeping cars, meals, the works. We won't be able to afford it for this many people. And even if we could, we wouldn't get past the scanners at the gate. However, there is a train that leaves at 10 p.m. on certain days. And, to our advantage, behind the train yard is an abandoned Jewish high school. If we could wait there until the train arrives at around eight o'clock, I think I could pick the padlock on one of the empty cars. We could load up on the side facing the school while all the attendants are checking passengers."

Bart and John contemplated Micah's suggestion. "You think we could get all the children on there without being seen? What about bathroom facilities?" asked John.

"How would we feed the children?   Are the cars heated?" Bart inquired.

Micah explained, "The great thing about this option is that it is so new that it's not very well-monitored yet. Getting the children on the train will not be a problem, and they keep the cars partially heated just in case they have to haul something that needs to stay at room temperature. We'd have to take food with us for the most part, but the train makes at least one stop a day. It is a pleasure ride so it takes ten days. But when we stop we can find somewhere to wash up at least. We may have to make do with toilet facilities—it will definitely be crude."

"We've had to do that some already, especially on the balloons," John laughed. "I won't even explain how all that worked."

Bart snickered, "That's okay. We don't want to know."

"Samuel, I know that we're not exactly your crowd spiritually speaking. But I really believe that you and the other women need some allies at this point in your journey. And we want to help you get where you need to be," John said. "I think Micah here has an excellent plan to get us through several states quickly and undetected. I don't think any of us can afford to pass this up."

Samuel slowly sat up holding his ribs. "It's been hopeless . . . until now. If I'm honest, I have to say that. We had all nearly lost hope, and when you have no hope, you've got less than nothing. You see, this is not the first time this has happened," he said pointing to his bloody face. "I'm more weary every day, and what I think we all really need at this juncture is comrades. I know we don't agree on everything; I have a hard time with some of that. And I've got to reconcile it for myself, but," Samuel sighed, "I think it's time to suspend some of what divides us for the sake of this common goal."

A steady, frigid rain drenched the parallel t-rails on the platform as they leaned into one another in the distance. The creosote-stained crossties lay in their crushed white stone beds appearing shorter and closer together long into the foggy horizon. Though the locomotive was a standard Mountain 4-8-2 Passenger, it stood on the tracks like the first line of a patchwork quilt, sewn together with fabrics from different pieces of historical cloth. There were four sleeping cars with individual roomettes from the 1890's. The two long passenger cars mounted upon two six-wheeled swiveling trucks were made of stainless steel from the 1920's. The refurbished Y6 engine straight out of 1940 towered mysteriously in the dusk like an ebony, single-eyed knight in full armor. Two coal hoppers, filled to the top with jet-black shards, reminded joyriding passengers of the hard days when men spent their entire loathsome hours underground breathing dust that would eventually facilitate their deaths. Thanks to public awareness due to a string of unfortunate and fatal accidents and to recent technology that had put a welcome end to the need for living human workers in the mines, the coal in the hoppers did not arrive there at the expense of anyone's life or health. Two brownish red boxcars from the 30's that were used to carry a variety of products were connected finally to a red caboose complete with a glassed cupola protruding from the roof. The engineer had twice walked the length of the entire train checking for anomalies and spitting moist wads of Chaws Chewing Tobacco into the wet, gray granite beside the tracks. Finally, he glanced at his watch and walked away from the platform and into the station office.

Inside the station, a female desk clerk with brown hair pulled back tightly into a bun shuffled through a stack of forms and filed them methodically into a black fireproof cabinet. A couple of elderly passengers who had arrived too early were sitting stiffly in the lounge, drinking Zot from cans and browsing articles in the local E-news. The train, which was not yet running, was at this time occupied only by the engineer's assistant who was sitting in the caboose with his legs propped on a stool playing solitaire on a laptop computer.

Micah stealthily approached one of the two 40-foot boxcars. Hoisting himself up onto the lip of the car, he eyed the latch on the sliding door. There was no lock. He slowly pushed up on the latch and slid it to one side. Pushing the door open slightly while keeping an eye on the caboose, he peered inside. It was pitch black inside the train. Micah could see nothing. He reached into his satchel and found his flashlight. Sweeping the inside of the car with a narrow beam, Micah saw six sets of eyes. He shuttered not knowing exactly what he had found. Cautiously focusing the flashlight in the direction of the eyes he could make out six figures crouched in one corner of the train. Micah jumped and lost his balance for a few seconds. Calling into the car in a loud whisper, Micah said, "Hello?" No one answered. Holding the flashlight steadily into the corner where he saw the figures he could now make out faces, bodies. Six petrified, heavily clothed people with their knees up under their chins sat motionless smudged with dirt from the old box car.

"Who are you?" whispered Micah.

"Just travelers," said the younger man in what sounded like a New York accent. "Who are you?"

"Just a traveler, too, I guess. Didn't mean to scare you." The six people who seemed genuinely afraid stared at Micah as if they were waiting for him to say something. Micah only stared back not knowing what to say and thinking all the while of the Covas, the Becketts and the others waiting patiently in the parking lot against the school building in the rain. Finally Micah said, "I take it you people aren't paying customers."

The older man reluctantly said, "Yes, but if you are going to turn us in please spare my girls and my wife here. Just take me." He spoke in a smoothed-toned southern drawl. Micah sized up the women sitting next to this man. The three younger females, though dirty, were visibly beautiful and roughly the same ages with possibly only a couple of year's difference between them. Two of them were brunettes with shoulder-length hair and the other one had long, auburn hair pulled back into a ponytail. They were lean and tall women with interesting but striking features. Micah had been in the show business world long enough to know that these women, actually the entire family, had a presence about them which suggested that they had spent some time on a stage and were accustomed to make-up, nail polish, and coifed hair. The wife, who also appeared to lack the self-consciousness of people who do not live in the public eye, was round in every sense of the word. Her deep blue eyes were round; her pouting mouth was round; her fingers interlaced around her round knees were round, and her entire blonde head was perfectly round and accentuated by a rounded, cropped hair cut, tapered along the circumference of the face. The man, the father of the clan, had jet black hair, obviously dyed, large, capped teeth which were almost white and soft, slightly effeminate hands, gently manicured, a dead giveaway to the fact that whatever occupation to which he had devoted himself, it had not included much manual labor.

Sitting a few feet from the others was a man, possibly in his mid-thirties, who, next to the conspicuous presentation of the others seemed vaguely out of place. He was thin with angular features and dark, curly hair which, matted with gray dust, had the appearance of a powdered costume wig. He wore black plastic-rimmed glasses and was balled over into a hunch with the bony bends of his knees pulled up tightly under his chin. Beside him on the dingy floor were three or four thick hardback books and a worn duffle bag. As Micah studied him, the man glanced nervously up then back down at the ground in front of him.

Micah weighed his words, then said, "Do you think," he paused, "there is room in here for a few more?"

The question caught all six faces by surprise. Finally the wife of the older man said, "How many?"

"Well," Micah said, matter-of-factly, "about fifteen."

"Goodnight! That's an army! Who are you?" said the man, astounded. "I'm not sure we can all be comfortable in this one car. Where are you headed?"

"Pennsylvania . . . initially."

"You know, there are two," suggested the younger man.

"Two what?" Micah asked. He heard the door slam at the station office and the sound of men's voices.

"Two empty cars. The next car up is empty, too. What if your group splits up after we get going. There are doors at the ends of the cars—you can cross over, even when we're moving."

The woman asked, "All adults?"

"Some kids, too," Micah quickly added, "Really good kids. Well behaved."

"Well, boy, it ain't exactly our train so we can't exactly tell you that you can't ride. Bring 'em on in before they start loading the 'cattle.'" He smiled jokingly. The tension in his jaw relaxed.

Micah ran back to the school building in the dark. The group, which had shifted to the south side of the building, startled him as he approached.

"All clear," he said to Samuel, Bart and Rachel.

"There are six other stowaways already on board. They seem fine with the idea of traveling companions. And there are two empty cars, so we can spread out once we get going. Let's move—I heard the crew getting ready to board. Maggie, who had developed a kinship to Micah, held his hand as they walked to the train. The children were boosted into the dark boxcar. Simon and Maria were frightened and started to whimper. The man and his family stood up and turned on their flashlights. The younger man stood motionless in the corner.

"Name's James Freeman," said the older man, extending his hand to the others, offering firm handshakes and deliberate eye contact. "This is my lovely wife, Martha, but we all call her Marti. And these are my girls, Ruth, Becca and Eve." The door to the train was pulled tightly from the inside. James had invented a way to latch it using a flat, metal bar so that the railway personnel would assume it was locked. The young, slender man, who John discovered was from Queens, was Levi Heschel.

"Inspections are usually about 30 minutes after passengers get off at the stops," said James. "We found that out the hard way. Now we try to get off before the passengers do. Obviously, we have to take everything with us. But it's not so bad. Gets you from A to B."

Everyone found a place in the boxcar taking up less space than what Micah had originally thought. The children sat together in one corner around a flashlight talking about model train sets they had seen and sketching trains in their drawing books. Simon, who was playing with a plastic car on the floor, was getting drowsy. . The sound of an engine grinding silenced them all.

"What supplies do you have and what do we need?" Rachel asked the woman. "I think we've got enough bread, bottled juice and water, and dried fruit to last us until we get to Pennsylvania. But if you want more than that, we probably will need to hop off at the next stop and pick up a few things." She paused and smiled. "We do have toilet paper, though."

Rachel looked a bit worried, especially with all the children having to go every five minutes. "I'm not sure I even want to ask."

"Trust me, you don't," Marti smiled, loosening up a bit. "But we'll walk you through it.

In the opposite corner Becca, Ruth, Sarah and Miriam were talking quietly. "I never got to finish either," sighed Becca. I did complete a few classes at a two-year community college in accounting, but then we had to move. I hate it!" I always wanted to be an accountant. I'm good with numbers."

"I was studying Music," Ruth said. "I took a few basic theory and music history classes as well as private piano." She brushed the dust from her pants. "It doesn't help when you can't stay in one place long enough to practice, though. I ran out of money anyway."

"We know just how you feel," Sarah commiserated. "Deborah, Samuel and the two of us were . . . . " The gravelly sound of the engine silenced them all.

"They will board soon," said James. "You'll feel the train vibrate a little when the people step on."

The train's whistle blared loudly as the conductor called out, "All aboard," swooping up stereotypically at the end of the phrase as if he had been cued for a scene in an old movie. The train began to rumble as people walked the ramp into the train. Simon's toy car jittered up and down on the wooden floor of the boxcar. Without changing expressions, Simon watched it edge awkwardly down one of the planks.

Marti spoke, "Once we stopped in a town in Oklahoma. When we were getting back on the train we discovered they had filled this car with boxes. Kitchenware. We had to ride in the other one. You never know when they'll haul a load."

"Where are you from, originally?" asked Rachel.

"Texas. But we've been everywhere."

"May I ask what you do?"

"You mean before, what we did before.... ? You ever heard of Southern Gospel music?

"Of course. When I was a girl we used to listen to the Statesman, the Blackwood Brothers, you name it. My dad was a fan," said Rachel.

Marti smiled reminiscently. "Well, we're the Singing Freeman Family. "We've sung in every church east of the Rockies, and even a few in California and Utah. The girls have been singing with us since they were old enough to stand and hold a mic. I home schooled them so we could be on the road all the time. We traveled around in a green MCI bus. Called it Henry. Then we lived on it."

"You lived on it?" John asked.

"Yes. We had to sell our house in Abilene to pay bills after the Tolerance Amendment put an end to so many churches. No Quartet Conventions. No all-night sings, anymore either. Too much hootin' and hollerin' for the government. Pentecostals like us ain't never been big on moderation or meditative-type worship, if you know what I mean." Marti winked at Rachel and Isabel. Isabel kept observing Marti like one would observe an orangutan at the zoo, with a sort of baffled curiosity of a species somewhat peculiar but uncannily similar. Marti continued, "It got to the point where because we don't have the chip we had to park the bus in this town in North Texas out in a field and just live in it. You know it's got a bathroom and all." Rachel nodded, half grinning in amusement. "Then after awhile as we watched things in the country go from bad to worse, we decided it was time to get while the gettin' was good. We don't exactly know how but we're leaving here. We just don't belong anymore."

Rachel, knowing how Marti was feeling, laid her hand on top of Marti's hand. "Well, you've got friends here. We're all coming from different places—our family, the Covas, Samuel, Miriam, Sarah, Deborah—but we all follow Jesus. We all just want to be able to be who we are without question or restraint. We're all worried about our kids, jobs, everything." As waves of light from the from flashlight beams passed over Marti's face, Rachel could see that she was crying.

"Praise Jesus," she whispered. Then she was quiet. She simply shook her head almost in complete disbelief at having found compatriots in such an unlikely place.

Chapter 14

Sleeping on the train took some adjustment. The antiquated boxcar moved roughly down the rails. Every imperfection, pebble and flaw in the tracking, with so little shock absorption, rattled everyone to the bone. In addition to the jolting ride, the sound of the boxcar on the tracks, the rumble of the steam engine and the train whistle that sounded at every intersection, made the journey incredibly noisy, even deafening at times. Often the travelers had to shout to communicate.

Everyone decided after about thirty minutes down the line that at least for the night they all would sleep in the same car. It was obvious to John that the Freeman's and Mr. Heschel were familiar with the locomotive, the route and the routines of the personnel on board. The fact that these veteran stowaways had gotten from Texas to Kentucky undetected was a great comfort to John and Bart. Deborah nursed Samuel's cuts and bruises and changed his bandages. He had taken some of Rachel's pain medication, so he was not in the mood for conversation, atypical behavior for Samuel. Eventually, he got comfortable enough to sleep. Miriam, who was likewise concerned with Samuel's wellbeing, seemed overly reserved, not wanting to shout over the noise. Maggie had fallen asleep in between Micah and Rachel. John held Simon as he slept, and he, Bart, Sarah, Rachel and Micah talked with the Freeman's and Mr. Heschel.

"What is your story?" he said addressing Levi. "I mean you don't seem to be James' long lost nephew or anything." Micah had gotten used to reading behind the eyes, and Levi, Micah surmised, was the type of person who had "a story," not just your run-of-the-mill, everyday life, but something unusual and interesting.

"We're not related," Levi spoke. "We only just met two days ago on this train."

Micah asked, "Here on this train? Just traveling?"

"No . . . leaving. I'm leaving, too."

"Why?"

"Same reasons as all of you, I assume. Plus I don't have anywhere else to go."

"No family?"

"Oh, I've got family. We're just not on good terms right now." Levi shifted uncomfortably. The train veered around a corner sliding everyone to one side of the car.

John, who had been eavesdropping on the conversation, finally got the nerve to ask a question that had been gnawing at him since they had met Levi. "I notice that you have a copy of the New Testament there. But . . ." John hesitated, "I guess I thought you were Jewish with a name like Levi Heschel."

"I am Jewish," Levi asserted. The comment elicited the full attention of the others. "I'm a Jewish man who believes in Jesus. My great-grandparents were Lithuanian Jews who came to the States years ago, to New York. My whole family lives there still. My Jewish heritage has not changed. I mean all the customs and traditions are extremely important to me. I carry the Talmud and the Torah everywhere I go. I've had a thorough Hebrew education, the whole thing." He pushed his glasses up on his nose. "It's just that I had an experience with Jesus that I cannot deny or ignore. It changed my life forever. My family has been mourning me like I'm dead for three years now."

All John could manage to say was, "Wow." Micah, who seemed to be lost in thought, as he pondered Levi's words, said nothing.

Finally Rachel spoke, "Are you associated with Jews for Jesus?"

Levi's face warmed at the question, "Yes. . . or I was before I left. I had been out in L.A. visiting a man I met in that organization when I decided that God was telling me it was time to leave the country."

Rachel and John continued talking with Levi who, as it turned out, had been a philosophy professor at N.Y.U. and had several interesting theories on the state of Christianity in America, the Tolerance Amendment and the recent emigration of believers.

"Unfortunately," Levi expounded, "much of the goodness we attribute to our founding fathers, their patriotism, their level-headedness, their unwavering reason is exactly what has lead to the dilemma Christians find themselves in today. I mean, our country was literally nursed on enlightenment thinking. When you base your religious beliefs solely on what is reasonable, when you ignore the mystery, the miracles, the emotion that is inherent in the way God has always worked, you reduce God into that which you can see, touch, prove. You take away the power of it. When Jesus gave his speech to the woman at the well about believers worshiping in spirit and truth, he was acknowledging the balance that must reside at the core of all worship, the knowledge and the power. Unfortunately, I think the United States has never seen the full potential of God's power in the lives of his people. The Age of Reason brought us advances in science and technology that ushered in many great things. But it also stripped us of the glue that could have, in the end, preserved us all."

"I agree," said Marti, "and when you do put your faith in the power of God to do miracles, to most people you look like a buffoon. I'm not denying all the falseness that has been done in the name of Jesus. I've seen plenty of it myself. I'm just saying that when it is real, most people don't believe you. It's not that way in other countries. Our missionary friends have told us that most tribal religions have several levels of 'spirits' that they call upon for help or else avoid because of trouble. And unfortunately, the first thing most Christians do who go to 'minister' to them is convince them that spirits don't exist at all and that it is uneducated or 'unreasonable' to think they do."

John was secretly glad that Samuel and Deborah were not part of this conversation and that Sarah and Miriam seemed to be keeping their opinions to themselves. He knew that there were many differing and potentially warring ideologies represented on this train, and he was glad to see that at least during these times of getting acquainted the dissentious opinions had been kept silent.

Slumped in a corner booth and fiddling with a French fry, Hannah observed a waitress in a light blue cotton apron wiping the stainless steel counter with one hand and scooping cups and plates into a brown washtub with the other. The waitress accomplished this task with all the feeling of a robot programmed to finish an assignment. Hannah sighed loudly, "What are we doing here?"

"Indiana. The Flat State," Tim added sarcastically.

"Let me see the map—the one with house churches marked on it," Hannah demanded without glancing up. Tim spread the wrinkled map out on the table. The bell on the diner door clanged and in walked nine women with matching lavender shirts. They were all speaking at once to each other. Two of the women had their arms around one another's waists and were laughing at a joke another woman had just told. They asked the hostess for a table for nine in the smoking section. None of the women looked at Hannah or at Tim as they made their way to a large, red table in the rear of the restaurant. As they passed, Tim read the words on their shirts: "Gay Pride March—D.C. or BUST!" The word "BUST" was spread ironically over the left breasts of all nine women. Hannah glanced at Tim as she read the word and covered a smirk with her hand. Looking out the window, Hannah noticed a school bus that had been painted bright yellow with a rainbow logo. All of a sudden she noticed a devious look on Tim's face.

"No, no way!" Hannah said reading Tim's expression.

"Yes, Hannah," Tim goaded her. "We could do it. We're actors. They won't care about us if we pay our way. They just want warm, lesbian, protesting bodies in the seats."

"You have got to be kidding. Tell me you are kidding. What if we get caught?"

"What are they gonna do, look under my dress? We won't get caught."

"There is no way I'm going along with this. I don't feel good about it on any level."

"Don't you wanna see the kids?" Tim asked. "This is the most promising solution I've seen. We are good at this, Hannah. They won't suspect a thing and we will be further down the road."

"I don't know, Tim. It's weird."

"Okay. It's weird—I'll give you that. Let's at least follow them. See where they're staying tonight. I know it's not ideal, but Hannah, I've got to see the kids."

Tim and Hannah were ready when the bus pulled out and into the town of Guion. It was not difficult to keep up with the yellow giant as the streets were narrow and short. The bus made several stops and starts and wide turns before it arrived at the parking lot of the Comfort Inn. In the restaurant they had overheard three women talking about the stops they would be making on the trip: King's Island in Cincinnati, Wayne National Forest near Portsmouth; Charleston, West Virginia; Hot Springs, Virginia near the Homestead Ski Area and Hot Springs, and Jefferson's Monticello. Tim jotted it all down and had already located places where he and Hannah could stay, some houses, some abandoned churches. The hope of seeing her children soon was materializing in Hannah, and she grew fonder of Tim's outlandish idea with each passing minute. The couple had not seen or heard of the whereabouts of their children for several days, and they were beginning to worry that something unfortunate had happened to them.

Tim and Hannah reassessed their cash reserve and finding a nearby costume shop invested a hundred Euros in costuming, stage make-up, and a wig. Tim figured it would not do to spend much on clothes since most of the D.C. or BUST women were wearing t-shirts, jeans and tennis shoes similar to what Tim wore on a daily basis anyway. The James' had actually taken a course in costuming and makeup during Tim's last sabbatical and had done the make-up and costuming so often in plays at the university that they were experts in the field. They found themselves grateful at this juncture in their lives that the university's curriculum had demanded so many Shakespeare performances and that the wily bard had written into his plays so many cross dressers. Tim's small-boned frame and small feet made it easier to disguise himself as a woman. Soon he had breasts, long, black hair, make-up, which they kept to a minimum, and a "voice" which Tim had adapted from a character he had played once.

"Won't they wonder why we aren't staying where they stay?" asked Hannah.

Tim answered, "I think if we explain that we're night owls and that we like to camp they'll buy it, so long as we're here on time when the bus leaves."

Striking up a conversation in the lobby of the Comfort Inn was effortless. Most of the women were passionate about their causes and were eager to discuss politics and policy with anyone. Tim had become adept at cocktail party conversation being in the academic, meet-n-greet world for so long. In no time Tim and Hannah had established good rapport with several of the women who seemed to believe that Tim and Hannah were, indeed, a lesbian couple.

"Why don't you come?" asked one particularly tall, fair-skinned woman. "You seem to know how to articulate your own causes. We need people like you in the march."

Tim, trying to pretend the question caught him by complete surprise, squeezed Hannah's hand. "I'm afraid we cannot. As much as we'd like to march with all of you, we don't have chips. I'm afraid we'd be stopped."

All three of the women to whom Tim had addressed this comment began to laugh. "Are you kidding? No cop stops a yellow rainbow bus with 'Gay Pride' written across the front. We've got our rights and they know it. The authorities will show up in Washington to keep the march peaceful, but they're harmless really. Our lobby groups are too powerful. We've driven all the way from California; four women on our tour have no chips, and nobody cares. Hell, we even got a police escort in downtown St. Louis."

Tim said, "Give us a few minutes to discuss it. Oh, and we're campers. We aren't much for hotels, so we wouldn't be staying with all of you."

The tall woman winked at Tim, "That's fine. We've all got our . . . preferences. Some women aren't into hotels. And some have families close by. We never see them at the hotel." Tim gave Hannah an incredulous glance.

"Well, we've definitely got a camping preference," Tim said winking back at the tall woman. "Can we see the itinerary?"

"Of course." The woman handed them a lavender folder and two lavender t-shirts. "You don't have to wear them all the time, but the publicity never hurts, especially in public situations."

Hannah and Tim walked over to a sofa in the hallway of the inn. The itinerary explained that each woman had to pay a nominal fee for fuel and wages for the driver but otherwise they were responsible each day for their own food and hotel room. The stops were ideal with the exception of a few where there were no house churches they knew of. They could stay with the tour until they caught up with Rachel and John. They'd have to leave the bikes behind, but the women seemed agreeable with the idea of hauling their tent and camping supplies.

Slowing gradually then grinding to a halt with a belch of gray steam, the train arrived at a station around 3:15 a.m. not far from Lexington. The itinerary that Micah had obtained showed this stop as the Lincoln Homestead and My Old Kentucky Home for the morning tour with continued travel to Daniel Boone's grave near Frankfort in the afternoon. James Freeman woke his family and the others at around 5:30. "If we want to get outta here without being seen, we need to leave now. On these early stops they inspect the train at around 6:30 before the passengers get off at 7:00.

"Where do you suggest we clean up?" Rachel asked yawning.

"The sinks in the public restrooms will have to do for this stop," said James.

"Usually it's not too difficult to find a truck stop. Every now and then they have showers. We'll see."

Waking the children was formidable task. Andrew and Jesse were nearly impossible to rouse; Simon, Maggie and Maria were whimpering with exhaustion, and Thomas was simply irritable. Samuel was feeling the stiff pain in his ribs. Deborah and Miriam helped him off the train, and he moaned as his feet landed in the loose gravel by the tracks. It was still dark, but the promise of the sunrise filled the air. Micah and John stood guard until everyone had vacated the car.

"Don't you think we look a bit conspicuous all walking around together?" asked Bart.

"Good point," said John. "Why don't we have a little separation time today. Let's all meet back here at noon. The train pulls out at one. Micah, maybe you could hang with Samuel and Deborah in case Samuel needs help getting around."

John could tell by Samuel's face that the idea did not sit well with him. "That's okay," said Samuel, limping away from the others and giving Micah a wary look. "I think I can manage fine with my sisters, here."

Micah nodded in resignation, "Suit yourself. Levi, you like sushi?"

"Yeah. I haven't had sushi in . . . forever. This ain't Brooklyn, you know. You think we can find some out here?"

"Well, let's look around. I'm in a zone for sushi," Micah said, slinging his satchel over one shoulder.

John and Rachel took the children to a nearby café for some breakfast. They found the restrooms first and, using only paper towel and dispenser soap, cleaned up the best way they could. One man came in while Thomas and Andrew were washing under their arms, their bare bellies exposed, and threw them a disgusted glare. The boys giggled as he exited the restroom.

This part of Kentucky was breathtaking, the rolling, green hills, the morning mist, the bright sun on the naked trees. It was not a warm day, but the temperature was bearable with jackets, and after the children had eaten, they were in much better spirits as they explored the streets of the small town, called Lincolnton.

"Nice looking group you got there. They all yours?"

"John wheeled around and saw an officer in a black uniform walking behind him. Simon immediately became fixated on his Glock in a holster on his belt.

"No actually," John began casually, "These two are mine and these three are my sister-in-law's children."

"Looks like you guys are on some sort of an expedition with all those backpacks and bedding. You from around here?"

"Not far from here. We just like camping this time of year," said John.

"Little chilly for that with young-uns isn't it? School day, too. These kids in school?"

John hesitated then said, "We are in the process of moving to a new place, both our family and my wife's sister's family. So we were allowed a couple of weeks before the kids start up at the next facility." Rachel, afraid that Simon would blurt out something, pulled a bulbous, grape lollipop from her purse and handed it to him.

"So where are you from?" asked the officer.

"O.27!" The policeman's radio attached to a loop on his belt blared in a voice that could have been a man or a woman.

The officer held the radio up to his mouth, "Yes, go ahead."

"There's a domestic disturbance on 1213 Oak with a firearm. Are you available?"

"10-4, on my way," said the officer. Turning to John he said, "You all take care. Have a nice break. Keep safe with the camping."

Simon popping the lollipop out of his mouth said, "Okay, 10-4," then smiled showing his purple stained lips and tongue.

As the officer drove away, Rachel leaned into John, "That was close."

"Yeah. Maybe we should stay out of sight for the rest of the day."

Rachel suggested, "I could use an hour or so washing clothes. You think I could find an O Rent? Everyone is filthy. Why don't I take Andrew—his leg won't last long on a hike—and Maggie? Leave the backpacks with me. You take the boys for a walk in the woods there."

"You think Simon can handle it?" asked John.

"Actually," Rachel interrupted, "I think it would be good for him to get out some of that pent up energy. Just keep an eye on him. He'll sleep better tonight on the train."

Rachel met Isabel and Maria in the O Rent. Bart had gone to get the supplies on the list. Maggie and Maria played with their dolls on top of the washing machines; then they made up a game called "Scare" in which they chased each other around the washers and dryers, dishwashers, and vacuum cleaners with laundry carts. Rachel let Andrew walk next door to an instrument store. He had been mourning the fact that he was not able to bring his guitar on the trip, though because of all the walking and his weak ankle he had been, at times, relieved. His ankle was almost as good as new. "A few more days," he told Rachel on the train, "and I'll be back to normal."

The boys and John trekked up a mossy incline into a thickly wooded area. It felt good to do something physical. John, who had been an avid basketball player used to working out everyday, had not had much of an opportunity so far to do so. The light shining down in streams through the black branches of trees onto the forest floor accentuated the variegation of browns and greens, dry leaves, twigs, pinecones and fir limbs. Jesse spotted a copperhead snake that, rustled from his slumber by the sudden foot traffic, slithered off into the briars. Simon kept up with the others, staying between John and Thomas, and singing, "Do You Know the Muffin Man." Now and then around the particularly steep or tangled areas, John and Thomas boosted Simon up and over, which provoked a "Wheeeee" from him every time.

At the top of one hill there was a level table, thick with trees, which Thomas suggested could have been the sight of an ancient Indian burial ground. The trees were sparser here. The group stopped to rest against a thick sycamore tree, all except Simon who tromped through the leaves searching for acorns and milkweed pods. John was bent over with his hands on his thighs getting his breath when he heard Simon say, "The baby! Come here. Come here, baby." John turned his head just in time to see Simon reaching his hand out to pet a brown bear cub.

"NO!" John howled, leaping up and grabbing Simon. A guttural, gravelly growl sounded in a thicket about fifty yards from them, close enough to cause the hairs on John's neck to stand straight up. "Follow me, very quickly, boys," he whispered holding Simon next to his body. They sprinted toward the hill, Simon bouncing violently with John's every step. Jesse and Thomas understanding fully the imminent danger ran twice as hard to keep in step with John. They heard another growl and sticks breaking in the woods behind them. "Faster boys! We've got to get back to the street!" They could hear the cars below. Jesse and Thomas bolted ahead of John leaping with long strides down the side of the hill. They emerged from the woods and landed on the shoulder of one of the side streets in town. John made the boys continue running back into the heart of town, their hearts pounding heavily in their ears. Glancing back toward the base of the hill, John saw the object of their terror-- a thousand pound mother bear lumbering down the side of the street. The bear slid to a stop when she saw the oncoming traffic on Main. Stunned for a few seconds by the sight of automobiles, the noise of motors and the gasps and screams from pedestrians, the bear turned tail and ran back up into the woods.

John let out a heavy sigh, his legs shaking with anxiety. Simon, who still had his arms tightly clasped around John's neck braced himself not two inches from John's face and said smiling, "You're kinda wobbly, Uncle John." Thomas was hyperventilating. John coaxed him to breathe deeply.

"It's over. We're okay," he kept saying. They walked into town and located the O Rent. Entering through the swinging door, the boys and John stood there wet with perspiration and panting rapidly.

"I saw a baby bear, Auntie Rae. I saw a mommy bear, too," Simon blurted out. Rachel looked inquisitively at John. "You don't want to know," he said, hugging her. "I cannot believe it! I thought the only ones that survive today were in captivity! It was SO close!"

"OH my gosh! Are you serious? " She grabbed Simon and hugged him closely "Gross, you're all wet. Must have been some hike." John rolled his eyes. "Why don't you give me the wet clothes and change into something clean. Then go next door and pry Andrew from the guitars."

Sitting back in the dusty boxcar, the travelers traded stories, talking excitedly. Much to the John's dismay the second empty boxcar had been filled with canned goods, so everyone had to resign himself to mandatory communal living once again. Bart had gathered supplies and had purchased several inexpensive games from a discount bin. The children were happy and occupied themselves with these fresh amusements. Andrew, who had been given two old guitar magazines by the sales clerk at the instrument store, was sprawled out in a corner with a flashlight reading intently. Thomas was perched next to Maria bragging about how he had outrun a bear in the woods, exhibiting to her in an animated manner, his near-death escape.

Micah still had not returned to the train. Levi had returned alone claiming that he and Micah had gotten separated in the stores on Hughes Street. John held his watch to the light. It was noon. Fearing the engineer would be returning soon to walk the perimeter of the train, John decided it was best to close and latch the door. He knew that if Micah finally arrived he would have the good sense to unlatch the door and come on in. The door shut with a clank, and the darkness hushed the voices inside. Everyone had learned that the cue to whisper was blackness. In town Bart had purchased miniature reading lights for anyone who wished to read. Those who had new games and old paperbacks from a bargain bin put the new lights to immediate use. Bart moved over near Deborah and Samuel.

"Are you okay?" he asked Samuel.

"Yes. It actually felt good to move around some and get a good meal," Samuel replied. "Thank you for asking."

"I brought you something. Nothing big." Bart handed Samuel a small rectangular icon with a picture of St. Stephen on it. "This reminds me of you because you are willing to suffer for your convictions."

Samuel grinned obligingly and handed the icon back to Bart. "No thanks."

Isabel, who saw this interchange whispered to Bart, "Why did you do this? You knew he would react this way. It's like casting pearls before swine with these types. He will never appreciate the saints as we do."

Hearing this last comment Deborah stood and spoke firmly to Isabel, "You have no idea what it means to be a Christian, to draw hard lines, and stand up for what you believe until it costs you something. You think just because you go to confession once a week you can get away with murder. I hate to break it to you, girl, but you can always tell a tree by its fruit. And most Catholics I've seen like to buy now and pay later. You all think if you can get a little upset about abortion and gay marriage, you can get drunk, see whatever movie comes into theaters, have no personal relationship that impacts your life!"

Isabel jumped to her feet with a fire in her eyes. Moving in close to Deborah's face she spouted, "What you don't know is a lot. You people with all your rules that you use to hammer other people make it bad for all of the rest of us. You love no one; you just want all the 'T's' crossed and the 'I's' dotted. Maybe you should have a little wine now and then. You're wound up way too tight!"

James Freeman evidently sensing the presence of something ominous in the train stood up and laying his hands on the shoulders of the two women began binding Satan in the name of Jesus and speaking rather boisterously in tongues. Samuel called out, "Hey, Freeman, you trying to get us all arrested? Save all the theatrics for Christian TV. No wonder the world can't take us seriously! You guys ruined it for everyone!

This comment caused James to stop short in his prayer and glare angrily at Samuel who was glaring back, clutching his side. "Well they should have told me," said James, "that I'd be sharing the train with a bunch of Mexican Catholics and a flock of fun-damn-mentalists!"

"Shhhhhh!," John interrupted, abruptly, holding the palm of his hand out toward the others. The train door rattled. Rachel hushed the children. Everyone could hear the voices of men outside.

Chapter 15

"I thought I heard something in here," one man said.

"Better check then. We load up soon." John motioned to everyone to back into opposite corners of the train, flat against the wall just beside the doors. The latch lifted with a creak. The door slid open. Rachel held her hand over Simon's mouth. The bright sunlight flooded into the box car. A man poked his head in and rubbed his eyes as the dust flew out.

"Frank!" a voice hollered from the front of the train.

"Yeah," the man answered still rubbing his eyes.

"Can you help me with this coupler?" the voice shouted.

"Be right there." The man coughed and slid the door shut with a bang. Nobody inside the car moved or said a word. Standing for several minutes along the wall of the car, the travelers waited in oblivion. The sounds of breathing were audible.

Finally Simon whispered into the blackness, "What are we doing?" Jesse and Thomas giggled softly. "Are we playing the quiet game?"

"Yes," Rachel whispered to him. "Just a few more minutes." More time passed. As they began to relax, the door rattled once again. Everyone halted, staring at the door. Slowly the latch lifted and slid gradually to the left. All eyes were on the door, muscles tensed, breathing grew shallow. A thin ray of light pierced the darkness and dusk inside the car.

"You guys in here?" It was the voice of Micah. The sighs of relief sent everyone to the floor.

"Hurry. Get in," said John. "The engineer could be back any minute to walk the train."

"I don't think so," said Micah. "They've already begun to board." Micah hopped on and shut the door. The travelers settled themselves in small groups around the car.

No one talked much once the train began to move. Micah could feel the tension, could sense that something had happened while he was gone, but was afraid to ask. The ride to the site of Daniel Boone's grave was long enough for an afternoon nap. Most of the travelers took advantage of the opportunity. James, Micah and Miriam remained awake. Miriam was engrossed in a biography, so James took the opportunity to acquaint himself better with Micah. "We've been to a couple of those studios in L.A.," James was saying. "They used our family once in a movie. We were singing at a fair. Directed by a fellow named Doyle. The girls had a blast, you know, at Disneyland and all. We used to be on a show every week when the girls were small. Out of North Carolina. Went off the air eventually."

"Yeah, I've worked in most of those places in L.A., some in New York, too. I'm glad to be done with it. It's a rat race. It's never been who I am. And actors are a trip, let me tell you," said Micah taking a bite out of an apple.

"Gotta say, I loved it. Every minute I've ever been on a stage. I really miss it. I don't think Marti does. Even the girls seem to be perfectly happy without that life. I love it, though. I guess those days are over." James wiped a streak of dirt from his delicate hand. "Why were you so late today?" he asked Micah. "Did you get messed up on the time?"

Micah glanced over at Bart and John, then at Maggie taking a nap on Rachel's lap. "No, I knew the time. I was in the middle of something, that's all. Lost track of the hour," Micah replied, his eyes darting around evasively.

The train came to a halt. The vibrations of the passengers disembarking woke the children from their peaceful naps.

"John," Rachel said running her hands over Simon who had been sleeping beside her. "Feel Simon's body. He's burning up!" John put his hand on Simon's moist forehead.

Zann Renn

"Good grief! As soon as we can, let's get him out of here. I hope there's a med center still open somewhere." Everyone jumped out of the boxcar. John asked Bart and Isabel if they would mind taking the other children somewhere to eat, to which they agreed obligingly. Simon was still asleep as John carried him into town. About a quarter of mile outside of town, Simon woke up and in a puny voice announced that his stomach did not feel right and proceeded to vomit down John's shirt.

"It's all this cold and traveling with so little sleep," said Rachel. "Not to mention we haven't exactly been eating or sleeping on any schedule. It's too much for a three year old." The first clinic they saw had closed at four, just ten minutes before they arrived. Rachel ran into a pharmacy on the corner and asked the cashier where they could find another clinic.

"About seven blocks south. Head down to the next stoplight, turn right. Seven blocks. Just past Hank's cleaners."

The waiting room at the clinic was full, but one woman, seeing the frenzied expression on John's face and the stains on his shirt had pity on him and traded her number for his. When John's number was called, Rachel followed John and Simon, who although he was awake, was limp and lethargic.

"Place your hand on the plate, please. We need your information," said a robust nurse in a flinty tone.

"Ma'am, I'm sorry, but we don't have a chip and we're from out of town," John pleaded. The nurse sighed in disgust, then called to another nurse in the back, "No chip, Flo! Bring a set of forms!" The nurse, without glancing up from her work, commanded them to take a seat. Another ten minutes went by, and another nurse emerged with a stack of papers in his hand.

"Fill these out, then we'll process them and get back with you," he snapped curtly. "Number 108!"

John stood to his feet, "Sir, excuse me. How long will this take?"

"Usually without chip around an hour for processing. Just make yourselves comfortable."

John felt the frustration rise up in his chest. He took several short breaths, then stood up and shouted, "NO!" All the nurses turned and for the first time looked at John, incensed at having been challenged. "No ma'am," he said to the robust woman, "we will not wait! This child is burning up. The fever is making him regurgitate. We have to catch a train in an hour or we will be stuck in this town indefinitely. You will see this child now!"

"Sir! You must sit down. Around here we tell people when they will be seen. We don't care what's wrong with you. There's nothing special about a kid with a fever. We've got other patients, too!"

John, feeling defeated for a few seconds, finally, said, "I guess our good friend Senator Dryden would like to know about this place. He's always bragging about the friendly and expedient health care in Kentucky. I'm sure he'd like to meet you, Ms. Wanda Jones," John said reading her nametag with a sarcastic tone.

Nurse Jones was dumbfounded. "Wait right here," she said to him quietly. She left the room and in minutes returned smiling and saying, "Dr. Bracken will see you now."

Rachel took Simon from John. "Honey, he's on fire," she said holding his body close to her own. "And he's trembling." She laid him down on the table while they waited for the doctor. His oval face prickly with heat appeared lifeless. A handsome, young, African American man with dark, disheveled hair entered the room.

"Dr. Bracken," he said extending his hand. "Simon . . ."

"James," Rachel added. "He's my sister's boy here with us on vacation." As she was speaking the doctor held a thermometer in Simon's ear.

"106," he said. "How long has he had this?"

"I'm not sure. It came on the afternoon." All of a sudden Simon's body began to convulse.

"Jenny!" the doctor called out, retraining Simon's spindly limbs in an attempt to prevent a fall from the table. A petite nurse entered through the rear entrance of the examining room.

"Ibuprofen! Get the tub ready!" The nurse observing Simon in tremors knew instinctively that they were dealing with high fever.

Rachel felt nauseous. "What's going on?"

"Febrile seizure, connected with high fever." Finally Simon's body began to relax. The nurse came back in with a blue, infant tub and began to fill it with tepid water. "Let's get this sweater off." Rachel and the doctor began removing Simon's clothes. His clammy skin felt like a hot water bottle as they laid him in the tub. The nurse stuck a syringe in his arm.

Simon blinked his eyes and spoke lethargically in a high-pitched tone, "Is it bath time?"

"No, honey. This is Dr. Bracken, and you have a fever. We're just trying to get it down, okay?" Rachel said reassuringly.

"I'm thirsty," Simon whispered. The nurse left the room and returned with a box of apple juice.

John pulled Dr. Bracken aside, "What do you think this is?"

"I'm not sure," said Dr. Bracken. "Most likely a virus. A child this age can get fever fairly easily. I'll do some blood work, and a throat culture—looks a little irritated."

"I hate to say this under the circumstances, but we're traveling with a group, and it's imperative that we leave here in an hour or we'll be stranded. I promise Simon will get rest tonight, but unless this is something very serious . . . . The seizure concerns me. We don't want to do anything that would jeopardize his health or . . . ."

"Don't worry. When a child runs a fever over 104, he can have a seizure like this. It's very common. Just watch him. This Ibuprofen should take effect rapidly. If this is bacterial, which we'll know shortly, we'll prescribe an antibiotic." The doctor and nurse gathered up their clipboards and exited the room.

Rachel and John looked at one another. "If this is expensive, I'm not sure we'll have enough to cover it without government chip insurance. We've been living on borrowed time without the chip as it is. We haven't had any medical emergencies until the past couple of weeks. What will we do?" Rachel asked.

"Pray," said John. They put their hands on Simon's slippery legs and their arms around each other. "God, we need a miracle here. Touch Simon's body, please. Help us find favor with this doctor. We need you now. Amen." John squeezed Rachel close to him.

The doctor and nurse came back into the room. The nurse worked with Simon and quickly got a throat swipe.

Dr. Bracken removed his glasses and said, "I understand you had a misunderstanding with Nurse Jones."

"If you want to call it that. I know you are busy, but I've never felt that busyness gave anyone reason to be rude or heartless," John explained.

"You were right to be angry. Ms. Jones will not be working for us much longer. This is her last week actually. I apologize for how you were treated." Dr. Bracken felt Simon's glands. "Do you know Senator Dryden?"

"Yes," John replied. "I used to work in Washington. Senator Dryden and I were close friends. Still are."

"He's a good man. Used to go to church with him. He's an honest politician with an extremely difficult job, and he's done so much for the underprivileged"

"Yes, I know," John agreed.

Dr. Bracken examined Simon thoroughly then told Rachel to dress him but to leave his sweater off. "Just a t-shirt for awhile, light blanket, until the fever breaks. Watch him. If he gets too hot he'll behave lethargically." Within fifteen minutes the results had come back from the throat culture, and Simon had tested positive for strep throat. Dr. Bracken called John into his office. "I have no idea what your situation is, but something tells me you need a break here. I'm giving you samples for the antibiotic and some fever reducer. The office visit is free. I will get in trouble with the AMA if they heard me say this to you, but let's scrap the paperwork. If you will agree to leave quietly, I'll pretend you were never here." Dr. Bracken winked at John.

John was astonished. He found himself trying to hold back tears. "Thank you. This is kind. God bless."

"Some have entertained angels unaware. God be with you and your family," said Dr. Bracken standing and shaking John's hand.

John and Rachel knew they had little time to spare in getting to the train. They moved swiftly through the streets of town carrying Simon. The sun was setting behind them, and the air was growing cooler. When they reached the train station they realized by glancing through the window at the empty lounge that the passengers had already boarded. John glanced at his watch. "Great! They're scheduled to pull out of here in two minutes." They sprinted down a long chain link fence until there was an opening. Running back toward the train they heard the familiar whistle and the call of the conductor signaling departure. Rachel ran ahead of John up to the side of the train. Thankfully Bart was standing with the door open just inside. The train edged forward.

"Give Simon to me, then hop on quickly," he yelled at Rachel. Rachel raised Simon up to Bart who handed him back to Isabel. Rachel grabbed the lip of the train and swung her leg up and over, panting breathlessly on the floor. The train began to pick up speed. Turning, Rachel saw John running at a clipped pace beside the box car.

"Oh, God! Honey please grab onto something here!" Rachel cried.

"I'm trying! The ground is so uneven!" John grabbed at the floorboards, but his hand slipped ramming splinters into his palm. Lagging behind briefly he quickened his pace and moved again beside the opening in the boxcar. Bart stood at the door trying to find his balance.

"I'm bracing myself here, John. Grab my hand."

John lunged forward and caught Bart's thick arm with both of his hands. Holding tightly John swung out and around, afraid to let go.

"I got you man," said Bart. John saw the darkening Kentucky countryside spinning like a globe before him. Then with a thud that shot pains through his knees he landed on the floor of the train. Rachel rushed to his side.

"Are you okay, John?"

"I'm not sure yet," John said between gulps of air. "Never chased down a train before. I feel like James Bond," he said smiling.

A special palette was made on the floor for Simon. Rachel had filled a thermos with ice water for Simon to drink and for sponging his forehead when the fever shot up. For now he was sleeping. John saw Samuel talking quietly to Miriam. She had been reading to him a passage from the biography she bought. Samuel's face, which was usually serious and angular, seemed softened by the exchange. His eyes followed her eyes as they darted back and forth across the page. Marti moved over next to John who was attempting to dislodge the splinters from his hand.

"Let me see it," Marti said. John looked up at her soft, round face. She was pointing to his hand. He placed it into her hand, which was warm and soft as a pillow. In her other hand she had a pair of tweezers. She propped a flashlight up on a backpack so that the beam illuminated John's hand; then she plucked at the splinters quickly and effortlessly until each one was gone. Pulling a disinfecting wipe from her bag, she cleaned John's hand and folded it in his lap like his 3rd grade teacher used to do when he was fidgeting.

"I always carry a pair of tweezers for just such emergencies," she said nodding at John.

Jesse walked over to John and sat down beside him, laying his head on John's shoulder. "I was afraid you wouldn't make it, Daddy," he said in a voice like a toddler.

John put his arm around Jesse's broad shoulders. "I had to get back on here to go with you. I'm not gonna let you leave without me." Jesse wrapped his arms around John's waist and immediately drifted off to sleep. The rhythm of the train over the tracks which before had felt abrupt and jarring now seemed soothing to John, and a quiet serenity filled his heart. Rachel was sleeping by Simon and Maggie, her mouth open and her fist curled under her tawny cheek like a girl. Andrew and Thomas were lying on their backs with their hands under their heads staring at the ceiling and talking about girls they liked back in Kansas. It was strange for John, with all the uncertainty of his life, of this venture, even of their destination, to feel this kind of peace. Warmed by Jesse's oversized body he began to shift in and out of consciousness.

A factory appeared that had been operating in the same manner for a long time. The smoke from the extensive pipes protruding from the roof of the factory belched pollution into the air until the atmosphere surrounding the building was a murky gray, making visibility nearly impossible. People were walking up to John, but he could not make out their faces until they were almost next to him. He was an employee on the assembly line, but instead of automobiles or toasters, they were creating miniature factories much like the one in which they were standing, with miniature smokestacks that emitted miniscule curls of smoke.

The people who were walking in and out of John's line of visibility were somber and vacant—no one made eye contact. They walked past quickly wearing black workman's overalls and charcoal caps, but no one spoke or looked at him. Across the conveyor belt were other workers. Squinting he began to recognize faces of people he knew—the Covas, Bart and Isabel and sweet Maria covered with soot and putting parts onto the tiny factories. Samuel and Deborah stood there along with Miriam and Sarah, all in overalls, working the line. He saw Tim and Hannah and their children, even Simon who was coughing, red with fever. He saw Levi and the Freeman's and Micah all laboring at various tasks. He turned and saw Rachel beside him as well as Andrew and Jesse. Everyone seemed unhappy and sickly and vacant. As the sooty air began to coat John's lungs, he started gasping and choking. He fell to the ground with his hand around his throat, heaving. One by one, each of the others began to drop to their knees trying to breathe. John looked around him and all of his family and friends could be seen on the floor under the conveyor belts and machinery.

Bart moved in close to John's face and with a pinched voice said, "I think if we stay on our knees we can crawl out of here. If we don't, we're all going to die." Bart led the way across the dingy factory floor and out a side door. Even outside the air was thick and polluted. They all continued to crawl. John and Rachel helped the children when they lagged behind. Samuel and Deborah helped the Freeman's who were growing weaker. John turned and saw Micah lying on the ground. He shook him until he came around, then carried him on his back. The sounds of coughing and sighing could be heard throughout the ranks, but everyone continued to crawl until it seemed that the smoke was dissipating. John paused for a moment and peered up at the sky. Every now and then he could actually see through the smoke, and he was able to catch a few rays of sun shooting through. The coughing began to cease and breathing became less labored. John took a long, deep breath. The clean air extricated whatever had been contaminating his lungs. Under his hands he felt sand. He scooped up a handful and let it run out through his fingers. Something inside of him told him it was safe to stand. As he stood, he saw his friends and family all around him, his children, Rachel, all of them rise to their feet. In from of him was the shore of an ocean more beautiful than North Oahu. Overhead, a flock of seagulls flew, calling to each other. Palm trees hovered in the warm breeze. The sun was so brilliant, brighter than he ever remembered it. He put his hands on his hips and taking in long breaths, in and out, he felt that somehow he was breathing more than just air, for with each breath his body, his mind, his spirit felt sounder, more at peace.

John woke with the sweaty body of Jesse plastered against his trunk. His shirt was wet with perspiration. Jesse was in a deep sleep, his mouth gaping open. The train had stopped. Glancing around the car, John saw that Micah was also awake. He looked down at his watch and held it under the beam of his pin light. It was 5:17 a.m. He tried moving his legs without waking Jesse and realized that his knees and hamstrings were sore and tight. He moaned. Rachel walked up to him and lifted Jesse off his body, laying him gently onto a mat on the floor.

"Where are we?" he asked Rachel still blinking his eyes.

"I'm not sure. Somewhere in West Virginia, I think."

Micah moved over next to them. "James says we're near Charleston. Got any idea what we can do here for fun?"

"This is all a new adventure for me," said John stretching. He stood, unlatched the door cautiously and edged it open. A fresh wind moved across his face. He took a deep breath. Inhale. Exhale. The air was clean and cold.

Chapter 16

"What is it that you do in the real world?" Hannah turned around to see Gretchen, a trim, muscular young woman with long, jet-black hair and ivory skin. Her eyes were amber spears of penetrating intensity.

"We are both in theater," said Hannah, "or we were, back in Kansas. We're professors." Gretchen grinned mischievously then changed expressions altogether.

"This is what's afther comin' on me for nursin' you day an' night...I was a fool, a fool, a fool! Get me a dhrink o' wather, you jade, will you? There's a fire burnin' in me blood!"

Hannah laughed out loud. "O'Casey! Not a bad Eire brogue for a white girl. Were you in 'The Plough and the Stars?'"

"Yes, Bessie Burgess. Did a lot of community theater in Boulder. You got anymore of those cheese crackers?"

Hannah handed her a handful of crackers. "I miss the acting," said Hannah, taking a swig of iced tea. "Teaching was great when I got a sharp class, and directing, too, but every now and then I get the itch, you know?"

"Something freeing about becoming someone else, forgetting who you are for a few hours, exploring other people's psyches, even trying to find the right 'look.'"

The bus ground to a halt and Carol the tour guide's fuel stop announcement over the loud speaker bludgeoned Tim out of a peaceful slumber, and he forgot where he was for a moment. His long wig had gone flat on one side where he had been sleeping on it rather heavily. Hannah tried to straighten it as everyone was exiting the bus.

"Nothing makes you wanna pee like a bus," said Gretchen, scouring the rest stop for the toilet facilities. Heading into the women's restroom took some discipline on Tim's part. He nearly always anticipated the screams of offended ladies, forgetting for the moment he was one of them. He longed for a decent urinal, or even the privilege of standing while urinating, but neither luxury was plausible in his current situation. It was important for him to maintain appearances, so he sat, tinkling like the rest of the women.

Back on the bus, Hannah began to read. Eventually she grew tired and slightly nauseous. Thoughts of Simon began to present themselves in her head, memories of his mannerisms and the interesting way in which he pronounced certain words. Then she remembered the time when he cut his foot and had to get stitches. The memory was strong; then it became overwhelming. In the past when particularly vivid thoughts of people whom she loved arose into her consciousness, Hannah's habit was to pray for them. She had discovered that in nearly every case, the thought had been divinely placed, and she was a serious intercessor. She began whispering a prayer about Simon, asking for his protection and safe keeping, praying specifically for his body. She prayed that God would send his angels to stand guard over him and minister to him. She prayed until she felt a release in her spirit; then she drifted off into sleep against the cool window pane.

She awoke in the middle of the night. The bus had stopped.

"Where are we?" she asked groggily.

"On the border of Ohio and Pennsylvania. We are here for a couple of nights," said Gretchen. "You guys hungry at all?"

"Yes, actually," Tim said in his feminine voice. "I could eat a horse."

Hannah gave him an amusing glance.

"Come hang with us," said Gretchen. "Melinda, Bet, and me." The only thing open at midnight in the little town of Hodgkins was a pub. Bet, a dark, stocky Italian woman from New Jersey was bound for a career in comedy. As they devoured club sandwiches and cold beer, Hannah and Tim laughed harder than they had in a long time. Hannah learned that Bet and Gretchen had been together as a couple for nearly seven years. Though they had not been married officially they had made a commitment to each other, which had remained unbroken.

"What brought you two together?" Hannah asked.

"Gretchen replied in her most gravely voice, "Her hands—dey was skinny and white like dey wasn't real but painted on somep'n. Dere was a million miles from me to her—twenty-five knots a hour. She was like some dead ting de cat brung in. Sure, dat's what. She didn't belong. She belonged in de window of a toy store, or on de top of a garbage can, see!"

Tim cackled so hard he spit out a mouthful of beer. "That's the best Yank I've ever heard. And I've had to sit through a lot of O'Neill, trust me!"

"I like how O'Neill's characters speak. It feels natural to me," Gretchen said leaning her face on her hand and yawning. She let her eyes rest on Tim and Hannah, glancing back and forth at each of their faces. "Can I ask you a question?" she said finally.

"Sure." Tim wiped his mouth with a napkin.

"Are you guys . . . how do I put this . . . are you Christians?"

Hannah grinned, "Yes, we are. What make's you ask?"

"I don't know—the way you look and act mostly. There's a peace about you that I've felt before around other Christians."

"You aren't those rigid types, are you?" Bet asked in a direct manner.

Tim snickered, "Not sure what you mean by rigid. I'm feeling fairly flexible at the moment." Hannah rolled her eyes. "Truth is we wouldn't think of navigating through his world without Jesus. Everything's too complicated without him; it's complicated enough with him."

Gretchen pondered Tim's comment; then spoke. "It's all interesting to me. Really. I find Christianity fascinating. I used to go to church with my Grandma when my parents got divorced. I was about seven. Her church was small, not more than thirty people, but they had this thing called testimony time. I always liked it because people would just stand up and start talking about God and how he had worked in their lives that week, big things like healing someone of cancer who had been prayed over and little things like helping someone find a lost ring or a wallet that was missing. I've run into some Christians since then who seemed to be just talkin' the talk, if you know what I mean. But at Grandma's church, those folks seemed sincere, like all that stuff meant something to them. There was this one old man—everyone called him Brother Pete; I never knew his last name. Every week when they'd start singing, he'd yell out, 'What a Friend!' It was a song called 'What a Friend We Have in Jesus.' They'd all start singing, and Brother Pete would sing louder than everyone, and slightly ahead of everyone, if I remember correctly. Eventually, he'd begin to cry and his nose would run and his thick voice would crack. And one by one everyone would start to weep and raise his hands. It was confusing and wonderful to me all at the same time. One day I asked my Grandma why Brother Pete cried like that, and she said, 'Darlin', he's been touched by the love of the Master's hand.' I'm still not sure what she meant by that, but I loved the poetic way she phrased it. It stuck in my mind like a line from a play. Anyway, it feels good to be around women like you. I feel like I'm home, in a way."

A miserable cold front had moved into that region of Pennsylvania. The icy rain mixed with 20 mile per hour winds sent a chill into Tim's bones as he erected the tent in a nearby family campground.

"I hate that there were no churches around. I'm not feeling all that holy . . . just cold." Hannah shivered.

"Look at it this way: we're not likely to run into anybody here at this campground tonight," Tim said yawning and removing his wig. He pulled Hannah in close and zipped up the sleeping bag. His cold body soon felt the warmth from Hannah's toned legs. They held each other a long time before making love.

"Let's pray for Bet and Gretchen and Melinda. I like those women. And Gretchen in particular seems to be searching for something deep spiritually."

"I agree," said Tim, "and also Simon's been on my mind so much today."

"Me too!" said Hannah. "I'm so sick in my heart, needing to see the kids."

Chapter 17

The Kanawha River evoked an almost dingy quality under the morning sun. John and Rachel passed a man fishing with his son, both silent, chewing wads of pink bubble gum. The man nodded at John, then checked the tension on his line and began to reel in slowly.

"We need to talk," said John sitting on a bench. "I think it's time to break from the train now." Rachel listened as he laid out a plan. "If we're in Founder's Fork, we can follow river systems all the way to the West Virginia/Virginia border, Pocahontas County. Sixty miles down this river," he said pointing to a map, "is a house church, farmhouse church, actually. Remember the Sarios talking about Greenway?"

"Yes! It's legendary! The house that sent out hundreds of people into the mission field, but always remained under the government radar."

"I don't think it would hurt to stop down for a couple of days. Rest. Eat a few decent meals. Jesse and Thomas were both complaining of sore throats this morning."

"So was Maria," Rachel agreed.

"I think we're all going to be ill if we don't get out of the cold and dust and give our bodies some down time."

"Have you run this by the others?" Rachel asked.

"I mentioned something to Isabel, but I wanted to get your take on it first. When we meet at the café in town this afternoon, I'll run it by everyone."

The Pit Stop Café was famous for its biscuits, homemade, over-sized, flaky biscuits that most patrons ordered with thick sausage gravy. Wicker baskets of brown, piping hot biscuits were delivered to the tables by waitresses in pink uniforms.

"I've heard of it," said Samuel, "certainly have. We all have." Deborah, Sarah and Miriam all nodded.

"I've heard of it, too," Marti Freeman added spreading some grape jelly on a biscuit and popping it into her mouth.

"Greenway. How do you hear about such places?" asked Levi.

Bart sipped some hot tea and said, "When you've been underground as long as we have, but you still long for community, you begin to seek out places where you can find believers, even if it's miles from where you are. The grape vine, so to speak, in the home church circuit is an effective vehicle."

"So do we all agree?" John was posing the question when into the café strutted four men, two with guitars strapped to their backs.

"Jimmy Freeman! I'm not believing this!" one of them exclaimed.

James jumped up and an expression of shear delight spread across his face that none of his fellow travelers had yet seen.

"Oh, my gosh! What are you boys doin' here?" James asked as he gave them all manly bear hugs.

"Touring, man. Got a deal last week."

"You serious?" asked James.

"Serious as a judge, man. We're headin' back to Nashville tonight. They got us in the studio all next week."

Rachel, who was digging through her purse for a tissue, noticed, for the first time since the intrusion, Marti's face, which, in contrast to her husband's obvious enthusiasm was somber, almost pained.

The taller man with the guitar case lit a cigarette and said, "Man, you gotta come hear us play tonight. It would be like old times. We're at the Rider, a new club outside of Charleston."

James glanced around for a moment at his traveling companions. "Oh, I'm sorry. I need to introduce you to my friends." He introduced each one in the group to the musicians. "And you remember Marti," he said tentatively.

"Yes, Ma'am," the shorter man said, "always a pleasure."

Nonplussed by his mannerly demeanor Marti replied under her breath, "Sure is."

"We go way back," James said, addressing the whole group. "Collectively they're called 'Texas.' That's where they're from. Sounds like Nashville's where they're going, though." James winked at the band and grinning mischievously. "Honey, you wouldn't care if I caught a little bit of the show tonight, or at least some of sound check, would ya?"

"Yes, Ma'am," the taller man added. "We're in the old MCI. He won't get scanned going that far. One of us could drive him back here you know . . .whenever."

Marti said nothing, but feigned a smile.

"See, she's okay with it. Will you be here John?" James asked.

"Sure, James. I was about to ask if we could try a new plan anyway. We need to think it through and come up with the travel arrangements. But we'll probably head out in the morning."

"Oh sure, yes, I'll be here by then," said James grabbing his jacket and abruptly kissing Marti on the cheek. The café door slammed and he was gone. For a long time Marti and the three girls stood looking out the window. Rachel could feel the anguish in their spirits, though she did not fully understand what was happening.

Everyone agreed to camp for the night. A couple of extra tents had to be purchased, but the weather was mild, especially for this time of year, so they agreed to make do with a few tents and some travel pillows and thermal blankets they had been carrying all along. Micah, who had missed the entire café incident, located the group at a nearby family campground. When John asked him if he was confused about the meeting time he quickly muttered something about miscalculating the distance to a store in town where he needed some supplies. John knew he wasn't getting the whole story but asked no further questions. Toward evening, Simon's fever broke almost instantaneously. Rachel had been watching him very closely all day, forcing liquids down him and giving him fever reducer. He awoke from a late afternoon nap in a thick sweat, and his eyes and face appeared almost normal. Simon woke up hungry, which to Rachel was a good sign since he had eaten next to nothing for several hours. She breathed a thankful prayer as they set up camp for the night.

Marti had been uncharacteristically quiet and somber since they had left the café. She worked setting up her tent in silence, her girls helping with the stakes and the blankets as if they all knew the same secret but were not at liberty to share it with the others. Though the night was not too terribly cold, most everyone got very little sleep. John and Rachel were speculating about how to get to southern West Virginia without spending too much of their reserved cash which was dwindling; the Covas were also thinking about ways to get to the next destination and worrying about Maria who was restless with a sore throat and a fever. None of the children slept soundly in the tent as they were unused to the ground; Samuel had not slept well since his ribs had been injured, and his tossing and turning kept Deborah awake most of the night. Each traveler unbeknownst to the others wrestled with sleep. Around five a.m. Marti and her girls finally fell into unconsciousness for a couple of hours. Marti awoke at 7:35 to a sore neck and the sounds of crows overhead. She sat up, yawned and stared at the girls who were sleeping soundly beside her. Glancing down, she saw lying next to her blanketed legs a note scribbled on yellow legal paper. Immediately she recognized James's handwriting, and one tear ran down her flushed cheek.

By 8:15 everyone was roused and ready for the day. The travelers sat around a fire gulping coffee and juice and talking about the agenda which John had jotted down in the middle of the night.

"I don't think we all want to be rowing all the way to the border. Besides we'd have to get so many boats to make it work, and I don't think we can afford the rentals with our funds the way they are," John stated plainly, poking the fire with a stick.

Isabel set down her cup, "Exactly what is the situation with our funds. I think we need to assess that right now. Has everyone anteed up at this point? Have we pooled everything?"

"I've been keeping a log. Everyone's in the books, and we've got money, enough. It's just that the way we've been spending—food, rentals, necessities—we're at the point where we need to go easy. It's the unknowns that I'm worried about." John closed his notebook.

"Like what?" Samuel asked.

"Like we need to start getting realistic about this voyage over the Atlantic. We don't even know what vessel we'll be needing. We don't know how much money we'll need when we get there. We don't know who else is going to get hurt or sick and need medical attention. We all left in such a hurry, none of us had time to plan this all out completely. I wish Tim were here. He's the 'Plan Man.'" John took the last bite of a banana and folded the peeling carefully. "I hate to recommend this, but I think we need to cut back on food. Of course we need to keep some snacks at hand for the children, but if the rest of us could cut down to one big meal a day, I think it would really help with the financial situation."

Bart thoughtfully spoke, "John, you're right. I think we could all manage that. It wouldn't hurt for me to lose a little weight anyway." He patted his stomach. "Plus, I think if we go over all the gracious surprises over this past couple of weeks, I think we can see where we're being cared for by someone supernatural. There are too many coincidences, too many free gifts. God is providing; that's the truth of it."

John, who had been flipping through his notebook, landed on a page scrawled with ideas. "Can anyone besides me and Rachel navigate a sailboat?"

"I can," said Micah.

"Me, too," Miriam said. Samuel grinned as he discovered this new aspect he had not known.

"I can a little," said Levi.

"Good, well that makes five of us. Five boats. Four to a boat . . . ." John looked over at Marti as he made this last statement. Her eyes were red and puffy. She stared at the ground as she ran her fingers up and down the birch log on which she was sitting. John's face turned visibly sympathetic making everyone in the circle focus on Marti. She sat weeping, staring down into her hands as they fidgeted with a linen handkerchief.

Quietly John asked, "He isn't coming back, is he?"

"No." The three girls beside her wiped tears from their faces.

"What do you want to do, Marti?"

"If it's alright," she said closing her eyes for a moment, "If it's alright, we'd like to go on with you. He won't be back. He's not coming back this time. The temptation's too strong and . . . he's a weak man."

Rachel put her arm around Marti's shoulder. "We'd love to have you with us. We're gonna take care of you, don't worry. This is church," she added pointing to the people around the circle.

"We haven't prayed, you know, at all together, I mean," Levi said standing by a tree. "Is there any reason we can't do that now? There are too many unknowns—always makes me want to pray."

"Deborah, would you pray for us all?" John asked.

Deborah's prayer was powerful. Her vulnerability and her certitude in God's hand working in this and all situations made Deborah a warrior when it came to prayer. Everyone in the circle could sense a holy presence, and a feeling came over each one that in spite of the pain and the unknowns, everything was gonna be alright. When Deborah finished, she began to sing in a strong, alto voice, "When peace like a river attendeth my way, when sorrows like sea billows roll, whatever my lot, Thou has taught me to say, 'It is well; it is well with my soul.'" Bart, Isabel and Micah were unfamiliar with this hymn, but they listened as one by one everyone began to fill in the harmonies, beautiful four-part harmonies, "It is well, it is well with my soul."

Chapter 18

Bet pulled on a nylon parka as the women walked around Shaw's Lake. Some of the women had rented fishing gear at the tackle house and were already pulling in pike and largemouth bass. Tim walked with his arm around Hannah. They could see their breath frosty white against the blue sky. Gretchen stole up behind them and slid her arm into Hannah's.

"Hey, you," Hannah said playfully. "Is this a gorgeous day or what?"

"Yes." Gretchen didn't say anything for several minutes as they walked arm in arm around the lake. Finally she said, "That is not the question. What are we doing here; that is the question. And we are blessed in this, that we happen to know the answer. Ayes, in the immense confusion one thing alone is dear. We are waiting for Godot to come. . . ." Hannah looked into Gretchen's amber eyes, welling up with moisture. "Sometimes I find myself like Estragon, searching for enough rope to hang myself, hoping against all reasonable evidence to the contrary that Godot will show up before I end it all."

Hannah brushed the hair from Gretchen's face. "You don't have to wait. He's here. You just aren't looking with the right set of eyes." Hannah wiped a tear from Gretchen's cheek.

"I want to believe you. I want to believe you're right. I want to believe he's here. But there are so many bad things, so many hard, angry things. I've quit trying to talk to him about 'why.'"

Tim spoke almost in a whisper. "It's not always for us to know everything. We aren't God—He is. But I'll tell you this much, I know He misses your conversations, even the ones where you're asking him why. You know the Truth, Gretchen, deep inside yourself when you quit thinking for a minute about what's reasonable and what you can see, you know the Truth; now all you have to do is let it set you free."

"But I'm afraid. I'm afraid of what He will expect of me. I'm afraid to lose Bet. What will God make me do about her? For God's sake, Hannah, I'm a lesbian. I've heard all the teaching on that subject. I don't understand how the two of you can justify that either. "

"All God wants from you right now is you. Just come to Him, talk to Him, tell Him you want Him to have your life, because he loves you enough to do the absolute best by you. Then you and God work out what to do about Bet. I'm not going to give you some pat answer about your life," said Hannah.

"I wanna feel like Brother Pete. I want Jesus to be my friend." Gretchen began to sob like a child. Tim and Hannah sat with her on a log near the woods. Gretchen prayed a simple prayer asking God to be her friend again, asking his forgiveness for her sins and for her silence.

A grey heron floated over their heads landing majestically beside them near the water. With his slender neck erect and regal, the bird stepped lightly along the edge of the lake, followed the horizon with his slanted eyes, and bent gracefully to get a drink. Gretchen suddenly was overwhelmed with emotion and a deep warmth that she had never felt. She sighed, then laughed though the tears still streamed down her cheek. "Well, Brother Pete, I think I get it now."

Tim and Hannah looked at one another and smiled.

John quickly discovered that the sailing idea was not gong to be workable. The entire troop walked from marina to marina down the river only to discover that sailboats were far too expensive to rent and had to be returned to the place of origin. It seemed that getting from point A to point B by the river was quickly losing its appeal. The children were tiring as the hike was tedious; the day wore on. After talking with a portly gentleman named Max at Sails

Marina, the group collapsed around picnic tables on the lawn of the boat shop.

"Any fresh ideas?" John asked.

"Too tired to be fresh, Dad," Andrew said panting, his fair skin prickly red with heat. Simon who had not entirely recuperated from his infection was asleep on Bart's shoulder. The children were all sprawled out on the lawn like lazy dogs.

"Mr. Beckett?" The man named Max who had tried to help them with rentals approached John as he rested in the yard.

"Yes?" John said, standing slowly on his sore legs.

"I think I might have found you an option. Come inside with me." Micah and Samuel followed John into the boathouse. Max pulled out a map of West Virginia and said in a hushed tone, "I may have it all wrong, but I get the feeling you are . . . believers. Am I right?"

John hesitated for a moment as caution in these circumstances had become instinctive. Finally he said, "Yes, we are." Samuel nodded.

"There's a man I know who is moving his yacht down river today hoping to get to Florida by the end of the month. He's got a beautiful Viking 52 Convertible fully loaded. I told him about you, that I felt like you were believers. Tom's a good man. He's looking to sail out of the country, relocate in South America. You guys on chip?"

"No, none of us are, I'm afraid," John's face lost its enthusiasm.

"Well, that won't matter on the rivers. They don't run scans on motorized vessels until you reach the coast. You're only looking to go here, to the Virginia border near Greenway, aren't you?"

"Yes!" John breathed a sigh of relief. "Are there too many of us for one yacht?"

"You'll be in close quarters, but for few hours down the river, you'll be fine. Dress warmly. On deck it will be chilly." Samuel hugged John from the side and slapped Micah playfully on the back. It was the first time Micah had actually seen Samuel's teeth. He grinned with a pure joy that made Micah smile, too.

Tom Walsh was a gregarious, well-seasoned, sportsman with a thin frame and a salt water tan. He had Robert Redford-esque qualities, and Rachel couldn't tell by looking at him if he was forty or seventy. His hair was unnaturally blond and his smile, infectious.

"Welcome aboard the 'Cool Change,'" he said waving his arm in a grandiose manner toward the vessel.

Andrew shook his hand firmly, "Cool Change? Little River Band song, very cool."

The cockpit of the Cool Change was uncluttered and spacious; it was obvious that Tom ran a tight ship. The children walked around the forward deck, wide-eyed. Rachel was relieved to find the staterooms so warm and inviting. The children who were hours earlier complaining of hunger and fatigue felt that they had found an oasis. The u-shaped galley was situated opposite a dinette with windows all around. The kitchenette and refrigerator were well stocked with sodas and hot sandwiches. A cappuccino latte machine emerged out of the counter top at the press of a button. Rachel located a tin of Brazilian coffee and a gallon of milk and set out to make everyone Cuppa-style lattes. Classical music, mostly Debussy, was piped throughout the lower and upper decks. The children, especially Jesse, Thomas, Simon and Maria who had been popping pain reliever pills all day for sore throats, curled up on the beds in the forward and starboard staterooms. Maggie fell asleep by Andrew on the floor of the smaller stateroom on a palette under the thickness of a down comforter. Everyone else sipped coffee and gave silent thanks to God for the timely provisions.

Tom, as it turns out, had made a small fortune in an innovative automotive door locking system that caught on first with American manufacturers, then with foreign corporations, and now were used in virtually every automobile on the road. He was single, never married, and had spent the last twenty years and most of his money serving malnourished and physically ill people in third world countries. He had accepted the chip because he needed it to carry out his passions, but he had become increasingly disenchanted with the American government for its lack of monetary support to the poor of this world. He navigated the vessel like a tournament champion, his streaked, blonde hair blowing in the crisp breeze. "The sanctions put on Christian organizations who, let's be honest, do most of the charity work of the world, caused so many of them to close their doors and fold down due to lack of funding. The truth is that giving is simply not a national priority, or even the priority of the masses. It's the polite thing to do when you've got the extra cash, but it's not a mandate for most people like it is for believers. The sell-everything-you-have-and-follow-me line doesn't go over well these days with profit-minded folks."

Samuel smirked, "Forgive me for saying so, but isn't that easy for you to say. I mean, it appears at least to me that you are fairly set for life here. Got a pretty expensive little boat on top of it. It doesn't look to me like you've exactly followed the 'sell-everything-you-have' theology." For once Samuel had articulated exactly what the others were thinking, but were too afraid to say. Tom beaming from ear to ear was well acquainted with these accusations from fellow believers.

"I know what it looks like, but looks can be deceiving." Tom slowed the cruiser as he steered through a narrow passage. "When I became a believer everything changed--I have felt impressed to give away a large portion of what I make. For a while when I first started in the business, I bought into it all—the luxury home, the yacht, the vacation condos—all of it. Last year I sold the big house and bought a small ranch house in the country, liquidated all the rest of my assets. Last week I closed the sale on the ranch home as well. So all I got now is this boat and enough to buy some sort of car in Venezuela. I've tried to manage it well, put a good bit into foundations that will keep producing income for my 'habit.' There's nothing like the rush of seeing someone who has not eaten for days finally sit down to a meal, nothing like seeing the look of someone who's been hopelessly living with pain for years because they can't afford treatment finally get an operation or medical attention they need. It's life-changing stuff. Then you say to them 'Here is a cup of cool water in the name of Jesus. . . .'" Tom broke into a wide grin. Samuel, without responding, gave a steady nod, which let Tom know he understood and was in agreement with Tom's way of life.

Pin lights lining the doorways and walkways of the craft gave it a dramatic and magical glow as the Cool Change headed into the night sky. The sound of waves lapping against the boat and the even sway of the hull was a much-welcomed feeling after the jolting harshness of the train. One by one the tired travelers disappeared into the belly of the cruiser fell onto sofas or collapsed into berths sleeper divans and cots. John asked Tom if he needed any help in the cockpit and offered to stay up with him.

"No, thank you, John. You go ahead and get some sleep. I'm a night owl and this is my favorite time to talk to God."

Soaking in the soothing sounds of Debussy, John, full of gratitude, fell asleep on the floor next to Rachel.

Chapter 19

John awoke to the smell of Brazilian coffee. Rachel had toasted some bagels and the children were already on deck. Tom, who had dropped anchor for awhile in the night to get a few hours of sleep, exuded energy as he showed Maggie and Simon how to bait the small hooks on two pint-sized rods and how to watch the float for a signs of a bite. Isabel awoke with a sore throat and a low-grade fever. Rachel fixed her some hot chamomile tea and toast and handed her a couple of aspirin. In the cupboard of the washroom, Rachel found a bag of throat lozenges. Tom, after hearing the chokes and sputters coming up from the lounge, told her to take the whole bag.

"We are not far from Greenway. I assume you're going to the house church there," Tom said freeing a blue gill from Simon's line.

"Yes, that's where we are headed," said John.

"From here you can walk. It's seven miles southwest, but it's a nice day. You sure you wouldn't rather stay with me? Just ten days down the river. Several dams on the way that will slow us a bit, but South Americans are a friendly group."

"Actually, after traveling a day in these plush accommodations, it is very tempting. But my brother and sister-in-law would be fit to be tied. Simon, Maggie, and Thomas belong to them, and I know they must be dying to see their kids again. We're supposed to hook up in Virginia at some point, then head to the coast. We don't have a plan from there, but we're trying to find a non-motorized option. None of us has a chip."

Tom stood thinking for a moment then began to rifle through some papers in the compartment by the helm. He pulled out a cream business card and handed it to John. It read: Silas Alcon,

Ship Maker, 2319 Billow Lane, Virginia Beach, Virginia. "He's a man I met when I was looking to buy a boat. Good man, a little quirky, but he may have something you can use." Tom pulled out a sheet of white paper and began to sketch a map. "Here's how you get to Greenway. Be careful in Virginia. Strict on chip here."

"You are a Godsend, Tom. I've gotta say that one thing I've learned so far on this adventure is that there's more of us out there than I thought."

"As they say, 'next year in Jerusalem, brother.'" Tom's eyes gleamed as he pulled his tousled hair from his face.

Walking to Greenway was without difficulty. Tom's map kept the travelers off main roads and along some breathtaking routes. Eventually they came to a wooded area near an unpaved country lane. "This is it," John announced as they headed down the winding driveway. John thought about all the people who had been discipled and schooled at this place and what a difference those lives were now making in the world for Jesus.

The house, nestled in between two giant hemlock trees, was rustic and distinctive. It had the appearance of a Swiss Chalet, made of rough-cut lumber covered by a shallow pitched roof, and large windows all around. It was expansive, much larger than the 19th century Swiss versions, and it flaunted decorative motifs and heraldic shields. The landscaping was well thought out, like something out of Jane Austen, although it had not been manicured for some time. Out in front, a birdbath with sculpted crosses stood empty. Boston ivy had grown up around the window casements, and in the flower boxes were dried petunias and impatiens. Walking up the steps of the front porch to the door, Rachel noticed that several rolled newspapers, damp and yellowed, were strewn alongside the walk. The door itself was cut in an arch and brick red Hansel and Gretel- like. It had a wrought iron knocker in the shape of a fish. John used it to rap on the door. There was no answer. John rapped again, louder this time. Again no one answered. Micah stepped up behind a row of yews and peered into the expansive window, cupping his hands around his eyes to cut the glare.

"You see anything?" John asked.

"No, I don't think anyone is here." At this point Bart, Sarah and Levi were all gazing in the windows.

"I don't believe anyone has been here in months," said Rachel. "The yard is grown up; the landscaping is uncared for, and these newspapers are dated from May."

John sat down on the porch and put his face in his hands. "Did you try the door, honey?" asked Rachel.

"Yes," said John with an exasperated sigh." It's locked."

"Back one's locked, too," said Levi emerging from the side of the house. "Whole thing's locked up tight as a drum. No open windows, either."

Maggie and Maria began a game of ring-around–the-roses as the adults stood staring up at the empty windows or sat sprawled on the porch. Simon was bent over picking violets in the yard.

"One, two, three, four . . .," he said. Andrew stole up behind him.

"You counting flowers, Simon," he asked.

"No, not flowers. Fish!" Andrew looked at the ground where Simon was pointing and saw a series of small garden stones all bearing the ichthus symbol. They were spaced evenly about three feet apart and appeared to be leading into the wooded area to the east of the house. Andrew followed Simon as he stepped on the stones one at a time. Andrew began to notice that each stone had a unique symbol in the center in Greek with ornate designs around each one. The path wound around several oaks and maples in the thickest part of the woods until it ended at the base of a circular configuration of plain, round stones with a cement statue of Jesus in the center, his arms outstretched, and at his feet a wooden bench for resting. There was an inscription on the statue, which read, "Come ye all who are weary and heavy laden and I will give you rest." Just under the inscription in the center of the feet of Jesus was another ichthus symbol. Simon smiled up at Andrew and poked at the symbol with his index finger. When he did, a drawer below the feet popped open which made Andrew jump back and Simon giggle. Inside was a folded piece of paper that appeared to be a letter sealed in a plastic bag and under that, a skeleton key. Andrew grabbed the bag and the key, snatched Simon by the hand and ran back to the house.

"Dad!" he shouted, running to his father and handing him the bag and key. "We found these in the woods in a statue of Jesus."

Quickly everyone assembled around John as he began to read: "Greetings in the blessed name of Christ Jesus. If you have found this key, most likely you have heard of Greenway by reputation and you are welcome here. We regret that we are not present to greet you in person as we have gotten word that the authorities are on their way to our house even as we write this letter to take us to a rehabilitation facility. My wife and I are glad to suffer in this way for the cause of Christ. We can be partners with him in his suffering and this thought brings us great joy. However, we apologize to you who have worshiped here with us and to our children who will be apart from us for a time. We hope that all of you will continue to grow in the grace and in the faith in these difficult times. Our house belongs to any of you who find this key and who belong to Christ. Please use our home as if it were your own. May the peace of Jesus Christ be in your hearts forever. The Burton Family."

The key slid into the keyhole on the rounded door like a hand in a glove. Inside the foyer, the pine floors were shining with polish as if someone had recently been there. The great room smelled of lavender and coffee. The décor was sparse and open and the furnishings were shaker in style, blocky oak and pine tables and chairs. The colossal dining table just in front of them surrounded by a picture window along the rear of the house was girded with thick, wooden benches. The entire house seemed like it was built to accommodate an army. There was a cavernous hearth with photographs along the mantel identified by nameplates, all missionaries in the field of service. Around the corner was the kitchen. Rachel and Isabel explored it with envy—double ovens, large, porcelain sinks, built in countertop ranges with custom controls, a 10' x 10' walk in pantry fully stocked with non-perishable items, sub zero refrigerator and oversized freezer full of meat—all the amenities. "Someone must be paying to keep the electricity going," said Isabel. The walls, a pale lemon, showcased a collection of blue glass bottles, some antique, lined along the shelving over the cabinets. Levi who was surveying the bedrooms had already counted five on the first floor. A narrow staircase leading to a second floor revealed a library and four additional bedrooms as well as a greenhouse that had been used for growing vegetables year round. The children discovered an enchanting recreation room in the basement, containing four brightly colored student desks, a flat screened TV with several shelves of children's movies and educational films, a ping pong table, a mini trampoline, a loaded game and craft cabinet, and plastic bins, neatly labeled, filled with interlocking blocks, action figures, dolls and doll clothes, and miniature cars with race tracking which only needed to be assembled. Through a hidden door in the back of the room Jesse discovered an old fashioned bowling alley with soundproof walls. The pins had to be set up by hand, but Thomas and Jesse were elated to have discovered it. Andrew not only found an old workable turntable and a nice collection of classic rock albums, but in a closet he found a vintage Fender Stratocaster and an acoustic Martin D-15. Immediately he sat down and began to play. Maggie, Maria and Simon assembled a track and Simon began to line up cars for racing.

Bart built a fire in the fireplace that quickly eradicated the chill, and Isabel and Rachel began to prepare a meal with dry goods and poultry from the freezer. Deborah and Miriam walked around the backyard until they came to a garden swing in which they sat discussing the history of the Reformation. Everyone settled into a room; the children were exploring a jungle themed room adjacent to the playroom, with vines hanging from the ceiling and three sets of bunk beds shaped like palm trees. Samuel sat down at the baby grand piano in the living room and began to play. Marti lit candles then walked out the front door and into the woods. After a few hours of getting settled and locating the rooms, the tension, which had come from traveling together in such close quarters, began to lift.

After dinner, several of the guests reclined in overstuffed furniture around the living room. Micah and Marti retreated to bedrooms, while Ruth and Becca were enticed by the thoughts of a hot bath.

"It's been a labyrinth so far, but amazingly protected. I mean in spite of all the close calls, I have felt a presence of . . . I don't know, protection," John said. "Granted, the money situation could be better, but we have not gone hungry or been without shelter these past few weeks. Even roughing it has not been all that 'rough' . . . yet."

"Maybe in a strange way our steps have been ordered," Bart said as he massaged Isabel's shoulders.

Levi fiddled with a tassel on the sofa pillow, then said, "I can't stop thinking about the Burtons. What was it they did that was so threatening to national security? It boggles me. They sent dozens of purpose-driven people out into the world to give them some hope, some healing, and tonight we are in their house and they are in a Center. What in the hell goes on in these Centers? How do they think they can change people's belief systems with a series of classes and personal conditioning on moderate behavior?"

"It's not always just that," Eve muttered.

John turned to her, "What's not 'just that?'"

"The Centers. Depends where you go. We knew a man from Georgia in that DARE movement. You know, the group who believed if they spent hours, days, weeks on their faces together in one place praying in tongues that our nation would be healed? Well, he was arrested, taken to a Center with several others we knew. But we were told that he never stopped—kept right on praying with fervor, even in the Center. They tried to 'condition' him--private therapy, hypnosis--you name it. Then onto isolation therapy where he was forced to meditate on the greater good of the people and 'positive' symbols like the American flag, the peace sign, but he never stopped praying. Finally they experimented with some shock therapy, heavy medication, and God knows what else, until the state warden inspected one day and decided that shock was inhumane and medication was getting expensive. So they gave him a partial lobotomy."

Isabel gasped. "Are you sure? How do you know about this?" John asked.

"We ran into him this summer. He was living with his sister who has to care for him now around the clock. She had been arrested, too, and admitted to the same Center, but when she saw what was happening to her brother, she became compliant. Did whatever they told her. Signed all the proper documents assuring them she would not 'disturb the peace.' She left quietly and lives reclusively in West Texas."

A troubled hush fell over the room.

"Maybe, since it's the eve before Sabbath, I could pray the Sabbath prayer," Levi said.

Samuel shook his head, stood up, and started to leave. "I've made a mistake."

"Where are you going?" asked John.

"I can't do this. THIS," he said pointing to Levi who sat with his mouth gapping wondering what was going on. "There's only ONE way. That's why that man in the center was punished. It was a God thing—Paul warned us of the abuses of speaking in tongues. There's one way to do it."

"No, Samuel, not one way to do it . . . one way to heaven through Jesus. Lots of ways to do it," said Bart.

"That figures coming from you. I'm sorry. We've got everything here from speaking in some unknown gibberish and calling it prayer to kissing some guy's ring in Rome and now this Hebrew ritual—isn't this what has divided us, all these 'ways?' Are we going to start admitting Muslims? Let them pray to Allah and called it some ancient word for 'Jesus?' We should have all just stuck to the Word in the first place, to the fundamentals. There are no fundamentals with you people. We're going to be judged for this, you know. God doesn't like watered down religion or misinterpretation or compromise."

Rachel stood up and walked over to Samuel. "I understand where you're coming from. I understand even what you're saying to a point. But as a believer, I've gotta tell you, I'm offended by you. You hurt people; you stand at the gate like a Gestapo, like the religious leaders of Jesus' day, and you won't let anyone in. That is offensive to me, especially when you're doing it to people who genuinely love Jesus, who have sacrificed just as much as you have, or more, to be here."

Levi who was still shocked at this outburst from Samuel said, "Let's talk about fundamentals. God started HIS work way before you came along. He started it with the Jewish people. We were chosen, Samuel, and THAT'S biblical. Don't talk to me about acceptance of others coming into the fold. That's what my people have had to do their whole lives. We've been persecuted by every group of so-called followers of Jesus, including good protestants like Hitler and the well-meaning, Catholic Church who decided it was Godly to slaughter our people in the Middle Ages."

"Hold on," said Bart raising a hand, "Let's talk seriously about the poor Jewish population here in the States, you know the ones who make all the money, have all the education, hold all the top positions in all the top corporations. Hitler's been dead for years—I think we all can agree that he certainly does not represent the views of the majority of believers today. He's gone—the terror of his reign is gone. I say it's time to get past some of that. It's unseemly in light of the current status of Jewish people in this country and the strong voice they've had in government for decades to keep dwelling on persecution that happened ages ago."

This last comment sent everyone in the room into open argument, all speaking in raised voices, out of turn, the volume growing to an unbearable pitch, until Marti and Micah emerged from their rooms with their hands cupped over their ears and entered the living room which amidst all the standing, yelling, hand gesturing, crying and criticizing had turned into something quite frightening in light of their current circumstances. All at once, there was a piercing whistle from Micah who happened to be standing nearest to the basement stairway. Holding his hand up, everyone startled and shaking, grew quiet. "Listen," he said.

It took several seconds for their ears, still clanging with dissonance to adjust to the sounds. It was singing, the sounds of a strummed guitar and children's voices. John and Rachel began to recognize the tune; everyone heard the words, "Blest be the tie that binds our hearts in Christian love; the fellowship of kindred minds is like to that above." Then Maria's melodic voice could be heard teaching the children a song she had learned in Sunday school called, "Father, Son and Holy Ghost." Rachel wiped the wetness from her eyes and walked toward the stairs. John followed with the others behind him. They tiptoed down the steps where they could see without being detected. Maria was giving each child a broken piece of a saltine cracker. "Take, eat. This is my body, which was broken for you. Dominus Vobiscum," she said. The children, even Simon, were serious and reverent, as they had been taught to be during communion. Then Thomas passed around a box of grape juice. All the children took a sip from the straw. "This is my blood of the new Covenant which is shed for you and for the forgiveness of sins." Maggie stood slowly then said, "Do this for the remembrance of me."

The children, heads bowed, sat holding hands. They did not speak. Isabel and Bart began to weep. John, visibly remorseful, dropped his head in shame. However, it was Samuel who was most shaken by the scene. His shoulders began to tremble, and he broke into heavy sobs. The children, startled by the intrusion, looked toward the staircase. Bart put his arm around Samuel, who, at this humble act of kindness, fell into Bart's chest, weeping uncontrollably.

"What is it, Samuel?" Bart asked. "What is it, really?"

"It's not you. I'm afraid. I'm afraid God will punish us all for not keeping his word. I'm afraid he already is. I'm afraid if I let go of what I've always known as truth, there won't be anything left. I won't exist. I'm afraid that I'll never feel what some of you evidently feel. I'm afraid God won't love me if I don't do everything just right."

John moved next to Samuel. "That's not how it works. Not at all. You don't have to fear letting go of some of these ridiculous lines. Do you believe God is sovereign?"

"Absolutely," said Samuel.

"Do you believe he loves you so much that he would die again and again only for you, if he needed to?"

"Honestly . . . I don't know. I believe it in my head."

"Have you ever been in love?"

The question took him completely by surprise. "Why?"

"Have you?"

"Yes. Years ago. High school. I loved Alicia. I loved her so much that when she said she loved me, I couldn't eat or sleep for weeks. I thought about her constantly—I couldn't stop. I was crazy in love with her."

John smiled. "Okay, let's put out of your mind all the other stuff you think you know about God and think about how you felt with Alicia. That's you and God. That's it right there. He's crazy in love with you. He said, 'Do without Samuel? I'd die first.' You can let some of this go. He loves you enough to keep you where you need to be."

"Serve you with gladness and singleness of heart," Simon said, chiming in with only part of his line and giggling.

"Thus endeth the lesson," announced Maria resolutely.

Chapter 20

"Dad," asked Andrew, "do you think it would be okay to play some of these old records now?"

"Yes, that would be fine," he replied.

Andrew picked up the guitar and began to play along with the Rolling Stones, "Jumpin' Jack Flash." Simon wiggled and hopped, his version of dancing, shaking his head furiously to the music. Maggie and Maria held hands and spun circles around the room. Thomas and Jesse played percussion on the chairs and sofas with some toy magician's wands they had found. Inspired by the uninhibited exuberance of their children, Bart clutched Isabel by the arm and pulled her out onto the floor. Isabel could at least keep steady rhythm and her movements were smooth, but as Bart began to twist and gyrate to the music with his lumbering body in the most oafish manner, everyone, including Samuel, couldn't help but laugh.

"Go on and dance," John said to Samuel.

"Believe it or not," he admitted, "I can't. It's been too long."

"That's crazy," said John, "No one forgets how to dance. They just think they do."

John stood up and put his arm around Rachel. Leading her to the floor, they launched into something that somewhat resembled Voguing, which was even more hilarious than Bart's gesticulations. Micah, whose dark mood had lifted somewhat, asked Eve to dance; Levi asked Sarah. Andrew, who was acting the role of disc jockey, played The Who, Led Zeppelin, and the Doobie Brothers.

John had forgotten how much he loved to dance with his wife. Often in the past they would attend functions where dancing, mostly ballroom dancing, was part of the evening's festivities. He loved the sound that her gown would make as she moved in and out of his arms. When their lives had become a steady grind of working and making ends meet, it was as if his whole being had no air in it, like all that held their world together and kept them from drowning was his accumulation of hours at the end of the work day and his meager paycheck at the end of the week. Now as he spun Rachel around and around under the dim lights of the basement at Greenway, it was as if all the string that had bound him so tightly unwound with every turn. He had nothing to hold him down to a place, and the things in life, which he truly prized, were right there in the room with him. He found himself more present in the moment than he had been for a long time watching his children lost in music and his newfound friends howling at the random hilarity of the moment.

Out of the corner of his eye he saw Samuel finally stand up from his perch on the step and cross the room to the chair where Miriam was sitting, nodding contentedly to the music. Her blond hair, which was usually pulled back into a ponytail, was clean and loose around her face. She wore a plain green cotton dress with a white cardigan over it. Just as Samuel reached out his hand and asked her to dance, Andrew began to play "Best of My Love" by the Eagles. Everyone segued into a slow sway, even the children. Thomas put his thin, brown arms around Maria who was being watched very closely by Isabel. Maria stared shyly at the floor watching her own feet move. Thomas focused straight ahead at Maria's nose, trying not to smile.

Samuel, anticipating an up tempo tune, took Miriam awkwardly into his arms and stood frozen for several seconds. Miriam beaming with sympathy began to move slowly to the music, guiding Samuel's tall frame back and forth. Samuel's face was branded with confusion, as if all the elements inside of him were at war with each other. He looked to Miriam for help, to be rescued from his conflict, and she took the cue with tender authority. Full of longing, her eyes communicated what she could not, and John watched as the expression on Samuel's face began to soften. The feelings that had for so long been pushed down began to rise to the surface and manifest themselves in the lines and contours of Samuel's brown skin. His dark eyes became fluid as the music started to crescendo then fall. John watched with the fascination of a voyeur as Samuel's hand moved from Miriam's waist up to her face. He ran his brown thumb over the curve of Miriam's pale cheek and under her chin. He brushed a strand of blonde hair away from her eyes, and stared at her face as if he had never seen it before. Miriam pressed her slender hands over Samuel's as an act of affirmation. John was watching these moments of discovery as he held Rachel close, her head on his shoulder. Finally, Samuel leaned in close to Miriam and kissed her pink lips with his own pouting mouth, a brief gentle kiss which made John look away out of respect for the fragility of the moment. John glanced over at Bart and Isabel who had also been watching the scene with keen interest. Bart winked at John, and they all seemed as if they had foreseen this unfolding of events. Lost in the dance, they all soon forgot their despicable circumstances and the time on the face of the wall clock.

It was the first good night's sleep in days. The children, too exhausted to stay up late, went to bed without arguing with Rachel. Micah was sitting on the couch reading when Sarah, the last wakeful one, went to her room. Sarah had not been feeling well most of the day and finally lost her voice altogether. She spent the first couple of hours in bed coughing and kept Miriam awake next to her. Miriam was having a hard enough time sleeping as it was. She lay awake several hours grinning like the Cheshire Cat and staring at the full moon out the window. Marti, who was also wakeful, awoke around three twenty to get a glass of water. She was surprised to find Micah still awake in the north corner of the living room with a dilapidated laptop on his knees on which he was intently focused.

"Did you have trouble sleeping?" she asked.

Micah had been unaware of her presence. Slamming his laptop shut he hopped up looking a bit sheepish and disheveled. "No, I was just heading that way," Micah whispered nervously, and he tiptoed down the hall to the room he was sharing with Levi and Samuel. Marti stood a long time by the bay window in the living room staring at the moon. It had an orange hue and was enormous. In the yard she watched a cat dash into a thicket of rose bushes. Marti's hair, which was down for the night, drooped casually around her shoulders. Her white cotton gown was wrinkled. She ran her hand down the front over bulges and bumps which used to be an hour glass figure. The moonlight illuminated the lines in her face, but her eyes were full of the naivety of youth. She breathed a fog on the corner of the window and drew a small "m" with her finger, then erased it.

As the sun rose up through the branches of trees, the house itself seemed to awaken little by little. Levi had been up for an hour and was reading the Talmud in the wooden swing outdoors, swaddled in a thick, down comforter. Rachel laughed to herself when she saw him with his hair tossed every which way and his oval head emerging from the covering like a bulb. Ruth and Becca were making breakfast, instant pancakes with dried apples and bacon. Simon was sitting in Spiderman pajamas playing with miniature cars on the coffee table. Maria was brushing Maggie's hair and sweeping it into a haphazard knot with clips and bows that she had found in a jewelry box in one of the bedroom closets.

The day evolved into one of relaxation and recreation. Samuel, mellowed by his dance with Miriam, was conversing civilly with Bart, Isabel, Levi and Marti; Micah seemed somewhat preoccupied but found entertainment watching the children play kickball in the backyard. Rachel was acting as nursemaid to Sarah who by late afternoon was feeling much better. Ruth, Becca and Eve had warmed up to Miriam and Deborah—they played a long round of Monopoly then sung together around the piano with Ruth accompanying their harmonies. John and Levi had a long conversation about Israel and its role in apocalyptic prophesies. Levi had some interesting theories because of his years studying Jewish theology as well as his recent studies of the book of

Revelation. Marti sat out under the statue of Jesus with his outstretched arms, and she watched the squirrels scurry in and out of trees.

"Kinda chilly for squirrel watching, isn't it?" Marti looked up and saw Micah coming through the pines with of cup of tea in his hand that he offered her in a gentlemanly manner.

"Thanks. Yes, it's a little chilly. I find it strangely refreshing right now," she said sipping the tea.

"I love nature. I feel most at home breathing the air in a woods. You can actually smell the pine. I feel like Thoreau—always wanting to pare it down to the essentials. Real life is too full of . . . other stuff. Gets in the way of what matters, clarity. At least it does for me."

Marti watched him as he examined the bark on a white birch. "How long?"

"What?" he asked still focused on the tree.

"How long have you struggled with it?" she said in a hushed tone. Micah's eyes shot up and zoomed in on Marti who looked at him matter-of-factly over her cup of tea.

"What do you mean?" he asked.

"You know what I mean. Pornography. Sex. You're an addict. I can smell one ten miles away. James was an addict, you know." Micah shrugged trying to feign an expression of innocence. "Come on, Micah. You're too straightforward to cover this one. I can read you--the moodiness, the late arrivals, the staying up and slipping off by yourself. You hate yourself for it, too, don't you? I see how you look at Eve and Becca and Miriam when you think no one is watching. You hate that everything inside you tells you not to objectify women, to respect them, but when you're left alone with yourself, probably with some old wounds, you go back to your habit every time. Then you fall into the great addiction shame cycle. Trust me, I've read all the books."

Micah stared at her with his mouth open in shock as if her directness had unmasked him and left him standing naked in the cold.

"I don't know what to say," he said under his breath.

"Well, why don't you start by being honest? I'm over it with all the lies. Living with an addict makes you jaded. After awhile you don't take anything anyone tells you at face value."

"How did you know that my problem was porn. I mean . . . ."

"It's more of a feeling, Micah, like a spirit. I can feel it all over you every time I'm around you, every time you relate to other people. I know what I know."

Micah looked away, then down at the damp ground. "I hate it. I hate myself for it. And I'm afraid of . . . ." he trailed off.

"Of what you might do?" asked Marti.

"Yes."

"Well, it's a real fear, Micah. What you think becomes who you are eventually. I'm sure you probably already hit the strip clubs, 900 numbers, ran up your debt, and think nothing of it—it's part of your life. But it won't stay there—it will escalate. You'll need more and you'll cross lines you never thought you'd cross. Just like any other kind of addict. The drug begins to use you."

Micah began to weep. "I don't want to hurt women I love and care about. It makes me literally ill to know that a beautiful little girl like Maggie looks up to me. But you're right. Sometimes I'm already in a place before I even know I'm there—I don't even remember how I got there. I lose all track of time. I'm needing harder stuff on the net—last night I was on . . . kiddie porn before I realized it!" He began to weep. What's wrong with me?" He collapsed to the ground.

Marti set her teacup down on the bench and walked over to Micah who was leaning against the trunk of the tree. Tears ran down his nose and onto a patch of moss. She slipped her arm around him.

"I've heard you talking with John and Bart about the 'God thing' as you call it with a lot of distain. I don't know what happened between you and God to make you feel like that. I don't know that much about you at all except I know you're trapped under something heavy and you want out. And I'm gonna tell you something you're not gonna want to hear. The only way out from under this thing requires you to ask for God's help. People out there will give you all kinds of psycho babble, but the bottom line is that you're going to have to submit to Him on this and he'll give you the grace to get through it, to turn away from it. And I'm not gonna lie to you. There will be some hard work ahead on your part. You're gonna have to lay aside your desires and sweat it out, and at first it's going to seem impossible. But after awhile you'll find it has less and less hold on you. It may always be a vulnerable spot in your life, but it won't control you like it does now."

Micah stood staring at the ground. He nodded, but said nothing to Marti. Marti patted him on the shoulder. "You're alright, Micah. Stronger than you think. You can do this if you really want to. If you need me, I'll be here for you." She kissed her index finger and touched it to his cheek, then walked away.

Chapter 21

"It's not your turn! You already had a turn!" Jesse screamed.

"Say it again, and I'll . . . ," Thomas retorted.

"You'll what? Give it back to me!"

"Come any closer and I'll . . . " The strained voices escalated until Rachel was forced to call a halt to the bickering. She knew if she did not intervene the verbal sparing would segue into a physical manifestation. Both boys were tired. That was obvious. So Rachel made the executive decision that all the children should take naps. Isabel agreed on behalf of Maria who had been running hard outside playing tag with Maggie all morning and was hanging lifelessly on the arm of the sofa.

While the children napped, Rachel perused the bookcases of the house. Nearly every room had a bookcase, floor to ceiling, with the most eclectic collection of tomes she had seen in a private home, especially now when books were so scarce. In a small office beside the master bedroom, she discovered, to her delight, a few antique selections of American poets. There even a first edition of Whitman's Leaves of Grass. Beside it was Emily Dickinson, her complete works. Rachel removed both books from the shelf and was turning Leaves of Grass over in her hand admiring the binding when she glanced up at the vacant place the books had left and noticed a lever that was flush to the wall. She laid the books on the cherry desk and removed several others from the same shelf. The lever, painted to match the shelving, was nearly invisible and entirely so when the books were in place. Slowly she flipped the lever up. She heard a "click," then the sound of a motor. To her amazement the entire section of the bookcase began to turn sideways like something out of a Hardy Boys novel.

Beyond the shelves it was dark. Rachel squinted but could not make out anything in the interior. Quickly she ran down the hall to the kitchen where she found Marti washing some dishes.

"Come with me," she whispered, grabbing the flashlight from the pantry and heading back down the hall. Marti, covered in dish soap, looked intrigued and Rachel led her into the office. "Look at this," said Rachel.

"What is it?" Marti asked.

Rachel flicked on the flashlight. Both women gasped. Inside, there was a narrow passageway. Scriptures from the New Testament and the Psalms were written on the walls. They walked down the hall farther and discovered a slender, inconspicuous door. They opened it cautiously, their hearts beating with anticipation. Rachel shined the light inside. The walls were lined with shelves full of canned food and water. Three cots, set up on the far side of the room, outlined its dimensions that seemed to be about twelve by twelve feet. In the center was a table with a camp light, which, to their surprise, was flickering brightly. In the ceiling was an air vent. Rachel moved the flashlight across every corner of the peculiar room. In the far right there was a gray blanket thrown over something that appeared to be an end table or a desk. The women walked toward the concealed thing and lifted the blanket. Marti let out a scream that echoed throughout the entire house. Under the blanket were three elderly people, two men and one woman, trembling with fear. A pungent odor caught Rachel off guard as she jumped back dropping the blanket to the floor.

"Good heavens! Who are you?" The three people did not say anything. Bart and John came bursting into the room having heard Marti scream.

"What in Saint Peter's name is this room??" asked John. Then seeing the three people in the corner, he let out an, "OH!" The old woman began to cry.

Marti, who had been stunned to silence, finally came to her senses. "Don't cry. We aren't going to hurt you."

"Yes, y'will!" The man on the right, wearing overalls and a dingy flannel shirt and sporting a beard, finally spoke. "You say y'won't but y'will. Harm will come of it, sister. We know what y'all do in them thar centers. We know y'all."

"Oh, but we're not from a center. We're hiding here, too. Please don't be afraid. How long have you been here?" asked John bending down on one knee to speak to them.

"Not sure. Nearly a month, I believe it to be. Forgot to keep a count. We've heard y'all in the house. Sounds like the whole army! How many of ya are there?"

John laughed, "I'm sorry we've been so loud. There are several of us. We're believers. We've heard so many good things about Greenway and the house church that we came to stay for a couple of days. Then I promise, you can have your house back."

"Oh, this ain't our house. The Burtons took us in after the army came to the mountains and took our church and most our family to the center. We been hidin' here off and on ever since they came and took the family. We ain't bathed in awhile. Please accept our apologies for stinkin' as we do."

"That's okay," said John. The woman, who had finally stopped crying, looked at John with an expression of innocence.

"This is my sister, Dorcas and one brother-in-law, Phillip. My name's Mathias. We's from the mountains near Georgia."

With some difficulty they all three stood up to shake John's hand. Both men were unusually thin and bony. The woman was both thin and diminutive. The longer John and Rachel stood in the room, the more poignant was their awareness of the odor, a putrid mixture of body smells and urine; the smell was overpowering. Rachel and Marti began to back away into the office room.

"Let's get you folks out of here. We've got several men and some tough women in our group." John winked. "You'll be safe with us for the night."

"Seein' as we ain't got nothin' to fear, let me flush yonder toilet." The old man tiptoed spryly to the other side of the room where there was a hole in the floor. He cranked a lever on the wall and there was a loud "whoosh." "Can't flush when army men's around. Move it along, Dorcas." He took the woman by the arm and, followed by Phillip, they shuffled down the scripture hall and into the light of the office where all three immediately covered their eyes with their hands.

"Lands it's bright in here!" These were the first words from Phillip's lips who quickly wiped tears from his sunken face. Rachel walked to the windows and lowered the blinds.

"There. Is that better?" she asked.

The three elderly people blinked and focused on the others around them. Setting his eyes on Bart, Mathias said, "Why yer a big fella, ain't ye?" Bart smiled and chuckled out loud. "Now if y'all don't mind none we'd like to have us a nice bath. No need to fuss. We know where yonder washrooms is." Then Mathias cleared his throat with a blustering "Humpph" and the three of them shuffled out the door. They all went into the back bedroom where Andrew was sleeping, opened the closet, removed several items of clothing and towels, closed the closet door, and shuffled out. Andrew, who was still groggy with sleep, raised his head a little from the bed and squinted at the intruders with a confused look on his face, then lay back down as if resigned to the fact that strange things were always happening in this present company.

John heard three clicks of restroom doors, and the three strange newcomers disappeared from sight as quickly as they had emerged. Marti and Rachel agreed to bleach the "hiding room" while their new guests were bathing, shaking their heads in amusement as they thought of Mathias. "Well there you have it," John said to Bart grinning.

Dinner was an interesting affair. Phillip, Mathias and Dorcas were verbally grateful for a home cooked meal, and the warm, delicious food opened up a conduit of stories from the trio about their lives in the mountains, about the Burtons taking them in for almost a year, about their months in hiding, emerging only now and then to bathe and inspect or clean the house, about their assumptions and fears during the past few hours when they were invaded by this noisy group of people. "We heard ungodly music, devil music, comin' up from yonder cellar. Sent cold chills down m'spine."

Andrew smirked, "Sorry about that, sir. I was playing that music just for fun. I didn't mean to offend you."

Mathias raised an eyebrow at Andrew, then shook his head in disapproval. "So what kinda God-fearin' Christians are y'all?" he asked, directing the question to Bart.

"Well my wife and daughter and I are Catholic; Marti, here, and her girls are Pentecostal; Levi is a Jewish Christian, and Micah . . .we're not sure yet," he said winking at Micah.

"Micah is an environmentalist!" Maggie said taking Micah by the hand.

"And John and his family," Bart continued, "Well they're just your run-of-the-mill evangelicals."

"Run-of-the-mill?" Mathias asked questioning Bart's assessment. "What mill?"

John laughed out loud; everyone did until finally even Mathias, Phillip and Dorcas broke out into a wheezy laughter. Simon walked over to Dorcas and stood quietly by her chair. Finally she took notice of him.

"Well, hello there. What a fine fella y'are!" Simon beamed.

"I like your glasses. They're sparkly." She pulled Simon up on her lap.

"These here glasses are as old as the hills. Can't see much without 'em, though."

"I like your name, Miss Dorcas," he said with a shy smile.

"I like your name . . . what is it? Oh, yes, Simon." Simon giggled.

"Since we are all together," said Levi following the meal, and since this is my Sabbath . . . do you think it would be okay for us to do the Shabbat Havdalah together? I'll lead you," he stated looking at Samuel in a conciliatory way. "I mean, I don't want to offend anyone, but . . .."

"Why not," Samuel consented nodding at Levi.

Levi instructed everyone to use some square cloth napkins he found for head coverings. He explained to the children that the Havdalah was the service at the end of the Sabbath day and was to be taken very seriously. The children helped Levi set up the chalice of wine, the small box of herbs (mostly cinnamon and cloves) and a candle, which was not a genuine Havdalah candle, but under the circumstances, Levi felt that God would understand. When Levi and the children located three stars in the sky, they began the ceremony. Levi set the wine in the center of the table with his friends all around him. Phillip, Dorcas, and Mathias opted to sit in the corner of the room on chairs, but they were reverent and respectful as Levi said the first blessing over the wine. "Barukh atah Adonai Elohaynu melekh ha-olam, borei p'riy ha-gafen. (Amein)." Everyone together recited the translated phrase that Levi had given to them: "Blessed are You, Lord, our God, King of the Universe, who creates the fruit of the vine. (Amen)"

Then Levi set the box of spices in front of him and said, "Barukh atah Adonai Elohaynu melekh ha-olam, borei minei b'samim. (Amein)." Everyone said, "Blessed are You, Lord, our God, King of the Universe, who creates varieties of spices." The third blessing was recited over the two burning candles, which were set close together so that the flames overlapped. Levi spoke the words in Hebrew, "Barkh atah Adonai Elohaynu melekh ha-olam, borei m'orei ha-eish (Amein)." Together, everyone echoed in English, "Blessed are You, Lord our God, King of the Universe, who creates the light of fire." Levi moved his cupped hands over the flames, eyeing the shadows across his fingers. Finally, Levi said his next lines almost in a whisper, ending with the phrase, "Barukh atah Adonai, ha-mavdil bayn kodesh l'chol. (Amein)." When he finished, those around the table spoke quietly the translation, "Blessed are You, Lord, our God, King of the Universe, who distinguishes between the sacred and the secular, between the light and dark, between Israel and the nations, between the seventh day and the six days of labor. Blessed are You, Lord, who distinguishes between the sacred and the secular. (Amen)."

With that each person around the table took a sip of the wine until it was nearly gone. Then Levi used the few remaining drops to extinguish the flames. Everyone stood silently in the dark for several minutes. Samuel moved next to Levi and touched him on the arm. Levi looked at Samuel, and as the dim light of the sunset reflected off the picture window and into the shadows of the room, he noticed that Samuel was crying.

Chapter 22

What it was that had decimated the side of the building, no one knew. But the twisted metal and cement rubble were certain evidence that there had been an explosion. Pieces of former things—the fuselage of an airplane, the bumper of a car, the battered head of a rocket, a utility sink—lay strewn about the ground covering every trace of the natural; no blade of grass, no hearty dandelion, no tree. The wreckage still smoldered, the thickness of it rising up from enormous, irregular boulders, and in the center, one detached driver's seat from a passenger bus tottered precariously. Upon closer examination, one could make out the outline of a figure sitting slumped over in that seat. The figure, by all visible indication, appeared dead. But as the rubble shifted and settled, it jolted the hunched figure which began to rise to its feet taking a form not at all human, but half dragon, half beast, its clawed feet unfolding like cable, stretching forward, its long neck growing longer supporting a hideous, pronged head and jagged teeth. It had the forked tongue of a lizard and the hooded eyes of a serpent. Its body kept unfolding and expanding out of the wreckage until it towered over the entire scene. There was a sense that the cause of the collapse had unleashed the fury in the beast; it began to move forward on its huge talons, shaking the ground with every step. People who had been shocked to stupor by the explosion were now alive with terror, screaming, running everywhere. As the beast came closer to one of the fleeing people, a man in his mid forties, it unfurled its reptilian tongue and scooped up the man, devouring him in one bite. The scene happened over and over, the beast devouring the slower, weaker ones first, growling with delight after each meal and spewing fire from its nostrils. People sought out places to hide, under boulders, inside of cardboard boxes and abandoned car bodies. One couple found a door leading to an undestroyed part of the building. Jerking frantically at the handle, they realized it was locked and began pounding loudly and pulling at the door in hopes that someone on the other side would let them in. Time was ebbing away; the beast was closing the distance between itself and the frightened couple. Suddenly the beast raised its head and spoke. It uttered only four graveling words: "What you don't see."

John woke up trembling with terror.

In the darkness of the room John was keenly aware of his heart racing in his chest. It was still the dead of night—Rachel was sleeping peacefully beside him. He took a deep breath and rubbed his eyes hoping to fall back to sleep, when he heard a noise from the front hall which sounded like someone toying with the door. John sat straight up bumping his head against the headboard. Quickly he pulled on his pants and slipped on the tennis shoes beside the bed. On the way down the hall toward the door, he noticed the broom resting against the wall that Deborah had been using to sweep up the dust earlier that day. He grabbed it and slunk into the great room. Again he heard the sound—someone indeed was rattling the door. Isabel came out of her room at that moment and nearly scared John to death.

"Sorry, John. What is it?" she whispered.

"I don't know--someone is messing with the door." They peeked around the corner of the great room and stared into the shadows at the door. Moving quietly along the wall so they could get a better look, they stooped down beside the bay window facing the front lawn. From this vantage point they could see three figures standing in front of the door working with the lock.

Isabel whispered, "Good Lord, John. What are we going to do?"

"Isabel, can you get to everyone, quickly?" Isabel nodded. "Get everyone into the secret room as quietly as possible. I'll try to hold them off here. If it's the authorities, I'll try to make up something. It's going to look very conspicuous if they find this many people in one abandoned house. Maybe I can make them think I'm just a drifter. Go! Go, hurry!"

Isabel scurried down the hall, staying low to the ground. People in the rooms knew by the manner in which they were awakened that something was not right. They knew to keep silent, even the children who moved quite deftly down the hall and into the secret room. When the last one, who happened to be Samuel, reached the room, John heard the trap door click shut. John held his breath. It sounded as if whoever was on the other side of the door was trying to pick the lock. He waited for several minutes, huddled beside the door, the broom in his hand. Suddenly the knob began to turn and the door ever so slowly swung open. Three dark figures stepped cautiously inside. John rose without a sound to his feet raising the broom up over his head.

"Where is the light?" he heard a woman's voice whisper.

"Let me see if I can find a switch," whispered another woman, whose voice, even in the whispered tone, was oddly familiar. All at once the light hanging over the dining room table flicked on, illuminating the room in startling brightness. John stood blinded by the light for a few seconds, the broom still in his hand.

"John?" said the voice.

"Hannah? Hannah! Oh, thank Jesus, Hannah, Tim!" John dropped the broom and ran to his sister-in-law, squeezing her tightly. She began to cry. Tim grabbed John like a bear, holding him and smacking his back with the palm of his hand.

"I've never been happier to see anyone who was trying to hit me with a broom in all my life!" They all laughed and cried, frenetic with joy.

"Mommy?" Simon had appeared out of the darkness with droopy eyes wearing cartoonish pajamas. The others followed him.

"OH, Baby!" cried Hannah as Simon ran into her arms. Maggie and Thomas ran up to them, too, squeezing her and Tim around their necks. Simon jumped up into Tim's arms and kissed his father on the nose. Rachel rushed into the room in t-shirt and sweats and plunged into the embrace, holding her sister and the children and laughing uncontrollably. Hannah and Tim had been so absorbed in the reunion that they had not noticed that one by one the travelers had made their way cautiously into the great room. The couple had also neglected to introduce the guest who had come with them at such a late hour, who at the moment was standing by the coffee table eyeing a collection of Chekov plays on the bookshelf.

Remembering, finally, her manners, Hannah said, "Please forgive me; this is our friend, Gretchen. We met her on our way here—she's hoping that it won't be a problem for her to travel with us. Gretchen, this is my sister, Rachel, her husband, John and . . ." For the first time Hannah looked around the room at the myriad of faces. "Oh, my. Who are you all?"

John smirked and put his arm around Tim who also appeared shocked at the sight of so many strangers. "We're glad to meet you Gretchen," said John. "And since everyone is awake, we might as well introduce you to our traveling companions as well." John proceeded to introduce everyone in the circle starting with the Covas. Maria leaned wearily against her father's arm and muttered something in Spanish that not even Bart understood. When John finally reached Phillip and Mathias, Simon chimed in with ". . . and that's Miss Dorcas!" He gave her a sheepish little smile that she returned affectionately.

"How did you all . . . I mean where did you . . ." Hannah not knowing where to begin was cut off by Rachel who noticed that the newcomers appeared haggard and spent and were barely able to stand.

"Let's not discuss it now—these are long stories," said Rachel. "There will be time for that tomorrow. You three look exhausted. Tim and Hannah, you take our room. Gretchen, there's a day bed in the office no one has claimed. Please sleep as late as you like."

John added, "Tomorrow we make our next plan. We need to be moving on soon—I'm afraid of a group this large staying in one place too long." The others nodded in agreement.

Maggie who would not let go of her mother's hand asked to sleep with her in the king sized bed. Tim and Hannah agreed; in fact, the idea appealed to Simon and Thomas as well who ended up in the crowded bed with their parents, crammed up against the knees and elbows of their siblings. But Hannah and Tim didn't mind. They knew that their level of absolute fatigue would numb them to any tossing and turning, and they wanted more than ever to be near their children.

Morning came with a bite. An intense fog settled over the trees making visibility nearly impossible. The long, yellow grass in the front yard was coated with a delicate layer of frost. Around nine o'clock there was a knock on the door.

Micah answered it hesitantly. Peering through the peephole Micah saw a deliveryman in full postal uniform. Micah opened the door about six inches. "Here's your paper, sir," he said in a formal tone, then leaned in and said quietly, "Interesting article on page three." He turned briskly and vanished into the fog. Micah unfolded the paper. Levi and Sarah, having heard the knocking, came to see what had transpired. Micah gingerly opened the paper to page three, and there inside was note written on yellow legal paper that said, "Leave quickly. Authorities suspicious. United Brothers (sign of ichthus)."

"Let's get John. We need a plan," said Levi.

"Forget the plan," Sarah said. "We've got to get out of here, now!"

Within fifteen minutes everyone in the house was scurrying around, packing clothes, stocking up on food and bottled water, straightening up the house, burning papers which might incriminate them. The children darted in and out of rooms collecting their belongings and putting away toys. By 10:30 everyone was ready to walk out the door. For a long time Mathias, Dorcas and Phillip stood in the hallway of the secret room as if they were paralyzed by all of the sudden rush. Bart discovered them there and gently laid his hand on Mathias's shoulder.

"You coming?" Bart asked him.

"We will slow y'all down. We get along at a turtle's pace for all these achin' bones. Y'all get along well without us."

Bart smiled, "We won't leave you here." He pulled Phillip close to him who remained stiff and stared at the floor. "Trust us. God's going to lead us to the right places. You'll be able to keep up. We've been traveling with small children and one child with an injured ankle. Yet we made it here in one piece. We can't bear to think about leaving you behind in this dark room waiting in fear. Please come with us."

Mathias shuffled coyly back and forth on his worn boots. Finally, he said, "What y'all say Phillip, Dorcas? Y'all got it in ya to walk a bit with these folks?"

"Reckon" was all that Phillip said. Dorcas gave a quick nod and an impish grin.

"Okay, big fella," said Mathias, "We travel light. Carry our own belongings." He shuffled into the bedroom and removed a couple of antique looking travel bags from under the bed. "Come on, Dorcas. Let's not dally." Dorcas responded to his commands like an army private and moved gingerly along with Phillip who was pulling brown socks from a drawer and shoving them into a tattered bag. Bart shook his head in amusement and left to check on everyone else.

Chapter 23

"It's chilly," John was saying, "Wear your jackets. Layers work best. Let's head east toward Virginia. No use going in some other direction." The last one out, which happened to be Marti, locked up the house. John took Simon with him to replace the key in the statue drawer, and the entire conspicuous entourage commenced to walking east, keeping to back roads and wooded areas which was not difficult in this part of the country. Everyone seemed more rested and ready for the journey than they had been a few days before. Even Phillip, Mathias and Dorcas stepping lightly on the path, kept up well with the entourage of young adults and children. As they walked, John and Rachel took the opportunity to get to know Gretchen and to catch up with Tim and Hannah. Hearing about the escapes on the "D.C. or Bust Tour" entertained Rachel for nearly an hour.

"So which do you relate to better, Lawrence or James?' asked Gretchen.

"I've always gravitated to Lawrence. You do mean D.H. Lawrence, don't you?" Gretchen nodded. "I think he's got some thoughts in common not only with Freud, but also with Kant, especially his thoughts on the supersensible realm of speculative metaphysics." Rachel took a swig of water. "At least I think Lawrence touches on it with his ideas concerning our culture's overemphasis on the mind."

"I have never met Christians like you guys," Gretchen said grinning. "You are so . . . cool!"

Rachel laughed. "Well, if I had known that reading Kant was going to make me so cool, I'd have tried harder to make it to the end of The Critique of Pure Reason.

The group stopped twice for a twenty-minute break. John and Bart both felt they could not afford long layovers, even for meals. It was imperative to keep the pace. Deep down everyone seemed to have the awareness that danger might be awaiting him around the next corner, though they were not exactly certain what form it might take. The words, "authorities suspicious," rang in their ears as they made their way into the Virginia mountains. Hilly and winding, the back roads formed an endless labyrinth, and the way began to wear down even the fittest hikers. The ground was rough and frozen solid. The cold air nipped at their necks and faces, and brittle branches tore at their sleeves and legs. Each step grew more difficult the colder they got. Their feet went through the motions of walking even though they could not feel them. At nightfall they rested at the edge of a pasture surrounded by forest with dark, foreboding mountains on either side.

"We stop here for the night," John announced. "Bart and Tim are going to set up the tents. Everyone else needs to help find firewood. It's going to be a cold night."

"Dad," said Jesse in almost a whine, "I can barely feel my fingers."

"Where are your gloves?" John asked.

"I don't know. Think I lost them."

"Here, take mine," said Levi overhearing the conversation.

"Thanks," said Jesse, pulling the gloves over his stiff hands.

Everyone worked silently stacking loose branches and fallen logs. It took an hour to set up the tents, and there were not enough blankets for everyone.

"We'll have to make do for the night," John said. "Some of the smaller children can share. We'll all have to sleep in close tonight for heat—might be a little strange for some of you—I apologize for that. But it beats freezing to death." Marti prepared some hot noodle soup in cans she boiled over the fire. Everyone ate the meal with a few crackers and bottled water. For most of them it was not enough, and they laid down their heads still hungry and extremely tired.

The night offered little respite from their rigorous journey. Noises of coyotes and timber wolves, barn owls, cicadas and the desperate moaning of naked trees interrupted their slumber, frightening the children and forcing John to assign an hourly watch. The wind was bitterly cold, and, in spite of the lively fire that kept burning all night in the center of the camp, the dropping temperatures kept everyone from peaceful slumber. Twice the travelers heard aircraft overhead. Around 2:30 a jet boomed through the dark sky like a thunder bolt; then, almost at dawn, a whisper copter flew by so low that Rachel felt it might land right on top of them. Peering out of the flap on his tent, John eyed the copter that seemed to be unmarked. He recognized the make and model as those used in covert government operations and surveillance. Throwing on some clothes he immediately awoke the others, and in twenty minutes they all dressed and pulled up camp, burying under a thin layer of mud and leaves the remains of the fire.

For the next two days, they stayed in the thick of the woods, avoiding the most overgrown areas, but keeping undercover of trees most of which had lost their leaves. There were twenty-three of them, now, in all: twenty-three sets of footprints; twenty-three colorful jackets and coats; twenty-three voices and twenty-three distinct rustlings through the leaves. Their choice to stay in wooded areas helped to cover them somewhat, but it also slowed them significantly as the ground was uneven and full of brambles.

At the end of the third day, the food rations began to dwindle. Nearly all of the canned goods were gone since, because of their weightiness, there were few to begin with. Each person had a couple of pounds of beans and rice, a few crackers, several small boxes of raisins and a few wormy apples which they had procured from an orchard they had passed by. All of the bottled water was gone, which though it significantly lightened the load, burdened the minds of the present company, especially since it had not rained in over a week. As they approached a relatively clear stream, John suggested that they fill all the empty bottles they carried but refrain from drinking anything until the water could be boiled. Maggie and Micah picked up two small bagfuls of walnuts from an obliging tree and squirreled them away in their backpacks for later, winking at one another as if they had discovered something that no one else knew.

That night as they tried to sleep in the bitter cold, a misty rain began to fall and gradually turned into sleet. By morning the tents were rigid with ice making the folding of them nearly impossible. All that day as they walked down back roads along the dense woods, sleet mixed with rain pelted their bodies and faces; the children and the older adults were forced to stop several times to rest and warm their extremities. Rachel, Hannah, and Isabel feared the children would develop frostbite in spite of their gloves. A few cars passed by, but no one seemed much concerned. John reasoned that it would be rare for a government vehicle to patrol such remote back roads, and at this point, because of the denseness of the woods and the ice, which had coated its branches, and the inclement weather, there were not many options. It appeared that they would be relegated to back roads until the weather let up at least.

The one bonus was that they were able to use their travel bowls for catching water as they walked, and they filled several bottles with cold rain. They reached, finally, a particularly mountainous area and the road began to wind sharply around the peaks. The trek would have been difficult for anyone in tiptop shape; needless to say, it was nearly impossible for the travelers. At one point, as they were resting on the side of the road, they voted unanimously to stay for an hour or so, find shelter in the brush wherever they could, until the rain let up a bit. Everyone split up into smaller groups and crouched under broad-leafed trees and beneath ridges. Marti and Hannah actually found a small cave, or what had been the entrance to one, and taking three of the children, waited there, listening to the rain and ice beat rhythms against the roof. Phillip, Dorcas and Mathias huddled with Bart and Isabel under the ledge of a slab of limestone, rubbing their hands together for warmth.

Bart noticed that Phillip's eyes had sunk into the white pastiness of his face; he seemed paler than usual and his eyes were glazed and lifeless.

"Are you okay, partner?" Bart asked him patting him on the knee.

"Okay, mister. Just short o' breath, that's all. I'll be right as rain directly." But Bart could tell that the hike had taken too much out of him and that he would not be able to continue at this pace much longer.

The woods seemed eerily dim with the cloud cover and trees pressing in around them. They started out again once the rain slowed to a drizzle, clopping through wet brush and moss for nearly three quarters of an hour. They came to a long, hollow oaken log, which lay dead as a corpse across the forest floor. Phillip, Dorcas and Mathias sat hunched over the long of end of it wiping their foreheads, rubbing their legs, and catching their breath. Dorcas pulled a half full water bottle from her satchel and slowly gulped it down in little swigs, then replaced the cap and stuck it back into her pack. One by one, travelers sat along the log, wordless, clawing through backpacks and gym bags for water and snacks. Maggie, Jesse and Simon collapsed like rag dolls lengthwise along the damp log, their mouths open and their eyes half closed with fatigue and cold. Levi stood apart from the group pacing and staring at the ground.

Finally he stopped. He raised his hands to the sky. Then he called out in a loud voice: "Barukh atah she'asah li kol tzoiki. Min ha'meitzar karati Yah, anani va'merchav Yah!" (God, blessed is the One who provides for all my needs. I have called You from tight places. You answered me with expansiveness).

The children sat up at this jolting, foreign sound coming so unexpectedly from the silence. Simon leaned in close to Hannah. "What is he doing?" he asked in an almost whisper.

"He's praying," whispered Hannah.

"Why is he walking around with his eyes open and praying loud?" Maggie whispered in Hannah's other ear.

"That is how Jewish men pray, Maggie. Be quiet now." Hannah covered her head with her hood. Maggie watched her mother bow in reverence and covered her own head as well.

"Va, ani t'filati l'kha Adonai ayt ratzon, elohim b'rov chasedkha, aneini." (Hear my prayer, now, and in Your compassionate ways, please answer me). Levi spoke these last words with his face, streaming with tears, to the sky and his hands in the air.

"Halt!" The voice came from somewhere on the other side of the woods, a voice which no one recognized, the voice of a man. Then came the rustling sound of footsteps.

Chapter 24

Quickly John said, "Tim, Samuel, you guys stay with me. Everyone else hide there in the thicket. Lay low, no noise, no movement. We'll handle this."

Hannah, Rachel, Bart and Marti hurriedly split everyone into four groups and scattered into the thicket. Hannah held Simon and Maggie close and whispered that they must not speak. Dorcas, Mathias, and Phillip hovered with Bart behind a boulder surrounded by briars that snagged their sleeves and pant legs and scratched lines in their thin skin. They could hear the footsteps coming closer.

Then finally a hearty voice spoke, "Officer Downey, hold there. What is going on?"

"I don't know what you mean officer," said John emerging from behind a pine. "My buddies and I are on a hike."

"That's not what I heard, son. What I heard sounded an awful lot like Jewish prayin'. This is public land. Are you folks aware of that?"

"No sir, we were not," said Tim, apologetically.

"Well, boys, I'm not sure where you're from. But you're in Virginia now, and we adhere to the law in this state. And it's against the law to have any out loud prayin' on public land. You boys alone?"

John glanced around innocently, "Appears that way, sir."

The officer gave John and Tim a scrutinizing look, then his eyes darted this way and that into the bushes and thickets that surrounded them. He walked over near to the place where Marti and her girls were hiding with Miriam and Sarah. Samuel held his breath, knowing that they could be discovered. But night was descending on the trees, which made it difficult to make out objects in the shadows. The officer bent in close to where the women were hiding until his face came within three or four feet of them. They held their breath, staying perfectly still. The officer swept the beam from his flashlight around the area, focusing in on one place for a moment. Then to his right there was a swish and several leaves flew into the air and landed gracefully on the ground. He turned his attention to the sound momentarily. The eyes of a raccoon lit up under the beam of the flashlight then the animal lumbered away into the brush. A crow cawed overhead and swooped down low before it ascended into the trees. The officer turned and looked once again at John.

"Who did I hear?"

"What sir?" asked John.

"Who was that praying in Hebrew?" John tried to think up an answer.

Levi appeared to the right of the officer. "It was I, sir."

"What's your name?"

"Levi Heschel."

"Figures," said the officer and spit on the wet mulch. He stared at John who was surprised to see Levi coming out of hiding. "So what's your name? Must be the ringleader."

"John Beckett. Ringleader of what, sir?"

"Squadron spotted camp up in the mountains, seven or eight tents. Too many for just the four of you. So where's everyone else?"

"What makes you think those tents were ours?" asked John.

"We've got an eye on you. Been seeing some others from the air. You all having church on public land? Disturbing the peace with out loud prayin'?" He grabbed John by the shoulder. "I've had it with you religious boys. You all come with me. Usually when we get the ringleaders, the rest will turn themselves in eventually. C'mon!" The officer removed his side arm from his belt and shoved the four men through the woods and down a ravine where, to their alarm, there was an army jeep waiting. Bart slipped out from his hiding place and watched behind a tree near the top of the hill as the officer cuffed the four men and shoved them into the jeep.

Rachel and Hannah overheard the entire exchange and remained hidden for nearly half an hour for the sake of the children who were petrified with fear of what the authorities might do to their fathers. As she crouched down, her knees throbbing in pain from the pebbly ground, Rachel's mind was racing: What to do, what now? Since she was a little girl she had always possessed the ability to process the events in her life very quickly and come up with viable solutions to problems way before others were able to absorb the initial shock of them. Mentally she began calculating: people, resources, feelings, supplies, possibilities, everything.

Slowly Bart emerged from his spot behind the boulder, helping up Dorcas and Phillip who had fallen asleep. He went from thicket to thicket arousing everyone from their uncomfortable hiding places. Standing in the clearing at the top of the ridge, no one said a word, partly in fear of being heard and partly from shock. But everyone was thinking about what should be done. Bart put his arms around Hannah and Rachel. "I'm sorry. I didn't know what to do. I thought of coming out of hiding to go with them, but then I worried about all of you, and . . ."

"It's okay, Bart," Rachel interrupted. "You did the right thing. We need you here."

"What are we going to do?" asked Micah. It was the question of the hour. Everyone felt paralyzed. Jesse couldn't stop crying—all the children were trembling from fear and cold.

"I'm not sure," said Gretchen. "That was frightening. It's okay, Jesse." She put her arms around him.

"Should one of us follow them?" Deborah asked standing at edge of the ridge and looking over.

"It depends on what they plan to do with them," said Becca. "It could be dangerous."

Finally Bart said, "I know almost for certain that they won't do anything with the guys tonight. Most likely they'll keep them in lockup for a couple of days. With the weekend coming up, there won't be a hearing until at least Monday. That buys us some time. I don't know Virginia State Law, and our one 'law expert' has been detained. But I do know that in some cases of misdemeanor like this they won't hold them if they don't have the space . . . may not hold them anyway. It's different from state to state. Why don't we bed down for the night? Then in the morning we'll make our way toward town and see what we can do to get them released."

Rachel and Hannah, as if growing accustomed to unfortunate events, quietly began to set up tents as if they were resigned to the decision out of shear exhaustion and grateful they didn't have to make it themselves. Hannah and her three children slept that night in extremely close quarters with Rachel, Jesse and Andrew. It took a long time to get the children calmed down enough to go to sleep. But thankfully, sleep finally came for everyone, though it was hard to put the circumstances out of their minds.

Rachel awoke before dawn. Bart found her cross-legged on a large, flat rock, her worn Bible gapping open in her lap and her hood pulled up over her head. "Good morning," he said handing her a cup of coffee.

"Hey," she said in a cryptic tone, taking the coffee from him and returning to her thoughts.

"Maybe I should get everyone moving so we can get an early start looking for John and the guys." he said moving up next to her and sipping coffee from a collapsible mug.

She sat pensively for a moment or two, then said, "No."

"No, what? 'No' let's not wake everyone up or 'no' let's not go into town?" Bart was perplexed by Rachel's mood.

Finally she closed the Bible in her lap and turned to face him. He noticed that her eyes were swollen and red as if she had been crying.

"No, I don't think John would want us to go find him. That's not how John thinks, Bart. I've been thinking about this for hours, praying about it, going over and over it in my mind. And I had a thought that gave some peace."

"What's that?" asked Bart.

"I feel we need to press on. Keep heading east. John will find us."

"What do you mean? How will he know where we are?"

"The same way we got through Kansas in a balloon. The same way we found you. The same way we made it through Illinois undetected and the same way we found Tom and the Burton's house and the same way Tim and Hannah found us. This seems like a horrible thing that has happened. Looking at it from the outside, from just the facts, that's the way it seems. But there's a reason for it, just like there's been a reason for everything that has happened to us. As haphazard as it might seem to someone else, there hasn't been a mistake or a coincidence. Something in my spirit tells me to keep moving. "

Bart nodded his head at Rachel and threw out the dregs of his coffee. "Let's wake the others and tear down the camp. Let's start east." He took her hand and cupped his other large hand over the top of it giving her a wide grin of understanding. Then he walked away to wake the others.

Oddly enough, when Hannah heard the plan she seemed relieved. But Thomas and Andrew were more of a challenge to convince. Thomas said flatly, "I'm not leaving Daddy," and it took nearly an hour to convince him that this was the wisest course of action, that his daddy would sooner or later find them.

Miriam also seemed especially quiet, her way of questioning the wisdom of the choice.

Deborah reasoned out loud. "You know, he's always known somehow how to get out of scrapes. Also, if everyone shows up in town, it could be the end of all of us."

"I agree," said Ruth. "I think the best chance of us all surviving is for all of us to stay together, first of all, and secondly to stay under the cover of these woods. It's going to take all of us to take care of these kids and the older ones."

"Samuel is used to persecution. He's unaffected by it in some ways. He will rise up out of it no matter what they dish out."

"John is no dummy," said Isabel. "He knows a lot of people, too. He seems to be very diplomatic with the authorities; they seem to like him. He'll do whatever it takes to get back to us. "

"All those years in politics . . .." added Rachel. "Might be worth something when it's all said and done."

At 7:30 they began to walk though the sun had not appeared on the horizon. The light of its coming arrival had illuminated the ground enough to start the trek, and Isabel wisely suggested that they begin to seek out private properties to walk along even though they ran the risk of being evicted. Public land seemed, in the state of Virginia, to be the hazardous selection—the officer had made that point quite clear. They decided to take a narrow and slightly worn path down the side of the mountain and walk along an expansive tobacco field. The day, though the temperature hung just above freezing, was clear and refreshing. Three times they spotted deer grazing in pastureland, once, a red fox. By noon, everyone was hungry, but the rations had nearly run out. They made a meal of beans and rice, their last, and savored it slowly and gratefully. Marti's girls took turns carrying Simon on their backs in a makeshift sling while he slept after lunch.

By nightfall, the temperature dropped again below freezing and the dormant wind found its life and began to whisk wildly through the wheat field where they walked. Maneuvering the hills had tired everyone beyond belief. An old, wooden shed, empty as a tomb, was the most welcoming sight, and since it stood far away from any visible buildings, the exhausted crew thought it to be abandoned. They made camp for the night. The children complained of hunger; the older folks, too breathless to complain, wheezed and coughed, collapsing into piles on the shed floor. Little was spoken; angst filled the frozen air, worries of every kind. But their aching bodies could do no more to rectify the situation. Finally, Bart, fearing any fire would attract unwanted attention, blew out the lamplight. Rachel pulled Andrew and Jesse in close to her and tried, despite the cold that had entered her spirit and body, to sleep.

At three in the morning, she woke, restless and sore. Hannah, Gretchen, and Miriam likewise were awake, sitting up, rubbing their hands together for warmth. Miriam watched Gretchen out of the corner of her eye as she zipped her coat up around her neck and coughed. Miriam had not yet spoken to Gretchen other than to say "hello" and "goodnight." It was as if Miriam was uneasy with her—she studied her, not knowing what to make of her or how to process her past. Gretchen, somehow knowing her thoughts, smiled and nodded at her. Miriam quickly nodded back and turned away, straightening her bedding and pulling on her gloves.

"We've gotta do something," Rachel finally whispered to them. "I've got to get some food at least for these people."

"We're coming, too," said Miriam nodding again at Gretchen, and the four women stole feebly out of the shed into a field of overripe tobacco under a full moon. They didn't know what else to do but walk. They moved through the rows of frosty tobacco, careful not to crush the plants. They walked nearly six miles before they came to a house. Rachel thought it to be the plainest house she had ever seen, though it did not appear to be very old. A basic cement foundation supported a white farmhouse with small, symmetrical windows, long and rectangular. The structure was devoid of ornamentation, no finial or scroll head, though the place seemed sturdy and carefully crafted. The pitch of the roof was so slight it was almost flat. A chimney flue protruded unaffectedly from the roof, and the entire house was painted white. The yard had been landscaped for practicality, everything useful and in its place, pots of dry herbs, stakes where tomato plants had been, a blanket of brown grass that glistened under the moonlight.

The barn, built from thick timbers and located adjacent to the house, was capped like a schoolboy with a rounded roof. Miriam, Hannah, Gretchen and Rachel tiptoed around the house and approached the rear of the barn. Rustling noises could be heard inside which made Rachel hesitate before peering through a knothole in one of the boards along the backside. All she could see was the pitch-blackness and her own breath rising up before her eyes. Noticing that they were not visible at this angle from the house, Rachel flicked on her flashlight and shined it through the hole so that Hannah, who had found another hole, could see into the barn.

"It's chickens and pigs," she whispered. "And several horses. Wow. This guy's serious about farming."

A voice behind them suddenly made them leap. "Who are you?" Rachel dropped the flashlight, which hit the ground with a thud and rolled sideways illuminating the brown boots of a tall, dark man. Drawing the eyes of the women to the ground, the boots stood brown and featureless except for a couple of muddy smudges on the toes. "Please give me an answer," said the man, not gruffly but insistently.

Chapter 25

Rachel stepped forward, "Please don't shoot us or anything. We weren't going to steal your things from you. We . . .," she hesitated, "We have children in a camp near here. We didn't plan our trip very well, you see. And the gist of it is, we have run out of food. We had no intention of taking anything. We just . . . ." She took a deep breath, "We just wanted to see who might be living here and who might be willing to help us out. You see, it's cold and . . ."

"Come in, all of you," said the man. The women looked at one another. Gretchen shrugged. They trailed the man several steps behind. Rachel whispered to Hannah that the man did not appear to be armed.

"Let's just stand here," Miriam said pausing on the porch, "see what he wants first."

"Good point," whispered Rachel.

When the man stepped up onto the porch he reached for some object hanging to the right of the door. Under the shadows of the roof, the women could not see what it was. Suddenly there was a "tick" and a flame at the end of a long match ignited the wick of a kerosene lantern. As their eyes adjusted to the light the women were relieved to see a man, about sixty, dressed in simple black trousers without pockets held up by suspenders, a white, simple shirt, black coat and a dark hat with a wide brim. He had a full beard without any mustache, and his face was wrinkled with age and weather. His brown eyes, though, betrayed him with a sparkle of innocence not often seen in a man his age.

"What are your names?" he asked in a hushed voice.

"I am Hannah James; this is my sister, Rachel Beckett and our friends Miriam and Gretchen. And you are . . . ?"

"Silas Yoder." He nodded but did not extend his hand. "My son is here with me. He sleeps now. He is Amos." Rachel detected a slight Germanic brogue. "Please come in," he implored.

The house was comforting and utilitarian. An open hearth with a fully stocked fire blazed a focal point in the kitchen. The flames licked the rough wood, which crackled and popped with heat. In the far corner stood a Franklin stove on which sat an iron kettle. Silas lit another lamp on the table and two on the mantle. Hannah, Rachel, Gretchen and Miriam began to feel instantly the warmth in the room. An oak trestle table with arched feet rested on a braided rug in the center of the cozy kitchen and eight slat back chairs stood like soldiers around it swaddled with flame stitch chair tape. Over the table lay a blue and white gingham table cloth and on it, a wooden bowl full of golden delicious apples and Bartlett pears. Next to a mission hutch made artfully of maple, a kerosene cook stove stood out because of its shiny blackness against the natural oak cabinetry, jelly cupboard and dry sink.

Silas Yoder opened the jelly cupboard and removed an old fashioned Ball jar from what looked like dozens, all full of color— green beans, yellow peaches, orange carrots, red beets, black strap molasses. He lit the stove, took an iron pot from the rack directly above it and twisted off the top of the jar that made a suctioned "pop." He worked without speaking, except turning once to notice that the women were still standing, he invited them politely to sit down at the table. He hummed softly an unrecognizable tune, then ladling the ingredients of the pot into blue, metal bowls and slicing three thick slabs of dark bread, he served the women who smiled graciously at him at the sight of warm peaches with a sprinkle of ground cinnamon. Wordless, Hannah and Miriam grew teary and clasped each other's hands. Rachel prayed, "Lord, we thank You for Your faithfulness, for supplying our needs, and for this kind man who you have sent to us. Amen."

For several moments the room was quiet apart from the sounds of spoons against metal bowls and swallowing. Silas, who finally pulled up a chair and sat down near the stove cleared his throat, "I knew you were Englishers, but I did not know you were followers of Christ."

"That's why we're here, Mr. Yoder," Hannah said wiping her mouth. "We are believers not exactly at home in the world. At least not the world we know. We're traveling, looking for . . . something better."

Silas stared at the floor for a second; his serious face softened. "How many are there in your number?"

Rachel answered, "I have two boys, Jesse and Andrew; Hannah has three children. Then there are the Covas, three of them, Deborah and Samuel Bradley, Sarah, Miriam, who you have met, Micah." Rachel was counting on her fingers. "Marti Freeman and her three girls, Levi, and three older folks who are sickly and tired. My husband, John, Hannah's husband, Tim and our friends Samuel and Levi were taken by the authorities just yesterday. We are not sure what will happen to them or where they are. We are. . . " she choked and began to weep, "We don't know what to do."

Silas shook his head and mumbled the words, "strangers and pilgrims," several times to himself. Then he said, "Before day breaks, you rouse the others. Bring them all here. We will make room and feed them. You are all welcome here."

The women full of joy nodded humbly at Silas. They were about to stand when Silas placed his hand on their shoulders, closed his eyes and prayed, "O Herr, wir sagen Dir Lob und Dank fur Deine heilige Speis and Trank, fur Deine vielfaltige grosse Gnaden and Gutheiten; Herr, der Du lebest und regierest, ein waher Gott bis in Ewigkeit. Amen." Then he recited the Lord's Prayer in English. The women spoke the words in unison with him until the final "amen."

"Jesse, Thomas," Hannah whispered.
"What time is it?" Jesse said yawning.

"It's 5:30," Hannah answered. Jesse flopped back down on his hay bed and turned over. "I'm serious," said Hannah. "Get up. We found a place to go, some food, too. Where's Simon? I thought he was right here."

"Check over by Mr. Bart," said Maggie adjusting her sweatshirt. "Or with Ms. Dorcas, there." Hannah swept the flashlight around the shed, but saw no trace of her son.

"Dorcas, Bart, have you seen Simon?"

"No ma'am," said Dorcas.

"I thought he was by Jesse and Thomas," Bart added.

Thomas answered, "He was right here by me." There was a hint of panic in his voice. He jumped up and began searching the corners of the shed, calling for his brother. Hannah, Rachel, Bart and Isabel trudged around the outside of the shed, calling for Simon and shining their flashlights up and down the rows of tobacco and into the bushes and tall weeds. Isabel found a section of the tobacco field where the plants had been broken and trampled.

"Look at this," she said to Hannah and Rachel. "Looks like a struggle, maybe. I don't think one little boy could break down a section of plants like this."

"Good, Lord!" Hannah gasped. It was still too dark to see anything farther than the end of a flashlight beam, but Hannah began to follow the trail of mutilated plants to the end of the field that lead her to a dirt road, but no sign of Simon. "Rachel! Where is he?" she said in a tone of controlled hysteria.

"I don't know, but I say we should not jump to any conclusions. Let's get the others, head toward Mr. Yoder's house, then come back out here when we've got some light. He probably just wandered off and fell asleep in the field somewhere." Hannah reticently nodded and gathered up her belonging as well as her two remaining children, and helped Dorcas and Mathias up from their beds on the floor of the shed.

The group followed Rachel through the damp tobacco up to the house of Silas Yoder. Each one searched the rows of plants for a sign of Simon. The other children called out to him, their breath forming steam as it hit the cold air. Hannah was becoming more visibly frantic and began to race up and down the rows of tobacco all the way up to the house.

After the women had left the Yoder Home, Amos, who had been listening to the conversation between his father and the women, emerged from his bedroom with a glare of disapproval. He spoke to his father in German as he had been taught to do when Englishers were not around. "Father, I heard what these women were saying, what they want. Why in the world did you tell them to come here?"

Silas cleared his throat. "Something in me went out to them. They are believers, Amos. I want to help if I can."

"But Father," Amos interjected, "You bring trouble upon us. We must stay separate from these Englishers these days more than ever. How long will they be staying here? Do you even know? People are desperate in these times. What if we lose more than we already have?"

"Amos, these people are in the same danger as we are. They have already lost some of their group to the authorities. These authorities want them for the same reasons they took your brothers. And your mother, God rest her soul, would agree with me if she were here. These people have chosen to be set apart, too, except they don't have the resources we have. We must do what we can to help them now. If we don't have charity, what have we?"

The women ran through the tobacco fields calling for Simon. The others followed behind searching in all directions for the boy. Rachel and Hannah arrived first to the front porch of Silas Yoder's home. Hannah knocked rapidly on the door. As Silas opened the door and raised his lantern to see his visitors, he realized quickly that something had gone wrong. Immediately he invited them all in, making a special place on the cushioned chairs for Dorcas, Mathias and Phillip who dropped like rocks onto the soft cushions. While Amos began serving everyone tea and warm bread, thick slabs of bacon, stewed tomatoes and seasoned green beans, Hannah and Rachel neither sat nor ate as they explained to Silas about the missing boy.

"Take me to the place where you were staying so that I can see these indentations in the field." Leaving the others in the care of Amos and Bart, the women lead Silas to the campsite and showed him where the plants had been broken.

"Yes, it is as I thought," Silas said eyeing the plants.

"What?" Hannah demanded.

"Six."

"Six, what??"

"Six- -they are a cult. Happened a couple times before. We don't have time to lose," he said following the path along the crushed tobacco plants.

"A cult?!" exclaimed Hannah. "What do you mean?"

"Meets secretly up here in the mountains. They are known, though some think it's rumor, for human sacrifice and bizarre rituals, but the authorities have been unable to catch them or at least they don't seem to try very hard. These people are evil. They prey upon the most innocent. We must find Simon right away." He stomped through the field until he came to the dirt road. Then he veered off to the left as if he knew where he was going. Rachel and Hannah followed fighting off tears and the sick feelings rising up in their throats. As the sun broke over the mountain peaks, they came to a thick grove of pine trees. Silas, as if driven by instinct, parted the branches of several scrawny saplings wedged in between the tall conifers and walked into the densest part of the woods. He stood for a moment examining the branches and forest floor, then he slowed his pace and began to creep silent as a cougar through the trees. Without being told, Rachel and Hannah stepped as quietly as humanly possible over the top of the dried needle bed.

Chapter 26

Silas slowed as he came to a grove of ancient shagbark hickory trees. Pulling his body in behind a massive trunk he motioned to the women to come closer to him. Hannah and Rachel tiptoed closer and hugged with their backs against the rough bark of a tree near Silas. Silas cautiously peeked around the curved trunk. "Sure enough," he whispered. Hannah and Rachel simultaneously stretched their heads around the sides of the tree. Hannah gasped.

"Baby!" exclaimed Hannah, cupping her hand on her mouth. Beyond the tree was a clearing. A makeshift camp had been set up there with tree tattered tents and a lean-to. The remnants of a fire smoldered in a pit surrounded by an odd configuration of stones. Another stone circle laid not far from the pit, eerily formed in black rocks, and in the center, the image of a pentagram. Off to one side, shackled to a sapling was Simon. He had obviously been crying for some time for he was heaving wearily with his red, swollen face flush to the ground. Around the tents empty beer cans and liquor bottles were strewn haphazardly and other than Simon, there was no one present in the scene.

Hannah started to rush out from behind the tree, but Silas held her back. "No. They're all just asleep. Been drinking all night though. That's in our favor. You stay here." Silas crept like a cat toward Simon who, upon seeing a strange man in a black hat inching toward him, began to cry again. Silas immediately slipped in beside him cupping his hand over Simon's mouth. "You'll be okay, Simon. I brought your mommy." Simon's eyes darted over the grove where he saw Hannah, wet with tears, waving from behind a tree. He started to jump up, forgetting he was shackled and tripped, falling face first to the ground. Silas picked him up and set him down on the grass gently. "Simon, you have to be very quiet so I can help you here, okay?" Simon nodded obediently. Silas could hear stirring within one of the tents. A man's deep voice let out a hollow groan. Silas began to work quickly. He removed a pair of metal cutters from leather pouch strapped to his belt. He clamped it to the leg iron on Simon's ankle. Click. The broken cuff fell off and hit the ground.

"What?" said the voice inside the tent. "What the hell was that?" Sounds of clanking bottles and rustling reverberated in the still cove. The tent visibly shook. Silas gathered up Simon and began to walk away when a hulking man in black pants and a black maxi coat, tattoos covering his face emerged from the tent. His hair was so black that it was apparent that it had been dyed and an AK-40 dangled in one hand. Silas froze, his fingers still over Simon's mouth. Rachel and Hannah were paralyzed with fear and trying to breathe, their hearts pounding so fiercely they were afraid the man might hear them.

Just as the man was about to turn around and face Silas who was still standing motionless at the corner of the camp, there was a loud noise on the opposite side of the camp that sounded like the footsteps of a large animal. The huge man cocked his weapon and called out, "Who is it?" Stumbling through the saplings and into plain view was Micah!

"Oh!" he blurted, appearing surprised at the scene. "Oh, I'm sorry. Am I anywhere near Lookout Peak?" He had a backpack on one shoulder and his headphones on as if he had been hiking all morning. Rachel and Hannah looked bewildered. The man lowered his weapon.

"Why in the hell are you here? You're in the wrong, fuckin' place!"

"I thought . . . uh . . . .," Micah stammered and began fumbling around in his back pack from which he pulled out a map of Colorado and unfolded it noisily and with exaggerated gestures in front of the man. "Let's see, I was here, then. . ." He continued rustling the paper. The man in black started to speak, but got something caught in his throat and began coughing. Micah quickly glanced at Silas and simultaneously winked and nodded and continued fidgeting with the map. Another man emerged from the tent, also dressed in black with hair that gave the impression of railroad spikes. Silas began to make his way with Simon, one step at a time, into the nearby bushes. Micah kept talking continuously and shaking the tattered map, which was now in two pieces. When Silas reached the hickory tree, Simon nearly leapt out of his arms onto Hannah who held him tightly and whispered to him over and over again to keep quiet. Seeing their successful escape and watching until Silas and the women were completely out of sight, Micah wadded up the map and jammed it gingerly into his backpack. The two men moved in a little closer, obviously perturbed by the peculiar behavior of Micah.

Finally the huge man said, "Listen, Dumbass, Lookout Peak is that way. Ten miles south." He raised his gun to his side.

"You know," Micah said trying to keep his cool, "I always get lost like this when I'm listening to music. Love that Black Sabbath," he said diplomatically. "Tell you what, I've got a laptop here I was thinking of pawning when I get into town. You men wouldn't have any use for a 'previously owned' laptop would you?"

The men looked at one another. The larger man cleared his throat and teased, "I don't know Mr. Black Sabbath, did the 'previous owner' save any good porn on there?" Both men began to laugh in husky voice.

Micah took a deep breath, "As a matter of fact he did. Have at it." He took the laptop from his backpack and held it out to the two men. The man with spiked hair grabbed it from him. Micah turned and started to go.

"Hang on, Black Sabbath, we need to see if you're telling us the truth." The huge man picked up an overturned camp chair and sat down with the computer in his lap.

"Look under 'gear" in the files." The man clicked and stared at the lit screen while the other man stared intently over his shoulder still keeping an eye on Micah.

Finally they both began to laugh lustily. "That's what I'm talking about." Lost in the images, neither man looked up from the screen. The huge man said, "Now get the hell outta here." Micah turned and slipped into the forest without turning back. The men did not notice as Hannah, her arms holding Simon tightly to her chest, Rachel and Silas bolted like deer across the fields and to the house.

Sipping the strong, hot coffee Amos had brewed, Bart said, "It's not as if we have many options. We have a business card. One contact on the coast of Virginia. A boat maker. That's it."

"A long way for you folks to travel on foot," Amos remarked

"Yes, plus we've got little ones, sick ones, older ones and no idea how to find John and the others."

Simon was sleeping heavily now across Hannah's chest. Her eyes were swollen and bloodshot. She was so exhausted. Rachel was exhausted, too. Dorcas and Mathias lay across Silas's overstuffed featherbed. Phillip was clammy, his skin sunken and sallow. Isabel could tell that he was unwell as she dabbed a warm towel around his forehead and fed him soup that he sipped slowly from a spoon like a toddler.

"I need to feed the stock," said Silas. "Coming, Amos?." The two men, one a mirror image of the other, especially in their plain clothes and hats, walked out the door and toward the barn leaving the rest of the company in silence. Marti finally stood and began to clean the kitchen.

"Come on, ladies, let's work on this house a bit. Looks like two men have been livin' here alone too long." Rachel understood this as Marti's way. She and Hannah stood wearily and joined Ruth, Becca, Eve and the others in the mindless task of tidying and cleaning, sweeping and dusting. Something to bring some order into the chaos. Forty-five minutes later, Amos and Silas returned to a nearly spotless house.

"Look at this, Amos." For the first time the company saw Silas smile a wide, toothless grin. "Come 'round the table, friends. We'd like to talk with you."

The women folded their rags and put away brooms. Micah, who had been polishing the upstairs windows descended down the creaky staircase.

"We are simple folks," Silas began. "Our community has never had much to offer the world. We have been content to remain separate . . .until now. But after talking with you, we see you are in the same position as we are. We have known for some time there is nothing for us here. This country will no longer allow us to remain separate. We have lost much already. We . . . want to help you." Silas walked over to the door and removed three skeleton keys from a high shelf. "Several of our people who have passed on left me in charge of their farms—crops, horses, barns, everything. We have twelve buggies and nearly enough horses to pull them. If I can trade the rest of the livestock for a couple more, we'll have enough horses to pull the buggies. As you know because buggies are not motorized, they are never stopped. We could be at the Virginia shore within three days depending on how much we stop." Silas cleared his throat and turned the keys over in his hands.

"What about the guys? Does anyone have any ideas about how we will find them?" Hannah asked in a worn voice.

Deborah laid down her broom. "John, Samuel and Jim know where we're going. They'll find us." She looked at Hannah who nodded and stroked Simon's matted hair. Rachel nodded, too.

Rounding up horses and buggies from five different farms turned out to be more of a chore than these former city folks envisioned. Silas and Amos tried to hide their frustration at the lack of equestrian skills exhibited by their new friends, but on more than one occasion Silas snapped at Rachel and Bart who were the least gifted with the horses and barked orders at the children who were trying their best to understand how to rein the animals and to ride the saddles. Maggie and Hannah, the only two who had taken actual horseback riding lessons proved to be the best assets.

Finally they were able to round up six buggies that were set up for two horses apiece. Twelve horses were hitched to the neck yokes, two on each wagon. Three of the horses were older and more worn for the wear, but Amos wisely paired them each with a young gelding.

Silas and Amos then began to assign drivers to the buggies. He and Amos would drive two of the buggies; Hannah was to drive one; Sarah, who seemed to catch on quickly during the brief training session, was assigned to another. Jesse was to drive one and finally, to everyone's surprise, Silas assigned Mathias to the last buggy because Mathias, as he discovered, had grown up on a farm much like Silas's and had driven many a horse-drawn vehicle in his day.

The next task involved gathering provisions that would be needed for the trip. With so many in the company, including three elderly people and several children, the provision list had to be carefully thought through so as not to underestimate the need. For this the company relied almost entirely upon the suggestions made by Amos and Silas who seemed to have an understanding about how to ration supplies and make good use of the available resources. Bart suggested they do most of the traveling between dusk and mid morning and between late afternoon and evening. Even though it was unlikely that they would be stopped in buggies, the sheer number of buggies in this particular caravan could raise suspicion in certain authorities. Both Hannah and Rachel were experiencing some waves of doubt in regards to leaving the area where their husbands had been captured. But their misgivings gave way every time to the consideration of what was best for the group and it was clear to both women that remaining in one place, where there was already suspicion among the authorities of their presence, was an unsafe gamble. For the company's sake, they resolved to press on, knowing that Deborah was right—the men knew the ultimate destination and would try every way within their power to reach it.

It was decided that on three of the buggies a small, flat bed wagon would be towed to carry trunks of oats, cracked wheat, canned goods, dried beef, kerosene, guns and ammunition, bottled water, blankets, tents, and matches. These trunks were secured tightly to the wagons by ropes. On their last evening in the house, Bart and Gretchen helped Amos and Silas herd their cows and other livestock to the nearest neighbor's farm. Though the herd trampled across the frozen ground, they were able to drive the livestock through the neighbor's farm gate and into the holding pen without detection, leaving only a brief note of explanation which read: "Had to leave town. Family emergency. Please see to my livestock. Blessings to you, Silas Yoder." That evening the company dined on the last of the beef from the previous winter's butchering—pork tenderloin, mashed potatoes, corn, seasoned green beans and raspberry pies which Marti, Ruth and Becca Freeman made from scratch. The children gulped the last of the fresh milk from Silas's recently departed milk cow, Nessie, and everyone else drank strong coffee with thick cream. After dinner everyone was so satiated and lethargic that, knowing dawn would come sooner than they might wish, they made the wise decision to call it a night and everyone, including Silas and Amos who were feeling the bittersweet sadness that comes from knowing a chapter of one's life is soon to end, went straight to bed.

Chapter 27

In the pre-dawn darkness, the travelers awoke to a familiar chill and discovering that the dark ground had been once again sprinkled in powdery snow they agreed to the extra coats and jackets offered to them by Silas who pulled the winter apparel from an oversized trunk at the foot of his bed. There was a tacit efficiency in the way everyone worked that morning packing their duffle bags, eating breakfast, gathering up the children and herding them into the buggies. The air in the roofed enclosures was replete with resignation mixed with fear, but soon Silas gave the word and the wagon train headed east along Sully's Creek down a rough, dirt road. In spite of the jostling and jarring of the ride, all of the children fell asleep on the shoulders and laps of the closest adults with the exception of Jesse who was focused intently on the long stretch of road and on reining his horses. Hannah found herself mesmerized by the sounds of the horses' hooves on the hard ground and their sneezes and grunts as they pressed forward.

The sun began to rise and Silas veered off the path beside the creek onto a winding mountain pass, which obviously had not been traveled by automobiles in some time. The turns and bends began to make some of the folks in the company queasy. Maggie asked when they were to stop. But Hannah just smiled at her and put her index finger against her nose, which Maggie took as meaning not much further. Around ten o'clock in the morning Silas pulled his buggy off into a wooded area along the side of the path. The others followed steering the horses deep into the glade.

"I think we should use these . . . just to be on the side of caution," said Amos pulling a large newly fallen tree limb behind him.

"Good idea," said Hannah spying a maple branch still holding on to a few of its dried leaves. Everyone stretched their legs and began to hunt for branches to cover the buggies. Amos snatched a narrow but long branch and returning to the road began wiping away tracks and fresh horse dung which he continued to do for nearly a mile stretch. He was glad to see that the brisk breeze began, after some time, to do the rest of the labor, blowing dust and leaves onto the road and covering some of the deeper grooves made by the wagons.

The children took advantage of the down time and organized games of tag and hide and seek among the trees. Andrew, who had nearly forgotten that he began the journey with a serious leg injury, ran faster than the others, routing out his cousins in their hiding places then bolting back to "home base." Jesse tried to take a nap, but with all the rustling and squealing of the children and the monotonous drone of adult conversation, he was unable to doze for long and soon joined the others in their frivolity.

Micah had been unusually moody and irritable since the group had pulled out of the farm that morning. Once he had snapped at Thomas simply for sitting too closely to him in the buggy. Marti watched him sulk around the camp pretending finally to sleep against a tree then wander aimlessly down a ravine and back again.

"What's up with him?" Hannah asked Marti.

"I think I know; he'll probably get worse before he gets better. Then, hopefully the big, fat wall he'll hit will wake him up." Marti shrugged leaving Hannah looking confused.

Suddenly they heard a snapping of fingers, a sound so loud the children stopped running and looked toward the road. Mathias was standing at the edge of the wooded area closest to the road and was holding one hand behind him motioning for silence. Instinctively, everyone froze and walked hastily toward the nearest trees and hid behind them. Eventually everyone heard it: the sound of popping gravel under automobile tires and the muted interruptions of a police radio. The car slowed as it passed the place where the buggies were parked, camouflaged with tree limbs.

The police radio got louder, and Rachel who was nearest to Mathias at the tree line could hear the phrases "possible perpetrators and deserters" and "companions of John Beckett." She held her breath and strained her ears at this welcome and disturbing mention of her husband's name. The car slowed briefly to a stop, and she could see the officer with dark sunglasses straining to see beyond the row of trees. He took a sip from a thermos, wiped his mouth, and spoke finally, "All clear. 10-4!"over his radio. As he began to drive away, Rachel swore she heard a voice on the other end say something about "perpetrators transported to Richmond." The words were like a knife against her tightening throat.

By four they were on the road again heading southeast. The horses, which were well watered and rested, made good time. Silas knew the back roads by rote or at least he knew of them. The moon rose full and bright, and the company were able to continue on in the darkness. By late evening they reached a kidney-shaped lake glimmering under the moon which, like a planet unto itself, shown its reflection in the dead center of the water. Making their way around the north banks, they came to a sign that read: "Lake Anna. No Littering." Rather than stopping for the night at a campsite, Rachel suggested they find a remote spot in the woods, camouflage the wagons and pitch their tents around the lake at some distance from each other. Micah found himself staying with Silas, Jesse and Mathias much to his dismay. He remained aloof and sullen as he unrolled his sleeping bag. Mathias and Jesse hardly noticed him as they zipped their bags shut and fell into a deep sleep, snoring like two hibernating bears. Micah looked at them, rolled his eyes and snuck out of the tent. He landed feet first in the middle of wet moss. Watching this display, Silas slipped out of the tent behind him closing the flaps and stood next to Micah.

"You have seemed unsettled in spirit today, Mr. Shaw," said Silas smoothing his beard. Micah said nothing, but turned his head away and fixed on the moon. Silas continued, "I saw you riffling through the waste bin today. What were you hunting?"

"Magazines," Micah blurted out without expression.

"What magazines?" Silas appeared perplexed.

"Just certain magazines, okay?" Micah retorted facing him, his eyes blazing. Gently Silas took Micah by the face and looked in his desperate eyes with his own piercing, dark gaze.

"The world, my friend, is too much with you, is it not? You must set yourself apart, Micah or you will never find peace; you will never be able to help another. Something weighs down on you, son. Break with the thing now." With these tenderly spoken words, the tears welled up in Micah's eyes.

"I can't. When people can't quit things, they are addicts. You know what an addict is, Silas? No . . . of course you don't—never sinned in your life, I bet."

"I know a good bit more than you think, son, both in what I see and in who I am. And I know this: there is no chain God cannot break. You want the broken chain, boy?" The tears dripped off Micah's cheek and onto his blue jeans.

In almost a whisper, Micah mouthed the words, "I want the broken chain. Help me."

Silas uttered one word, "Believe." He put his hands on the sides of Micah's head. He closed his eyes and remained silent for several minutes. Micah began to feel something he had never felt. It was a lifting, a weightlessness, a release; he was literally aware for the first time of something which could only be described as a "gripping," and he felt it, finger by finger, letting go.

"I want you to say these words out loud, Micah. Say them after I speak them." Micah nodded. The man kept his eyes shut and said, "God, Father, release my chains." Micah repeated. "Let me find freedom that comes from obeying You. Keep the evil away from me." After he repeated these last words, Micah gasped. He could feel that the oppressive feeling, the preoccupation of dark thoughts, the sexual movies that had been playing over and over in his head, all of it . . . was gone, completely vanished, and more than this, he could feel a presence of warmth, a fullness he could not describe and he began to realize how empty he had been before.

He began to see why he had been so desperate to fill the huge vacuum with cheap pleasures. But this new feeling was no cheap pleasure; this was something deep and real.

"Well, Micah Shaw," said Silas. "Are you washed clean?"

"I don't know completely what you mean by all that," answered Micah. "But I feel full, like I have a new chance."

"Do you want to be baptized, son? We are near a lake. We believe in getting baptized as a symbol of being washed clean."

Micah looked at the still lake and shivered. "It'll be cold." Then looking back at the lake under the moonlight he said, as if on a whim, "Let's do it!" They started toward the water then Micah turned and said, "Wait a minute." He walked back to the woods toward the tents and emerged again with Maggie on one side and Marti on the other smiling and winking at Silas who smiled back, his yellow teeth flashing. Wading out into the water in his t-shirt and shorts, Micah felt the numbness that comes with exposure to extreme cold. Silas didn't even flinch as he sloshed through the water sending ripples across the lake.

"I baptize you in the name of the Father, the Son, and the Holy Ghost." Silas spoke the words with authority and dipped Micah backwards into the frigid water with strength only a farmer could muster. The icy rivulets shocked Micah's system into a full awareness, an awareness he had never experienced. Without the pull of addiction on his senses, he began really to see the moon, the lake, the trees. He could smell the wet ground and the dry leaves. He could taste the lake water on his lips and feel the night air on every pore of his body. The water tricked down his neck and back and for the first time in years he felt truly clean.

Walking toward the bank, Marti, with tears in her own eyes, hugged him and told him that she loved him. Maggie, understanding that something important was happening, slid her small hand into his. Feeling something round and smooth against his palm he release her to see what she had given him. She grinned as he opened his hand and saw a shiny, brown buckeye with a miniature heart etched on one side.

Muted voices early in the morning before the sun began to lighten the landscape woke the travelers. Rachel had not slept well, plagued by nightmares about John.

"Mom?" Andrew asked in a drowsy voice.

"I'll feel better when we are moving," she reassured him, stuffing some rolled clothing into a bag. "Wake the others. I want an early start."

Andrew squinted at his wristwatch. It was 4:30 a.m. "Ughhh,." He yawned and turned over again.

"Now!" Rachel barked, pulling gently on his leg. Mathias and Dorcas were already awake, brewing some coffee over an inconspicuous fire.

Seeing Rachel taking down her tent through the flap in his own dwelling, Silas whispered forcefully to the others, "Time to go, now. Let us load the buggies." Nearly everyone woke coughing, sniffing and stretching sore muscles. It seemed like since the outset, at least one of the travelers had been ill. The miles, the weather, and the persistent stress of their circumstances were wearing down everyone's immune system. Hannah and Sarah awoke with pounding headaches that even the strongest medication in the first aid kit could not alter. Dorcas, Mathias, and Phillip were all coughing and wheezing more than usual. Becca and Deborah suffered from stomach cramps and Gretchen who had lived with herniated discs for most of her life was unable to rise and had to be carried to the buggy, wincing all the way. Bart had grown more and more silent the past several hours. Marti took Isabel aside to inquire about him.

"It's happened before," she answered. "He battles depression and we did not think to bring medication for it since he has been doing better for the past year and a half. I'm worried, though."

"Will he get worse?" Marti asked hesitantly.

"Yes, sometimes he can get very low." Isabel forced a grin and went into the tent to wake Maria. Isabel's beautiful daughter had developed a low-grade fever during the night and was clammy to the touch and somewhat listless.

"Mommy, do we have to go?"

"I'm afraid so," said Isabel, folding her blanket. "But you can ride with me and sleep in the buggy."

The weather that morning was nothing short of ominous. A motionless, chilly fog had rolled in during the early morning hours and visibility was almost at zero. Deborah and Micah quite literally bumped into each other before they saw what was coming. Mathias was groping through the briars, trying to locate one of the horses, which he could hear but not see. The entire atmosphere was permeated with a foreboding gloom that affected a somber mood in the travelers as they harnessed the horses to their buggies.

"Have we stumbled into a Thomas Hardy novel?" Miriam asked Gretchen.

Gretchen nodded slowly, her eyes surveying the lake, "Looks more like Poe to me."

The temperature continued to drop as the caravan passed through a fallow field strewn with remnants of tobacco leaves. About 9:30 the first snowflakes began to fall. Silas halted the horses so that everyone could find blankets and sweaters in the trunks. Multicolored scarves woven from hand spun yarn were wrapped methodically around the necks and faces of children. Isabel pulled Maria in close to her own body. Maria's cheeks were flushed with fever. Isabel poured some chamomile tea into a plastic cup from a thermos in her pack and told Maria to sip it. She gave Maria the last of the Ibuprofen, and within the hour Maria was asleep on Isabel's shoulder. By that time, the snow was falling steadily. Enormous, perfectly formed flakes landed on twigs of dry grass and on the few stubborn leaves still clinging to the trees.

"This is actually sticking," Rachel remarked, studying the ground. Silas lead the caravan up to a dirt road."

"It'll be easier for the horses here," he announced, bumping onto the path.

"Mr. Silas, do you think this weather will hold?" Andrew asked with a degree of concern.

"Not likely." Silas cleared his throat. "See those clouds over there?"

Andrew peered ahead. In spite of the fog, which had dissipated somewhat since the earlier hours, Andrew could make out something on the horizon. "Looks like cumulonimbus," he said. Andrew had loved studying weather in science class.

"Cumulowhat?" asked Silas, smiling his toothy grin. "Them's storm clouds, plain and simple."

"That's what I meant," Andrew responded. Then under his breath he added, "That's what I was afraid of."

Chapter 28

Just as the caravan had skirted two large potholes in the road, as if on cue, a lively gust of wind swept around them whirling the falling snowflakes into a frenzy and whisking away Silas's gray, flannel hat flinging it into a nearby blue spruce. Silas halted the horses once more, jumped off his rig, retrieving his hat and motioned to the other drivers to gather around.

"Friends, continuing on here is going to be dangerous, especially in yonder mountains there. Six miles or so down the way," he pointed toward the clouds, "lives a friend of ours named Phineas. He has a barn where we could shelter these horses until this passes over." Everyone agreed, trusting the good judgment and expertise of Silas.

Moving the horses and buggies down the road six miles was easier said than done with the razor-sharp winds and increasingly heavy snowfall. The sky grew darker with the impending storm. The winds began to tear at the canvas on the buggies. "Pull in here!" Silas called back as they came to a narrow drive. About half a mile down on the right stood a barn that appeared so similar in build to the one on Silas's farm it could have been mistaken for the exact same structure.

Silas jumped spryly off his buggy as they approached the building, and unlatching the huge door, he swung it open on its squeaky hinges. One by one the horses and buggies were drawn inside. It was a tight fit, but all except one buggy was wedged into the straw-lined chamber, and the horses were freed from their harnesses and ushered into stalls. It took both Silas and Bart to close the barn door as the wind howled through the cracks in the walls and jostled the loose planks.

"I'm going to make my way to the house to see Phineas," Silas shouted to Bart as he pushed open a small, side door. The travelers made seats out of hay bales that had been stacked neatly in one corner of the barn. Simon quickly climbed all the way to the top of one stack and sat there peering down on everyone settling in. The travelers moved in close together, making use of every coat and blanket to ward off the chill. Soon the side door of the barn swung open again, and Silas reappeared white with shock.

"What is it?" Rachel asked.

"He's dead! Phineas is dead!" Everyone was hushed.

"How did you find him?" Bart finally asked.

Silas glanced around at the children staring innocently at his shocked face. "I don't want to say . . . I . . . ." Bart walked over to Silas and put his arm around him. Amos and the other adults moved in close to him away from the children.

"He's been all hacked up," Silas whispered in a stutter. "It's so terrible! I can't . . . ." Silas turned his face away from the women. His voice cracked as he added, "Why would anyone do this to him?" No one knew what to say. Silas's words paralyzed Rachel and Hannah like a concussion.

Finally Bart said, "My feeling, at least for now, is that we should all remain here in the barn until this storm blows over. Then later on, Silas, we will give Phineas a proper burial and at least say a few words." Silas shrugged, the hot tears glistening on his wrinkled face. Amos reached out and hugged his father and led him over to a bale of hay to sit down. He routed out an old quilt from one of the trunks and wrapped it around his father's shoulders. They sat in silence for the remainder of the hour.

The force of the frigid winds made the old barn creak and moan like an abandoned ghost town. Occasionally a gust would slam up against the barn with such strength that following the assault the rafters would shake violently for a few moments. Now and then it would grow eerily quiet. At one such time, Thomas heard a faint whining at the side door. Opening it he discovered a slender bloodhound shivering in the snow. The poor creature was ushered in by the children who took him to be the orphaned pet of Mr. Phineas. Thomas begged Hannah to let him keep him. Hannah eyeing the protruding ribs along the dog's body simply replied, "We'll see." The children mashed up a little corn meal in some water and fed it to the hound who being utterly ravenous gobbled it down like it was sirloin. He drank nearly half a trough of water then lay down on the straw next to Thomas and fell asleep.

After what seemed like an eternity, the winds began to subside. Mathias and Gretchen pulled their coats up over their heads and ventured out. There under the half-clouded sky gleamed a white blanket about seven inches thick. Eventually Andrew, Thomas, Simon, Maggie and Jesse bounded out the door into the cold powder. Simon laughed out loud as he dove head first into a drift.

Hannah and Marti followed, inspecting the surrounding fields. As far as they could see in every direction there was stark whiteness. Bart suggested to Amos and Silas that they begin to find a way to bury the remains of Phineas. Approaching the house, Silas seemed increasingly unsettled. He opened the front door and the three men walked inside. The sight in the living room made Amos turn his head in disgust. The mangled corpse, butchered almost beyond recognition, caused Bart to question once again the divine reasoning behind such an atrocity. Bart stepped back out the front door and warned Isabel and Rachel to keep their distance and to keep the children occupied and away from the house while they dug the grave. Amos found an empty trunk in the attic which they used as a coffin, and five shovels that had been hanging on their assigned hooks in the barn were brought out. The men began digging. Phillip, who wanted badly to assist the other men picked at the ground for awhile, but he did not last long as he was not well and extremely weak. Rachel, seeing the other men laboring in the snow, grabbed Phillip's shovel and began to dig alongside them.

The work was difficult. The low temperatures had frozen the ground at the surface, but as they dug deeper the earth loosened somewhat, though not enough to keep the diggers from blowing warm air periodically into their cupped hands to keep them from frostbite. It took them the better part of two hours, everyone working without breaks, to dig a big enough hole to fit the trunk down into it. They lowered the remains of Phineas into the hole and covered it ceremoniously with snow and dirt.

Amos made a cross from some discarded paneling and etched "Phineas Lap: God Be With You" onto it with the dates of birth and death (as far as they could surmise) etched underneath. Silas called the others out of the barn to pay their respects. After a few moments of silence standing around the grave, Silas spoke, "This is the hour for men of courage, women of valor. Phineas was such a man. He was a good soldier in the army of the Lord. He stood against the world. He said 'yes' to the Almighty with his humble life. He was not proud. May the peace of Jesus be with us all, and we release you, Phieas into Jesus's hands."

Bart and Isabel made the sign of the cross. Amos got chocked up and walked off into the orchard. Slowly the travelers moved back into the barn except for Silas who stood a long time staring at the homemade cross over Phineas' fresh grave. Finally he gave an audible sniffle, cleared his throat, and shoved his hands into his pockets as he walked back to the barn.

Rachel had made him some soup out of canned broth and homemade noodles they had packed at Silas's farm. He sat down on a bale of hay to sip it. Simon came up and quietly sat down beside him. He patted Silas's knee with his grubby hand. "I found something funny," he finally said. "Wanna see it?"

Silas tussled Simon's hair and winked, standing up as Simon pulled at his hand. He led Silas through a horse stall to the backside of the barn where Phineas had stored some of his supplies and extra tools. "Look!" Simon pointed to what appeared to be several metal railings all in different colors stacked so evenly against the barn wall they looked like a rainbow.

As Simon had unknowingly predicted, Silas indeed began to laugh. "You're right, Simon," he chuckled. "This is funny. I forgot about this." Amos, seeing his father's apparent mood change, walked over to see what the fuss was about. He eyed the stack of railings.

Finally as if a light had come on in his head he said, "Are those what I think they are?" Silas smiled at Amos and nodded.

"I forgot that Phineas was in the buggy trade for awhile. He specialized in these converters." Simon looked puzzled at the two men grinning about colored rails.

"What is it?" Bart asked, coming up behind them with a mug of coffee.

"They are called buggy conversion sleigh runners," answered Amos.

"What does that mean?"

Silas answered, "That means we don't have to wait several days until this snow melts to get out of here."

Amos and Silas went to work right away removing the buggy wheels. Rachel and Micah would have loved to make themselves useful, but the two men worked so efficiently and quickly that Rachel realized that any outside help would in fact be a hindrance. Silas explained the process as he worked, "These converters here are built on buggy wheel hubs, and they have bearings to protect the axles' spindles. Phineas made some good money for awhile making these."

In no time the travelers were harnessing the horses to the newly converted sleighs. Simon was so excited he could not contain himself. The horses and buggies formed a line outside the barn, and Silas locked up everything just as he had found it. Though the time was already 4:15 in the afternoon they began to glide off into the dimming horizon and away from the descending sun.

Simon sang "Jingle Bells," every verse, all the way through at least seven times before Thomas, visibly exasperated yelled, "Enough!" Simon slumped dejected for all of five seconds then launched into "Over the River and Through the Woods." "I give up," said Thomas throwing up his hands. Bart laughed out loud for the first time in days, Isabel feeling grateful for even this small sign of joy.

They rode into the night, the moon rising above them like a cantaloupe. Amos reasoned that they were making up for lost time, but in truth he was thinking of Phineas and a primitive dread began to rise up in him. They stopped for the night at the top of a ridge near Bluefield. It was a remote location shielded in all directions by conifers. The horses sputtered and whinnied shaking their harnesses as they were fed and watered. The temperature was just below freezing as everyone staked down their tents and unrolled sleeping bags.

Both Phillip and Maria remained unwell. Phillip, who had barely spoken in several days coughed incessantly before drifting into a restless sleep, his brown eyes sunk deeply into their sockets, his pallor, a grayish white. "Phillip doesn't look good," Rachel whispered to Becca and Eve who were sharing her tent.

"I know. Poor guy. You can tell by his face. He really needs a doctor," Eve replied, sliding into her sleeping bag.

Rather than building a fire that Rachel and Micah agreed would attract unwanted attention, they relied on small battery operated space heaters, one per tent, that they had found in Phineas' barn. He had used them on cold nights when he had to clean the farm equipment. Rachel had grabbed them on the way out just in case.

The travelers slept, then, almost as a family would which had gotten used to the proximity of each other over time; Micah edged up against Mathias and Dorcas as a grown grandson might cozy up next to his aging grandparents; Maggie threw her arm around Maria like a sister might, with gentle nonchalance, and Maria cuddled Simon protectively as a mother lion. Sarah, Miriam and Gretchen lay next to each other, glad to be near the warmth of another person. Rachel, brushing Becca's hair off the pillow as she slept, began to feel the warmth of bodies, and finally fell into sleep. They were too tired, too preoccupied to think of any awkwardness. Tragedy has its way of peeling away nonessentials and sharpening focus. Whether it was calamity or terror or simply the necessity of cooperation required to meet goals, something profound and unspoken was happening within the hearts and minds of this group of sojourners. It was as if the disparities, the dissimilarities, the differences in background, gender, age, race, and locale had all broken away like dead, useless twigs, and they had become, over the past days and weeks, one organism with an unswervingly singular purpose.

Chapter 29

It was darker than he remembered. The floor, now that he noticed it, smelled of dry earth. Reaching down beside his cot he could feel it. The dust coated his fingers—he rubbed it around between the index finger and thumb. John figured he was underground as what little light that existed in this tomb came not from any window or door, but from a miniature grate in the ceiling. He moved his legs over the edge of the cot with a groan—they were stiff and sore, and a twinge of pain shot through his back where grooved gashes had begun slowly to heal. He winced. Deep voices could be heard from up above, but they were muted as if spoken through cotton. John strained his ears to listen but discovered that the dialect was foreign, archaic. The men were speaking . . . Latin. Glancing around the dimly lit room, he made out the form of a man sleeping on the cot against the wall. "Tim?" John whispered. The man stirred and turned over. John did not recognize him—he sported shoulder length hair, brown and matted into thick wads against his head. He wore an unkempt beard and mustache and had on what appeared to be some sort of costume, almost like a tunic in a period play. The man muttered something to John, which also sounded Latin. Once again John called into the darkness, "Tim? Levi?" But there was no answer. John began to realize that his surroundings seemed odd, that he was no longer in Virginia but somewhere in a distant past. He examined the barred door to his prison, its ancient lock indicating to John that this was no garrison he had ever seen in contemporary America.

Without warning, the ground beneath him began to rumble. John grabbed onto the edge of his cot and prayed aloud. Loose pebbles bounded across the floor like popcorn. The man in the opposite cot sat straight up and stared at John in fear. Suddenly, the hinges of the iron prison door came up and out, and the heavy door fell to the ground with a loud thud. All was quiet then except for the labored breathing of the strange, shaken man who finally got up the courage to whisper one word, "Paul?" He looked desperately into John's eyes as John immediately recognized him as Silas.

John awoke face down on a bare mattress that reeked of cigarettes and body odor. He pulled himself up to sitting and gazed into space. Levi was crumpled in one corner staring out the window.

"Did you sleep at all?" John asked him, trying to find his voice.

"Not really," he answered without turning his head. Samuel made an inhuman moan and turned over on his mattress.

"Dear God," he uttered.

"Let me see," John said. Samuel lifted up his shirt. John could see Samuel's brown body covered in bruises and cuts.

"Some things never change," Samuel muttered expressionless, pulling down his shirt and raising himself to sit on his bed.

Tim was pacing back and forth in front of the door. Now and then he would stop to peer anxiously down the hall. "Did they forget that we are here?"

"I don't know," replied John, standing and stretching his stiff legs. "Do we have anything to eat?"

"Are you kidding? Get some water out of the sink, if you can drink it," Tim retorted sarcastically. John walked over to the stained basin just in time to see a cockroach climb out of the drain and down the side of the pedestal. John cupped his hands under the faucet and took a few sips.

"Ugh!" he winced and wiped his mouth with a grimy shirtsleeve.

"You think you got through to them last night?" Samuel asked, addressing John.

"I don't know. I know a lot of people in this state, people in powerful positions. But that may not make any difference now. I dropped every name I knew, tried to argue it from legal angles. I don't know. I'm not sure if the same rights apply to people like us anymore." John walked over to the box-sized window and tried to look past the bars and through the dingy, bulletproof glass. He could see the town center and the top of St. John's Church, its three-tiered steeple like a white finger against the blue sky. He remembered that this had been the location where Patrick Henry gave his famous speech in 1779. "Give me liberty, or give me death," he had said, exploding with passion and conviction. St. John's, founded by Reverend James Blair, who became the commissary in the Virginia colonies for the Bishop of London, had evolved in those formative years into the heart and lifeblood of this city. The Virginia conventions were held in this church. John studied the new buildings which had risen up in this old city as he thought of his first year of American History in college, how the class had studied Thomas Jefferson's famous Virginia Statute for Religious Freedoms,s which was passed somewhere in the midst of those buildings on January 16 of 1786. Did Jefferson have any idea, John wondered, that this day would come? The Statute had forbidden religion or religious organizations from having any rule over citizens. The document provided insurance against the kind of tyranny, which the pilgrims had been subject to in England. It created the separation of church and state.

Over the years Americans had seen the face of religion change, but always the rights of citizens remained protected. And now? John thought about the "religion" of the current culture, the worship of majority rule and hedonism, the worship of easy access and digital money, the worship of moderation and status quo on one hand and excess and rebellion on the other, the worship of marginalizing those who believe something different and somehow threatening. John's thoughts were interrupted by the sound of a woman's voice talking to the two night guards. After a few seconds, the sound of footsteps could be heard coming down the hall. Levi and Samuel stood up and walked over to the cell door. John turned around just in time to see a familiar face.

"Shannon!" John exclaimed.

"John, how are you?" she said extending her hand through the bars.

"Levi, Samuel, Tim, I'd like you to meet Senator Casey."

Chapter 30

Rachel woke with a jolt. A bright light shone in her face. "Is it . . .?" she asked before recalling where she was.

"Miss, you need to get up and come with me," answered the voice on the other side of the light. A woman whose voice she had not recognized was speaking.

"Who is it?" She sat up rubbing her eyes.

"Officer Benson, ma'am. Please come with me." Eve and Becca were up now waking Thomas and Andrew. The lazy hound stretched out beside Thomas's sleeping bag stretched and gave a yawn as if the interruption seemed commonplace.

"What is it, Mom?" Thomas asked Hannah.

"I don't know. Get up and get dressed." Dorcas roused Phillip who began coughing incessantly. She poured him a glass of water from the thermos.

"Hurry up," said the voice of a man aiming a flashlight into her dazed eyes. She quietly stood, smoothing down her hair and pulling on a shabby coat. The campers one by one stumbled out of their tents. Five fully uniformed officers waited stoically armed with weapons and flashlights. Hannah and Rachel gathered their children in by their sides. Bart carried Maria who was weak with fever.

"Officer, if I may . . . " Bart began.

"No, you may not. Quiet, please! You have the right to remain silent. Anything you say can and may be used against you in a court of law. You have the right to an attorney . . . ." Bart looked over at Rachel standing resolutely, her arms around Jesse and Andrew. She glanced at him briefly then turned without expression to face the officers. Maggie began to weep and buried her face in Hannah's coat.

"What is it, Mommy?" Simon asked Hannah.

"Please keep the child quiet, ma'am," snapped one officer. The tallest man held his radio to his mouth and rattled off information in coded numbers that the travelers did not understand.

The woman leaned into the man on her right and said, "I think we have possible neglect here. How many children?" she recounted. "Six . . . and three older people. Okay, this many . . . we need the van. Bring it up!" An Asian officer quickly disappeared into the trees at her command. "Okay, people, let's see all your hands."

"We don't have chip, if that's what you need," Bart responded.

"None of you?" the officer glared at the group. "Unbelievable! Okay, any paper I.D.?" The travelers reached into pockets and purses producing various papers and licenses. "Fine. So, we've got Bart and Isabel Covas. This your daughter?" The Covas nodded and gave Maria's full name. "Then we got Rachel Beckett and . . . Andrew and Jesse Beckett." Rachel answered shivering. The moon had gone behind a cloud, and a chilling wind brushed Rachel's cheek.

The officer continued, "You are Hannah James and . . . . " Hannah gave the names of her children without feeling. "Then Deborah Bradley, Sarah Tucker, Miriam Cook, Micah Shaw, Marti, Ruth, Becca and Eve Freeman." The officer stopped for a moment sorting the papers and matching identification with each person. "Last we have Silas and Amos Yoder, father and son, I take it," she said eyeing their plain suits and hats. "And Dorcas and Phillip Lane and Mathias Childs. And . . . who are you?" The officer looked at Gretchen.

"I'm Gretchen Bertinelli. I'm sorry, but I've lost my ID."

"Great." She rolled her eyes and stuck the papers into a satchel. A plain, elongated white van emerged through the trees and the Asian officer jumped out and opened the sliding side door. "Everybody in," commanded the officer. Thomas's hound followed close at his heels as he walked toward the vehicle. "The dog stays here," the officer addressed Thomas.

"No!" Thomas screamed and clutched onto the dog's neck.

"I'm sorry, kid, but he can't go with you. Now step into the van."

Thomas shrieked, "No, you can't do this! What's wrong with you people? Leave us alone!" The woman motioned to two of the officers who proceeded to grab Thomas on either side and force him into the van against his will, kicking and screaming.

"Please don't hurt him!" Hannah cried.

"Ma'am, get your other two children and get into this van! It's too cold to stand out here all night." Everyone crammed obediently into the van, and the woman officer shut the door.

They huddled together shivering, partly from cold and partly from fear. The children were now all sobbing; even Andrew, who had tried to show a brave face for his mother, began to cry openly. The adults sat with arms around the children and began to clasp hands with each other, holding tightly as if their resoluteness were their only hope. The van bumped down the back road for several miles then swerved onto a state highway heading east. Hannah tried to make out the conversation between the woman officer who seemed to be in charge and the man driving. Since a glass partition separated the officers from everyone, she was able only to catch bits and pieces. She heard, "Richmond facility's full . . . Norfolk . . . limited space . . . long drive."

Hannah leaned over to Rachel and whispered to her that itß sounded as if they were heading to a facility in Norfolk. Overhearing her, Becca gasped. "I heard the punitive system there is one of the worst. Dear God! What is happening?!"

The van stopped in Roanoke for a restroom break. The female officer accompanied the women, and two male officers followed the men. No one spoke in the presence of these authorities, not even the children who eyed the uniformed officers not only with an attitude of distrust, but also with flagrant fear.

Winding around roads through the mountains began to make Maria feel nauseous. She vomited into her father's lap before Bart could help her. Then she began to cry in such a feeble way that Bart heaved a sign of frustration and held her so tightly to his chest that he muffled her sobs with his thick sweater.

The van stopped again in Lynchburg, then in Richmond. Just as they began to notice a body of water that they recognized immediately as the Chesapeake Bay, the glass partition was lowered. "We will arrive at our destination in fifteen minutes. Please be ready when we stop," recited the woman officer as if reading a script, then almost as abruptly, the partition was raised.

Rachel's mind was racing: Norfolk, where is that? What are we near besides the Chesapeake Bay? Where is John; what is he doing? What would he try to do? How do I protect the children? What will we do with Phillip, Mathias and Dorcas? Will we be all together? How long? What now? How long?" She could not end the obsessing; her mind worked almost independently of her other faculties to come up with answers.

Eventually, the van pulled up in front of a colossal modern building, angular and white as a mausoleum. Stepping out of the van, Dorcas, Phillip, and Mathias methodically stretched their cramped limbs. Phillip coughed from somewhere deep in his chest, and Gretchen handed him a lozenge she found lose in her pocket and patted him on the back.

"This way," the officer shouted over the roar of traffic. It had been so long since any of them had seen this many people, this many cars, or heard the sounds or seen the sights of a city. It was altogether overwhelming. The children had to be nudged toward the door as they gawked at LED screens across every building advertising everything from toothpaste to condoms. Noticing the overt nudity and profanity in several of the ads, Rachel, Hannah and Isabel gestured to one another as they hurried their children under the entryway marked "Admissions." The female officer leaned over the front desk. A gentleman in his fifties with an unnatural tan and exasperating nonchalance finally abandoned his paperwork and looked up over a pair of narrow reading glasses at the entourage.

"Damnit, Linda, what the hell are we supposed to do with this many? No SPACE. Did they not call you?"

The female officer retorted, "Yes, Bob, they called me. Said they had holding space until Wednesday. Said we could sequester. Three rooms."

"One moment," he huffed typing frantically on his computer. "Okay, I have a message here . . . ." he said after several seconds. "Rike Building, Rooms 42A, B, and C, only until Wednesday. Are they chip?"

"No," said the woman with disgust.

"Good God," he blurted. "This paperwork will take all night—give me what you've got," he stuck the papers which were handed to him into a file folder. "Fine. Take them down—we'll get to the paperwork later."

The woman motioned for the travelers to follow as she marched through a set of double doors and down a hallway at a clipped pace. Andrew noticed the mid-century décor—Le Corbusier chaises, Mies pavilion chairs, Andy Warhol prints, monorail track lighting with simple pendants and English rye grass, which was plastic but looked real. His ears were attuned to the contemporary blend of world music playing over the speakers in the halls. The color scheme, a flaxen gold hue complemented by sage greens, was intended to be soothing.

They passed several sets of numbered doors. Micah walked arm in arm with Dorcas and Phillip, helping them along. Silas seemed shell-shocked as Amos warily sheltered his father, walking closely behind Rachel. They came to an exit door following the woman through it and into a narrow alleyway, dingy with soot and lined with dumpsters. Hannah had to carry Simon who was struggling to keep up. Over the doors strange signs identified rooms: Operations, Legal, Grounds, Catering, Oversight, Insurance, Free Clinic. As they walked, the children, speechless, took in everything they witnessed. Passing one dumpster Maggie, without warning, let out a shriek. "Mommy! It's a baby!" The officer glanced around, but continued walking in a clipped pace.

"Mommy! It was moving! It was bleeding! Mommy, STOP!" Maggie was tugging on Hannah's sleeve as she tried to hold on to Simon. Hannah gingerly handed Simon to Rachel and swept Maggie into her arms.

Hannah stared into Maggie's eyes as she continued walking with an expression that Maggie had never before seen—her jaw was resolute, stern, and a single tear leaked out of the corner of her eye and down her face. Her voice possessed strength and reserve which silenced Maggie immediately, "Maggie, you must be quiet. You must ignore what you saw. You must keep up. You must obey me. Do you hear what I am saying?" Maggie nodded feeling the full weight of Hannah's message. She laid her head on her mother's shoulder and threw her arms around her neck. Hannah could feel Maggie's quick, warm breath against her cheek. The officer turned and entered another building through an unmarked set of double doors. The building they entered appeared much older than the other buildings. The paint on the dented, metal doors lining the gray hallway was chipped and worn. Some of the numbers had been scraped off—others were barely visible. The floors had not been mopped for some time and were marred with scuffs and smudges. A musty odor lingered in the dead air, and if the heating system was operational it had been turned down so low that the travelers immediately felt the chill.

Chapter 31

Approaching three doors at the end of the hallway, the woman in charge greeted a young guard. "They are to be here until Wednesday. Sequestered."

"Yes, Ma'am," he responded, signing the paper she handed him on a clipboard.

"You four in here," said the woman leading Dorcas, Phillip, Mathias and Silas into the first room. Amos looked desperately at his father.

Silas patted his son's arm and fixing his eyes gently on his son's face he said only, "God be with you." The thick, metal door closed with finality.

Then the woman announced, "Children under eighteen in here, adults in here." She pointed to the two remaining rooms.

Hannah immediately interjected, "Officer, you don't understand—these children cannot be alone. They need us right now. They are frightened; can you see that they are frightened? One of them is ill . . . ."

The woman cut her off, "Miss, you will do as I say. These children are in danger. They have obviously been in a neglect situation. From now on they are wards of the state. A representative from Child Services will be here at eight in the morning to take them to assessment. Now please, set the children down and back away." Thomas, full of rage, ran over and kicked the woman's shins.

"You are evil! You are an evil person from HELL!! What's the matter with you?" The security guard grabbed the boy and yanked him into the room. The woman radioed for backup on her phone, and within two minutes, three officers approached the travelers, their polished, hard soled shoes clicking noisily on the floor.

The children, including Maria, were separated from the arms of their parents. "You will be alright, Simon. Mommy is next door, just right here," Hannah spoke to Simon, all of them weeping. One officer pried Maria from Bart's arms, and Bart took a lumbering swing at the man, plunging his bulky fist into the man's jaw. The man stumbled back clasping one hand to his face. Instantly, the three arriving officers seized Bart and threw him forcefully into one of the rooms. Isabel screamed something incomprehensible in Spanish with desperation in her demeanor, her face flushed red, and tears steaming down her dark cheeks. Maria clung to her mother. Coming up behind her, the woman pried Maria's fingers from Isabel who in turn began to claw and grab at the woman, screeching like a wounded animal.

"Do I need to call for more backup, Ms. Covas?" asked the woman firmly. "This could get ugly. Really ugly. Do you want that for her?" She pointed at Maria still holding her back from her mother's arms. With visible reluctance, Isabel resigned.

She quickly turned, trying to locate Andrew. "Please take care of her for us," she pleaded.

Andrew walked over and took Maria from the struggling officer. Maria threw her arms around his neck, weeping. Thomas likewise lifted Simon and took Maggie's hand, and the children walked compliantly toward the room at the end of the hall. Andrew glanced over his shoulder at his mother standing outside the room, her hands covering her mouth trying to hold back the tears. She mouthed the words, "Pray." Andrew nodded and turned. The heavy, metal door closed behind them like a tomb. The other eleven women and three men filed into their designated prison. They slid quietly down on the wall nearest the children, hoping they could hear something, but the silence that answered them was deafening.

"What now?" Micah asked.

Becca replied, "I don't feel good about this."

"What time is it?" asked Miriam.

Ruth looked at her watch, "Mine is broken."

"Mine, too," echoed Deborah shaking her watch and holding it to her ear.

"I think around 7 . . . p.m., probably," Amos guessed.

The room redefined minimalism. A water-stained toilet and pedestal sink stood in one corner. As set of bunk beds with stripped prison issue mattresses stood in the other. There were no mirrors, no windows, no pictures, and the walls donned an off white hue with a gray tinge. Two folding chairs were stacked against the wall next to the door. Hannah set up a chair and motioned to Bart who was still holding his head and lying on the floor.

"You're bleeding," gasped Isabel examining him. Miriam pulled a wad of folded paper towel from her pocket and handed it to Isabel. The gash was long but not deep. Isabel applied pressure to it with her agile fingers. Bart simply stared stoically at the wall without speaking.

Rachel pounded the wall nearest the children's room. Three muffled raps could be heard in response. Clutching the wall she began to cry. "This is it," she muttered. "This is the beginning of the end." She ran her right hand down the wall and turned to Hannah. "I won't let them take the children. I'll die first. I have a strong faith . . . but not that strong."

"Don't say that," said Hannah. "There's gotta be a way out of this. God will show up here, too."

"Oh, yeah?" retorted Rachel. "At what point exactly is that going to happen, Hannah? How in the world can you be so optimistic at a time like this? What planet are you on?" She turned red with fury and glancing around the room at the others she added, "We are in the dead center of hell here. I don't believe God shows up here much."

Suddenly, there was a flicker and the overhead florescent light went completely dark. In the frigid cell, black and still, all that could be heard was breathing. A muffled set of knocks came again from the children's room. "Their lights must have gone out, too," Rachel guessed. "They must be so scared." Rachel and Hannah both pounded the wall three times hoping the signal to the children would imply that everything was alright and that they were loved more than they could ever know. Rachel sat on the floor. Now with the lights out, she noticed even more the musty smell combined with the body odor of her fellow travelers. She shivered with cold and closed her eyes. She tried to imagine what Hawaii looked like this time of the year: palm trees swaying in the breeze, the sea turtles crawling down the shore and into the water, the smell of fresh pineapple and coconut and the taste of miniature bananas from a road side stand, the glorious sunsets blazing red and orange illuminating the suntanned faces of her boys. As she closed her eyes she could feel the warmth of that memory, and she was thankful, at least for that, for memories that no one could take away, that she had devoted her entire life to making joy and peace for her children and for John, that she had known love.

The silence was interrupted by a whisper. It was Ruth who had been characteristically quiet since they had been placed in the room. She was saying, "God, we need you now to make a way." That was all she said. A few moments passed, and Rachel heard Deborah's voice, also in a near whisper, say, "Rescue us from these prisons." Silence again. Then Miriam spoke, "God, only you can save us." One by one each of the women spoke a sentence in prayer. There was a pregnant pause again before Micah spoke, "Thank you, thank you that these people found me, that I found you. This is enough answer for me." His voice broke as he began to weep. Finally Bart uttered a word, only one word, "hope," and then fell silent. Only Rachel remained speechless. She ran her fingers up and down the wall as if caressing the skin of a loved one. Hannah moved in behind her and touched her face. She pulled her long hair back into a bundle and ran her fingers through it gently. Rachel, as if in mindless resignation, laid her head on Hannah's shoulder. Gretchen and Miriam moved in by Rachel and touched her lightly so she would know that they were there. Rachel's thoughts began to shift and move like an ocean wave. One minute she rode in a horse drawn buggy, bumping along a country road. The next minute she drifted through the air under a multi-colored balloon waving at John on the horizon. Another minute passed and she was baking cookies for Jesse watching him take the first warm, sweet bite and moan with delight; then she was reeling in John's arms along the polished oak floor of an elegant ball room, moving, spinning, smiling as the room spun around and around her in a blur.

A thud jostled her into another reality. She caught her breath, still in the darkness of the cold room. Stiff with sleep, her neck having been bent resting on Hannah's shoulder she sat up and stretched it forward a bit. She could tell by her breathing that Hannah was still asleep against the concrete wall of their prison. Judging by the silence and the slow measured breathing, Rachel surmised that everyone had dropped off into sleep. "They are all so exhausted," she thought, and immediately her thoughts turned to the children. Down the hall she heard another thud. She stood up wondering where the others were and what time it was. She walked toward the faint light coming from the barely visible crack at the base of the metal door. She pressed her ear against the coldness of it. She was certain that she could hear footsteps though they lacked the intention and volume given off by the ones the officers had made earlier. The slivered light at the base of the door dimmed as if the ambling person or persons had paused just outside. Rachel could hear faint voices, then the rattling of a key. She backed away from the door and held her breath. She could feel her heart pounding against her chest. "This is it," she thought. When the door swung open slightly the flooding of florescent light from the hallway blinded Rachel. She saw the outline of two figures but could not discern the faces. She realized after a couple of seconds that the figures were staring directly at her. Still not able to make out their identities, she stood up a little straighter and pulled down her sweater, smoothing it with her hands in hopes of appearing somehow more presentable, more fit, less negligent.

Cautiously one of the figures lifted a hand and spoke in a soft tone, "Rachel?"

"John?" Rachel responded immediately. John!" her voice grew louder and she flung herself into his arms.

"Shhhhh," he quieted her. "They don't know we're here."

"How did you . . .?" John covered her mouth with his hand.

"Not now. We must move quickly," John cautioned. Rachel, this is Shannon Casey. She is a senator, so she has access here. But her being here with me is unlawful and incredibly dangerous for her. You've got to tell me now, quickly, where are the others?"

"Who is it?" Gretchen asked rubbing her eyes and standing to her feet.

Hannah awoke, too, her eyes adjusting to the light. "John, Good Lord, is that you?"

"Yes," John answered. "Are all of you in here? Where are the children?"

"No," Rachel cut him off. "John, they have the children locked next door and the older ones in the other room there," she said pointing down the hall.

Senator Casey spoke, "It's protocol. Most likely they will have the older ones euthanized within the week, and the children will be placed in the education center." She glanced nervously down the hall. "If they have sequestered the children they intend to put them in permanent state care."

"No!" Hannah and Isabel cried at once.

"Shhhhh! You MUST be quiet, all of you," John retorted firmly. "This particular building is not monitored electronically because it is so old, but that doesn't mean there won't be an inspection any minute now." He motioned to Shannon, "See if it works in that one." Shannon walked down the hall to the door where Dorcas, Mathias, Phillip and Silas had been ushered. The key turned easily in the lock.

"It works," she whispered. "Someone help here." Micah and Gretchen tiptoed hurriedly down the hall and into the room to assist their companions.

"Try the children's room," John commanded. Bart and Isabel who were now in the hall along with Rachel and Hannah followed the Senator to the door. The key was inserted into the hole, but it would not turn. The Senator removed it and tried again. The key would not budge.

"What's wrong?" John asked anxiously.

"It won't turn," said the Senator trying the lock for a third time.

Becca who was standing toward the end of the hallway called to John, "Somebody's coming!"

"Let me have it!" He grabbed the key from the Senator's hand and jammed it into the lock. He rattled it around inside, trying to manipulate the doorknob at the same time. The footsteps down the hall grew louder.

"Everyone back into this room!" John commanded. Everyone scurried into the larger cell, including the older ones who were relieved to be together with their friends. John pulled both doors shut firmly, and the Senator locked them with haste.

"Where do we go?" Shannon asked John her eyes darting up and down the corridor for a hiding place.

"There!" John quickly retorted pointing to a door marked "Maintenance." The door was, to their great relief, unlocked, and John and Shannon slipped inside pulling the door behind them. In their haste, they did not think to locate the light switch, so they groped the walls and shelving in the pitch black area which could not have been more than eight feet long and four feet wide. Skimming his hands along the interior, John accidentally brushed a tin can of window cleaner onto the floor. It landed with a clank. Both Shannon and John stood frozen.

Chapter 32

"What was that?" they heard from a voice outside the door.

"Came from maintenance," said another. The security guards began to fiddle with the doorknob. Shannon immediately slid in next to John behind the door, praying that by some miracle they would not be discovered. The door swung open letting in the light.

"Don't see nothing," said one man. "Where's the light switch in here?"

"I think it's on the left there below that shelf." John's thoughts moved rapidly. He knew that if he did not give the guards reason for the noise, his presence and Shannon's would be made known. Noticing the tin can just inches from his right foot on the floor, John edged it slightly forward. Just as one of the men bumped the door trying to locate the light switch, John shoved the can forward forcefully, causing it to roll out in plain view.

"Here it is," said one of the men bending down to pick up the can. "Must have fallen off the shelf when we opened the hall door."

"Well, put it back. We need to finish up here. I go on break in five minutes," said the other man exiting the closet. He set the can on a shelf, an arm's length away from John's nose, and without ever turning on the light, he shut the door. Both John and Shannon sighed and pressed their ears to the door.

"Let's check 42A," said one of the men. John heard the door to his wife's prison open up. For several moments there was no sound. John could barely breathe. Then he heard the man again say, "Looks like everyone's asleep. You check the kids."

"Dear God . . . ." John whispered praying that the inspection would be just that. He did not know what he would have to do if they had come at this early hour for the children. He wondered how they would react to the intrusion of these strangers.

"The lock's stuck on this one. Should work with this key. Maybe there's another key for this one. Wait . . . where are you going?" he asked.

"On break," the other man responded, his voice now somewhat distant.

"Ain't you gonna check the kids and these old ones?"

"Man," said the other man walking down the hall toward the door, "I don't feel like dealing with a bunch of cryin' kids right now before my break. C'mon. The door's stuck anyway. It's the middle of the night. They're asleep—they ain't goin' nowhere. We'll check 'em at five."

The other man's steps could be heard heading down the corridor along with his buddy. "Okay, but if Frix finds out, you can take the heat."

"Let's go," John said to Shannon reaching for the door. He unlocked the main cell door once again then tried the children's lock until at last he was successful. The children who had fallen asleep took a few moments to realize that John had released them. Andrew and Jesse threw their arms around him, squeezing him until he nearly laughed.

"Where's Daddy," Simon asked.

"He's fine, Simon. We'll see him shortly. Let's go!" he said motioning to the group gathered in the hallway. The entourage headed toward the exit door at the opposite end.

"Great!" exclaimed John as they came up to the door. "It's got an alarm attached to it!" Glancing up everyone saw the black control box and took a step back.

"Wait a second," said the Senator. "This building is on the old system. These boxes have not been converted yet."

"What does that mean?" asked John.

"That means that instead of a chip swipe this thing has an old fashioned keypad code. And if I'm not mistaken," she said opening the box to reveal a pad of numbers, "all of these old codes were the years of presidential births."

"This could take all night then!" Amos blurted out.

"No, maybe not. They always used the earlier guys. Fast, give me some dates . . . anybody," exclaimed the Senator.

"Washington, 1732!" said Becca.

"Adams, 1735," Deborah interjected.

"Madison, 1751," wailed Maggie, grinning.

"Shhh," Hannah silenced her.

"Try 1743," Simon straightened himself, rubbing the sleep out of his eyes. "Thomas Jefferson," he added almost in a whisper. Then a "click" was followed by a "buzz."

"Brilliant, Simon! We're out!," sounded the Senator. "This way." The weary group followed swiftly after the Senator who led them down an alley, then up a side street where a black, armored truck waited in the shadows. "It's used to transport valuables and national antiquities. The truck has its own chip. No one will suspect you in here. Your driver is Owen. He'll take you where you're going."

John hugged Shannon, then wiping away a tear he said, "God bless you, Senator. You have saved our lives. If you ever need anything . . . ." The Senator nodded.

She turned to face the other grateful faces. "God be with you all," she said. Waving a hand, she walked away into the night. Inside the truck, Samuel, Levi and Tim waited anxiously. Simon, Maggie and Thomas, upon seeing their father, ran into his open arms. Hannah clung to his neck, tears streaming down her face. Miriam kissed Samuel and Deborah held his hand saying over and over, "Thank you, Jesus." John sat with one arm around Rachel and his other arm around Jesse and Andrew. Marti interrogated Levi about all that had happened. The children, settled in the arms of their parents, fell back into a deep sleep as the truck sped down I-264 toward Virginia Beach.

Chapter 33

Because the days as they had stolen away into winter solstice had grown shorter, no dawning light rose up from the eastern horizon to greet them as the armored truck rolled undetected into Masthead Harbor. Sailing vessels stood languidly as monuments in their appointed slips as far as the eye could see. Closer to shore the smaller vessels bobbed idly; fishing boats and dinghies, dwarfed by the larger catamarans and cruisers farther down the docks, waited empty-hulled for their owners to come captain them. Two racer cruisers rocked beside a stunning, older, wooden, German Ketch. A Latitude 44 Motor yacht displayed a red "For Sale" sign. Sporting a roomy fly bridge and inviting sun deck, its features were listed on a placard spec sheet—two finished cabins with showers, top quality materials, sea worthiness in all sorts of weather, ideal helm positioning, glass fiber hand laid, mat and woven roving transverse—the list was endless. There was even an expedition yacht that had been used as a research vessel complete with eight guest cabins, chip communications and wet/dry labs.

The shoes of the travelers clopped along the wooden decking as John led the others with stalwart determination toward one singular goal: the Plymouth Grace, a majestic solid oak timber replica of the original Mayflower. The ship stood 106 feet long by 25 feet wide with four masts and six sails. It had been constructed from the somewhat sketchy specs taken from historical writings left behind by the Plymouth Rock community and had been deemed the most faithful replica built to this day. Its engineer and shipmaster, Captain Silas Alcon, leaned leisurely against a light post. Simon, who was by now wide awake, stared with wonder at the formidable vessel, inspecting with newfound intensity the mizzenmast topped with a flag bearing the symbol of a Celtic cross.

John extended his hand as he approached the captain. "John Beckett," he said eliminating the small talk. "We spoke on the phone."

"Captain Alcon. Pleased to meet you."

"Were you able to put together what we discussed?"

"For the most part with such short notice. The food wasn't much of a problem. But I had some difficulty with medical supplies. Just not enough time to pull it all together. As for the crew, we have six. We need ten. But if there are those in your party who would be willing . . ."

"We'll do it!" said John, Samuel and Tim almost in unison.

"Us, too," Rachel said pointing to Gretchen, Hannah and some of the other women. "Whatever you need."

"Been needing to give her a test run. This will give me the excuse," the Captain spoke as he moved a toothpick around in his mouth. "Did anyone see you coming down here?"

John answered cautiously, "Not that I'm aware of. But I can't be sure." John looked up and down the deck both ways. His eyes landed on a wooden bench resting under a hooded deck lamp. He made out the form of what appeared to be a man. Walking slowly toward the bench, he examined the sleeping figure for a few moments then made his way back to the Captain. "Who's that," he whispered pointing to the sleeping person.

"Big Chief. That's what we call him. He's Native American. Cherokee, I think. No one knows for sure. He never speaks. Sits on that bench all day watching boats come in and leave like he's looking for something. Occasionally he'll disappear for an hour or so, but he always returns right there. He's harmless; trust me. Certainly no threat to you. Most people just leave him alone."

"Alone," mimicked Simon staring down the deck at the sleeping man. The rest of the children gazed at the ship as if it were the dark ghost of some distant past. Phillip began to cough. John in his haste had almost forgotten about the older ones who, he suddenly realized, had to be extremely exhausted.

"We need to get them on board," John suggested, guiding Phillip to the gangway.

"Right," quipped the Captain. A group of brawny men stepped forward on the boat into the light as the Captain motioned to them. "This is Jim, the first mate. He will show you to your cabins so you can get settled. If I could borrow a few of you, John, we could finish loading these supplies. We need to set sail before dawn. We won't be tracked because the vessel is not chip detectable, but if they suspect us for any reason . . . ."

"I get it. Show us what you need." John kissed Rachel tenderly. She smiled and began to gather up the children and usher them forward onto the deck of the great ship. Within thirty minutes, the rest of the supplies had been loaded into the galley. The Captain suggested that everyone who might be assisting the crew stay on deck so that they could begin to pick up the terminology and the assignments.

The bow spring line was loosened, the anchor was hoisted up into the pocket, and the sails were unfurled. The ship began to rock and plunge forward into the blackness of the Atlantic. "Clear the deck lines and head aloft," the Captain shouted. The sinewy crew labored mechanically, obeying orders and heaving at the thick ropes. Jim, the first mate, began to give orders to John, Tim, and Samuel, basic tasks explained simply so that the men could begin to get a feel for the ship. In spite of their utter lassitude and their desire for food and uninterrupted sleep, no one, not even Phillip, Dorcas and Mathias, could stay below deck. One by one the travelers congregated aft, and as the brisk winter winds began to blow against the mainsail, the lights of the Virginia coastline grew smaller and smaller, until they twinkled like mere Christmas decorations. A warm tear welled up in Jesse's eye as Rachel embraced him and brushed away her own tears. Gretchen put her arms around Rachel; Micah wrapped his slender arm around Gretchen until one by one the travelers were embracing each other, watching the lights until they faded into darkness. Unbeknownst to them, the faint light of dawn, brilliant and beckoning, had begun to rise up before them in the east.

John, descending to the lower deck on an errand from the Captain, carried a crate full of bottle lamp oil to the hold. As he turned down the narrow corridor he saw something that made him stop stunned. There on the floor staring at one of the hand-colored maps near the chart room sat Big Chief. John set down the crate and walked over to him. The Cherokee raised his face to look at John. His expression was one of hope mixed with desperation. His wrinkled skin told the story both of his age and his experience. Each line spoke of trauma and heartache. His leathery hands suggested hard labor, and his matted hair, which had turned steel gray over time, hinted at an untamed, natural spirit. He lifted a finger and pointed to a plaque, which had been framed exquisitely in oak, the replication of a yellowed document. Moving closer to the frame, John recognized the wording immediately: "In the name of God, Amen. We, whose names are underwritten, the Loyal Subjects of our dread Sovereign Lord, King James, by the Grace of God, of England, France and Ireland, King, Defender of the Faith, Having undertaken for the Glory of God, and Advancement of the Christian Faith, and the Honour of our King and Country, a voyage to plant the first colony in the northern parts of Virginia; do by these presents, solemnly and mutually in the Presence of God and one of another, covenant and combine ourselves together into a civil Body Politick, for our better Ordering and Preservation, and Furtherance of the Ends aforesaid; And by Virtue hereof to enact, constitute, and frame, such just and equal Laws, Ordinances, Acts, Constitutions and Offices, from time to time, as shall be thought most meet and convenient for the General good of the Colony; unto which we promise all due submission and obedience. In Witness whereof we have hereunto subscribed our names at Cape Cod the eleventh of November, in the Reign of our Sovereign Lord, King James of England, France and Ireland, the eighteenth, and of Scotland the fifty-fourth. Anno Domini, 1620."

Under the document were the signatures of forty-one separatists fleeing religious persecution in Europe with a side note saying that this document was the foundation for the first laws of the colony in the New World. "Of these first colony members, only half survived the first winter. Those who remained were blessed with prosperity, happiness and a full life."

John Beckett's Journal—The Crossing

December 5, 20___

The first night passed by without difficulty; though it is powerfully cold, especially this morning when we were all on deck "learning the ropes" in a literal sense of the term. Captain Alcon made the suggestion during our morning meeting that we steer south in order to avoid icy seas that are common this time of year. That sounded like a plan to me. Simon, Maggie, and Maria (who is still not feeling well at all) spent most of the day 'tween decks with Phillip and Dorcas playing games and reading, while the older boys and the rest of us shadowed the crew members who are explaining to us the rigging and operation of this ship.   It is fascinating stuff, really. Rachel and Jesse have taken to it like a fish to water. Andrew seems a bit more out of his element but tries to do his part. I feel that we are all on the brink of something, which is at once exciting and terrifying. Standing on the deck looking up at the main mast and the blue sky beyond, I am experiencing something that can only be described as surreal. I pray for guidance and for the grace of God and mercies in our travels.

December 7, 20___

The first lessons begin. We now know what a "boatswain" is. Our appointed lord and master is Hollis Spenser. All day he has been barking orders in the most gravelly voice I've ever heard. Not only must we learn the operation of all six sails, but we must also master fifty-five different lines. My head is spinning and my muscles are sore. So much to remember.

December 8, 20___

Overcast today, eerily calm. The temperature continued to drop as the hours passed until it became nearly unbearable to remain on deck. Our winter coats and gloves have become our most precious commodity as we learn our designated tasks and understand more everyday about sea travel. Even in the staterooms below one can always feel the damp chill. We huddle close in the evenings 'tween decks and read, sipping hot tea or broth, until we doze off to sleep usually sitting up or slung across someone else's lap.

December 9, 20___

Last night a strong wind blew into the sails causing the ship to rock and plunge for the first time. It was suggested by Boatswain Spenser that we "clew up" the sails as so not to blow off course too much. Most of our group (including yours truly) spent the best part of the morning over the rails eliminating our breakfasts. One deck hand named Jack Branson ridiculed us mercilessly. At first most of us tried to laugh it off. But after awhile, all the taunting and teasing, compounded with the nausea, became slightly overwhelming. No one had either the stamina or the inclination to take him on. I hope this will not become a problem, as I know without a doubt this bout of seasickness will not be our last.

December 10, 20___

Sarah, Eve and Ruth have been appointed cooks and relegated to the fo'c'sle (kitchen) to learn the ship's system, which is, needless to say, antiquated. Mostly we will be eating fish, which must be caught daily, canned meats, and dry goods like pasta, rice, beans and oatmeal. We have canned goods aboard and a massive supply of drinking water. However, water for showering is prohibited. Instead, each passenger receives a small ration of clean up water each day to be used strictly for sponge bathing and brushing teeth. I can't wait to get a whiff of this crew in a couple of weeks.

December 12,   20___

Maria and Phillip continue to worsen. We are beside ourselves with concern for them, especially for Maria who has been nothing but sheer delight since we began this journey.   Bart grows increasingly silent everyday as he watches his little girl fight the infection that rages inside of her.   Isabel, always the nurse, constantly experiments with the medications we have on board and feeds her spoonfuls of chicken broth and applesauce—anything to keep her energy up to fight this illness. Isabel leaves her side only to tend to Phillip whose ashen complexion tells the story that none of us wants to say out loud.   He drifts in and out of sleep throughout the day.   Sometimes his speech is incoherent while other times he is lucid and wry as ever.   He coughs constantly. Isabel moved his cot into the infirmary so that he can get better rest and not disturb the others who are trying to sleep. I can tell, though she never speaks of it, that Isabel is more than a little worried about the limited medical supplies on board, and in spite of the fact that Maria is her only daughter, she tries very hard to use what supply we have sparingly.   She knows that under these conditions, it is likely that Phillip and Maria will not be the only two people on board to take ill.

December 13,   20___

We awoke today to the sound of the Captain's voice announcing that during the night one of the cross beams on the mainmast cracked.   Though I did not understand the specifics of the discussion amongst the crew members and the Captain, each man seemed to be brainstorming a solution that might serve as a stop gap until we dock somewhere and can get it fixed properly. The discussion went on for some time, which made me realize the seriousness of our situation and the unlikely event that we would be able to dock anytime soon. Finally, however, the men agreed that the ship itself was strong and could survive the fierce winds if the beam were repaired and a post were to be fixed securely from the lower deck up to support it. A proposal (and unanimous agreement) was put forth not to "overdo it" with the sails. So the crew and all of us set to accomplishing the job at hand, which occupied our minds, busied our bodies and kept our thoughts focused on something besides the bitter cold.

December 15, 20__
Another crisis. Leaks in the upper works brought on by high winds. In addition to the latest fiasco, most of us were once again "over the rails," while sensitive Mr. Branson barraged us with obscenities until Rachel kneed him in the groin and told him to shut up before she . . . . About that moment, she threw up on his boots. He was stunned for about thirty minutes, but within the hour he was back to his old, cantankerous self. I hate to say it, but I really dislike this guy. His jibes are demoralizing and have affected the spirits of each one of us negatively. He even pokes fun of the children when we are not watching closely. He's wearing on all of us, yet this Captain, for whatever reason, tolerates him and ignores his behavior. Samuel has nearly had enough, and there could be a serious confrontation soon, I feel. On a side note, the relationship between Samuel and Miriam continues to blossom. Samuel has been a different man since the incident at Greenway. He understands more about his freedom in Christ everyday, and his spirit lightens by degrees all the time. It is exciting to observe this transformation—he's a good man with a godly heart.
Tomorrow we caulk the leaks!

December 17, 20__
Today I heard a phrase that I never wanted to hear: "Man overboard!" Bruce Waller, one of the Captain's best men and a real workhorse, lost his balance during a brutal storm this afternoon and fell into the Atlantic! We were extremely concerned because of

the temperature of the water as we watched Bruce flail his arms waiting for someone to throw him a line. Our rescue efforts were thwarted because the ship seemed to have a mind of its own and the rest of the crew also had fears of losing their footing. But somehow, glory to God, Bruce grabbed onto a topsail halyard that was dangling in the water and, though he was under the surface waves, he held on with unmitigated determination. The crew, seeing his struggle, worked speedily to haul him in by the rope until he was able to grasp a boat hook and pull himself up. He's been in the great cabin ever since, drinking strong coffee (and some gin that he stashed away somewhere) and trying to get warm.

December 18, 20__
Because of yesterday's storms, the upper works began to leak again. We spent several hours caulking them as best we could. It was backbreaking work, but Rachel and the boys worked alongside me, so the time seemed to go by quickly.

December 20, 20__
Simon asked today what we were doing for Christmas. It was an odd question under the circumstances. Tim and Hannah looked at me and for the first time we realized that we had not given it a single thought. Furthermore, we had not celebrated Thanksgiving—as we discussed it, we were not even sure when it passed. We began to try to remember what we were doing on Thanksgiving Day, and not one of us had a clue. We decided that our last grand meal at Silas's farm was our Thanksgiving feast, and we agreed that's how we would remember it. We celebrated the day by enjoying the "last fruits" rather than the "first fruits" of the harvest. As I am able I've been reading bits and pieces of Williams Bradford's Of Plymouth Plantation. In particular the excerpts chronicling the voyage and the days leading up to it are, let's say, ironically familiar. As for Christmas, I don't know. All I know is that our celebration of it will be authentic and unprecedented.

December 21,   20__

Though I have not written each day about it, our thoughts continually turn to little Maria who is so wafer thin and pale that she can barely get up to go to the bathroom. We have each taken turns by her bedside. On Wednesday, Gretchen and the children wrote and performed a skit to entertain her. Today Levi spent the afternoon with her. He taught her a game with the dreidel in celebration of Hanukkah season. The mindless entertainment made her pluck up, a hopeful sign. Bart and Isabel do not say much about their worries or her condition. I think that Isabel knows more than she lets on, but the determination to cling to hope for Maria outweighs both the facts and the odds. I so wish that we had been allowed more time to plan for our medical needs. I cannot help but feel that I bear at least some responsibility in her illness. We are all constantly prayerful. Even Big Chief who seems, in these close quarters, to stay hidden somehow has been spotted now and then outside the infirmary where she's been sleeping. Thomas says he spied on the Chief yesterday and saw him mumbling something that sounded like a chant. These are the first sounds anyone has heard him make.

December 23,   20___

We are at a loss for Maria. She now sleeps so much of the day that even Thomas cannot keep her awake with his jokes. What will we do? Her blood pressure drops each day ever so slightly, measurable drops nonetheless. We all fear that unless God intervenes, we will lose her. Dear God, help us!

December, 25 20__

Last night as several of us (Bart, Isabel, Marti, Samuel and I) stood in vigil over Maria, we heard a tap on the door of the infirmary. Opening the door, we saw Big Chief standing there with an animal skin sort of duffle bag in his hand. We had not seen him for several days, and we had not until this moment ever seen the bag he was carrying. He said nothing to us as usual, but pointed to his bag then again to the girl on the cot. We realized that he wanted to give her something. I stepped forward to stop him or at to tell him she was too sick and tired to receive anything, but just as I started to open my mouth, Isabel stepped in front of me and pushed me away, making an opening for the Chief around Maria's bed. He opened the bag and pulled from it a stone bowl and grinder used for herbs. Then he pulled out several plastic bags all containing what looked to be dried leaves and flowers. Almost in a ritualistic manner, he began to grind combinations of the leaves with a grayish brown paste. As he moved, he hummed to himself a hypnotic tune none of us had ever heard. He leaned the girl's head back gently on his arm—she awoke groggy and weak. He spooned dabs of the paste onto her tongue. Maria made a dreadful face, but as she looked up weakly into the eyes of the Indian, she swallowed it down as if she knew that she should. He repeated the process time and again until the paste was gone. Then he heated up some water on the camp stove and crumbled a few leaves and flowers into a strainer along with some powders. Boiling her some sort of tea, he poured it in a cup and handed the cup to Isabel who was staring at him intently, warily almost. Big Chief held up two fingers that we all took to mean two cups—he closed the bag and walked out of the room. Isabel fed Maria one cup of the tea, then another. Afterward, Maria lay back on the pillow and fell into a deep sleep.

I was awakened this morning by the screams of Isabel, bellowing sentences in Spanish that I did not comprehend. Fearing the worst, I jumped out of bed, dressed in a hurry and ran down the hall followed by several of the others who had been 'tween decks and in the other cabins. When I got to the door of the infirmary, I saw something that immediately made me cry: Maria was sitting up, wide-eyed with a bowl of oatmeal in her hand, eating like a ravenous dog and laughing at her father. Isabel and Bart were crying, hugging each other. All of us, including the Captain, began to wipe away tears of joy. I felt a tug on my sleeve.

It was Simon still in his pajamas, holding a calendar he had made. He said, "Uncle John, look!" He pointed to the 25th day of the month. "It's Christmas today! It's Christmas!" I told him he was right. It certainly was.

January 1,   20___

Phillip passed away today. Mathias and Dorcas, upon hearing the news, stared into space all day like stunned sheep. We have no means of embalming him on the ship, so we had a short ceremony in which Silas and Samuel read some scriptures, and we sang a couple of hymns. Then we threw his poor, frail body into the sea. Mathias and Dorcas watched it float off into the sunset. They didn't say much during the service. Isabel says that they are in shock and that we need to give them time. Fortunately on this voyage, that's all we have. Phillip was such a gentle spirited man. Everyone grieves today.

January 6,   20___

In the night, Jack Branson developed an exceedingly high fever and excruciating headache. Isabel felt that it might be meningitis, especially when he began complaining of neck stiffness. However, she had no way of giving him antibiotics intravenously, and as the supply of oral antibiotics is so low, she knew what she had to work with would not have much effect. By two in the morning, Jack began vomiting like I've never seen a man vomit in my life. He was unable to quit. He kept on until there was nothing left; then he vomited rancid bile after that. Isabel felt completely helpless, and by four she had broken down and was crying, sitting in the floor of the chart room. She kept saying she didn't know what to do and that she didn't have enough supplies. At one point she said to Bart that she felt they had made a mistake in coming. For the first time in a long time we saw Bart take the wheel and say to her that this was no mistake, that he knew beyond a doubt they had come for a reason. Then he said something whispered to her in Spanish, so I'm not sure what it was, but Isabel quit crying after that and took his big hand and held it to her face. By seven this morning, Jack Branson was dead. His ceremony was much shorter than Phillip's. The Captain and a couple of the crew heaved his body into the water. I'm not sure how I feel about it all, and if I'm honest, I can't say that I'll miss him. I'm sorry about how he died. It all seemed so violent and awful. The children seem ambivalent and have gone back to their daily duties like nothing happened. Even Isabel seems to have moved on this morning and has been attending to Maria. Weird night.

January 8, 20___

Oddly enough Andrew has been assisting the Captain in the round house charting our course. He's become quite amazing with the quadrant and cross-staff as well as the other instruments. Because he's always been good at math, he's been calculating our longitude and latitude so that we can stay on course. I guess you never realize how much you miss computers and other instruments of technology until you have to do without them.

January 12, 20___

We have not noticed so much, mostly because it has been gradual, but little by little the air has gotten warmer. Without exact instrumentation it is difficult to tell where we are, but the Captain feels that with the exception of a couple of days where the sails did not come down soon enough and we were blown around a bit, we have stayed the course. On course for where I often wonder. With all of his certainty and bravado I don't think that even the Captain knows exactly where we will land. I think he assumes we will end up somewhere along the coast of Côte d'Ivoire. I find myself discovering more a different kind of navigation that has more to do with my spirit, a seeing with my eyes shut. I feel more everyday a twinge of something I cannot explain. Today as I swabbed the deck, I could hardly concentrate on my work. Sometimes you know what you know and where you are.

January 20, 20___

Last night I dreamed again. I was walking the length of a long plank. On either side of me the deep, dark water brooded. I was balancing like I did when I was a boy, walking across the old log at Pike Creek. But these waters seemed treacherous, dangerous, unknown. The dorsal fins of two huge sharks floated by along the surface of this water, confirming my suspicions about the depths. I started to panic. Turning around to go back I realized that I was not alone on the plank, but that all of my family and traveling companions were following me, trying to find their balance as I was. Suddenly I heard a voice, almost like a narrator at the end of a movie. It said, "For I have not given you a spirit of fear. . . ." Slowly the waters in the dream began to undergo a transformation. A light from somewhere deep inside began to glow, illuminating what waited beyond, solidifying the surface, hardening it, until it was as if on all sides of me there stretched a floor of glass, strong as iron and clear as a mountain stream. Below lay all types of beautiful ocean plants, corals, and anemones, an underwater garden. Its splendor took my breath. Then I awoke. It was still dark outside. Everyone slept. I walked up on deck, and under the light of the fullest and brightest moon I ever remember seeing, I witnessed an incredible sight: A humpback whale leapt up and out of the water several yards from the ship, and with the grace of an Olympian, dove back in again until all but his tail was submerged. Finally, he disappeared just like that, with barely a splash or a sound. Breathtaking!

January 26, 20___

The children grow more restless every day. The textbooks and leisure reading, which were supplied for us by the captain and packed 'tween decks for use by the children, have not been touched in days. They have been exceedingly patient and creative until now, drawing, writing, inventing games, fishing, learning basic seamanship. But now they are weary of being cooped up at sea. Though we are all feeling this weariness, it seems to manifest itself in a more obvious way in the children. It takes every bit of patience and grace in all of us not to snap at one another or blow up in anger. Recently it seems that in spite of our camaraderie as brothers and sisters, we are all getting on each other's nerves from time to time. The weather becomes warmer each day, which is a plus. I secretly wish for our travels to be over soon.

February 2, 20___

It was my turn at early morning watch (4 – 6 a.m.), the shift I most despise. I climbed the futtock shrouds as always and ascended to the topsail yard. At the top I closed my eyes, half sleeping, half swaying in the darkness and remained that way for I'm not sure how long. Every now and then I looked into the blackness, but could see nothing, not even the face of the sea as it was new moon and no light made the waters visible.

After some time, the light began to dawn in front of me and I could see what appeared to be something other than endless ocean. I squinted to discern what was out there, but the light was insufficient and I could make out nothing. I waited for what seemed like hours for the light to make its way up to the horizon and illuminate the stretch in front of me. By and by with the help of the emerging light and a pair of binoculars, I made out what seemed to be a landmass with mountains jutting out of it here and there. I stood trembling until I was finally able to shout out the words, "Land ho!"

In no time the activity on the ship escalated to almost a frantic pace; orders were given, and everyone was put to work. I have a feeling that this will be the last entry I will be writing for a long time. The duties and obligations here on the ship and . . . in the next place will no doubt fix my focus elsewhere. The words of William Bradford as he landed near Cape Cod haunt me now: "What could now sustain them but the spirit of God and his grace? May not and ought not the children of these fathers rightly say: our fathers were Englishmen which came over this great ocean, and were ready to perish in this wilderness; but they cried unto the

Lord, and he heard their voice, and looked on their adversity, etc. Let them therefore praise the Lord because he is good, and his mercies endure forever."

Afterword

Along a scaffold built by the travelers and the crew for the purpose, thirty-four toil worn pilgrims made their way onto the shores of a new world. The sea, tepid and serene, appeared to the travelers a brilliant color of turquoise they had never before seen. The powdery whiteness of the sand nearly blinded them with contrast, and schools of triangular fish darted nervously around pairs of foreign legs frightened at having their habitat interrupted. In the distance the mountains lay like sleeping titans. Around the coastline a dense forest of cotton and oil palm trees swayed in the gentle breezes. Out to sea, a pod of blue whales breached and cavorted before moving on south. Grass huts dotted the northern part of the beach, and a single hand-hewn canoe bobbed vacant in the center of an inlet.

Words seemed inadequate; no one spoke. The sounds of the silent lapping waters were soothing enough. John Beckett stood facing the wilderness and the mountains beyond. Samuel who stood next to him opened his mouth to whisper only one thing: "Free." John breathed in. His lungs filled themselves with the pristine salty air. In among the trees came a rustling and the brush of palm fronds. Slowly emerging from the brush, three natives dressed in animal skins with brightly colored embellishments, arm and leg bands, and carved spears strapped to their waists stepped out to see the new arrivals. The expressions on their dark faces spoke of wonder, curiosity and extreme distrust. John raised one hand as a gesture of friendship, but the natives kept their distance. For several moments, they stared at one another. Then the natives, as if they had the answer for which they had been seeking, began to edge guardedly away toward the north end of the shore. None of the travelers noticed Big Chief who at some juncture had also made his way down the scaffold and had joined them barefoot on the sand. Watching the natives recede up the coast, Big Chief moved forward as if the impulse to follow propelled him from somewhere deeper than he realized. Then he stopped just in front of the others and observed the dark men as they disappeared from view. His arms dangled at his side, a resignation. He wiped the remnant of an ancient tear from his weathered face.

About the Author

Zann Renn holds a master's degree and lives a quiet life in rural Tennessee. Zann enjoys family time, walking in the woods and making music with friends.

You can contact Zann Renn at
zannrenn@gmail.com